To Michael Walzer
with best wishes,
Roy Mottahedeh

Loyalty and Leadership in an Early Islamic Society

PRINCETON STUDIES ON THE NEAR EAST

ROY P. MOTTAHEDEH

Loyalty and Leadership in an Early Islamic Society

PRINCETON UNIVERSITY PRESS
PRINCETON, N. J.

Published by Princeton University Press, Princeton, New Jersey
In the United Kingdom:
Princeton University Press, Guildford, Surrey

Library of Congress Cataloging in Publication Data will
be found on the last printed page of this book

Publication of this book has been aided by a grant from
The Andrew W. Mellon Foundation

This book has been composed in VIP Bembo
Clothbound editions of Princeton University Press books
are printed on acid-free paper, and binding materials are
chosen for strength and durability

Printed in the United States of America by
Princeton University Press,
Princeton, New Jersey

To my Father

CONTENTS

PREFACE

This book attempts to describe the social structure of western Iran and southern Iraq in the tenth and eleventh centuries A.D. and to give an account of the social bonds that created this structure. The classification of social groups and of the variety of social bonds has been derived from the self-description of this society rather than from the language of modern social science. This self-description sometimes comes close to the established usage in the social sciences, and the reader may wonder why, for example, I do not call a certain kind of status "ascriptive," or a certain kind of social bond "dyadic." I have not done so because none of these modern terms fully corresponds with the terms used in self-description, and to discuss the degree to which the modern terms differ would add very little to the reader's understanding of the society with which this book is concerned. I have also avoided the vexed but fascinating question of continuity and discontinuity with the ancient Near East. The genealogy of social forms is a separate subject; and in my view, like the study of biological genealogy, it fascinates more than it explains.

I have tried to offer one or two representative anecdotes to support each point, and in the notes frequently give references to parallel anecdotes in the primary sources. To avoid encumbering the text, numbers for the notes have been put only at the end of paragraphs. Each of the references in the notes for the information found in the preceding paragraph or paragraphs is followed by a word or phrase in parentheses matching the reference to the information in the text. The reader will find comparatively few references to the secondary literature on this period. This is because the secondary literature on this period has rarely discussed the kind of social history that is the subject of this book. Secondary literature is cited only when, as in the discussion of ulema, the text directly argues with a view of Near Eastern social history that has been widely accepted.

I have, moreover, given only a brief account of the political and administrative history of this period. I hope to treat these subjects at greater length in subsequent books, which will also discuss the traditions of Islamic and pre-Islamic Iran that Buyid rulers and their officials sought to use in order to validate their authority.

I apologize for cluttering the text with transliterated Arabic words. Since the argument of the text depends on categories of self-description, the nonspecialist as well as the specialist will probably find it easier to have the appropriate Arabic words cited whenever they are discussed. In the index the number set off by solid carats (▶ ◀) refers the reader to the page on which the fullest definition of each Arabic term will be found. A standard system of transliteration has been used, except that I have written imam for imām, Koran for al-Qur'ān, ulema for 'ulamā', and Buyid for Būyid or Buwaihid. Familiar geographical names such as Medina and Baghdad are given in their common spelling; other geographical names are transliterated in agreement with Arabic pronunciation. I have followed the convention of using b. for ibn except at the beginning of names. In many cases, both the Hijrah and the Christian date have been given. The first century of the Hijrah roughly corresponds to the seventh century A.D., and the fifth century of the Hijrah to the eleventh century A.D. The citations of dates without equivalents for the first through the fifth centuries refer to Hijrah dates.

ACKNOWLEDGMENTS

This book owes a very great deal to several scholars who read it in part or whole and gave valuable advice for its revision and improvement: Margaret Case, Peri Halpern, William T. Graham, Andras Hamori, Albert Hourani, Abraham L. Udovitch, and Jeanette Wakin. The index is by Lois Gottesman.

Loyalty and Leadership in an Early Islamic Society

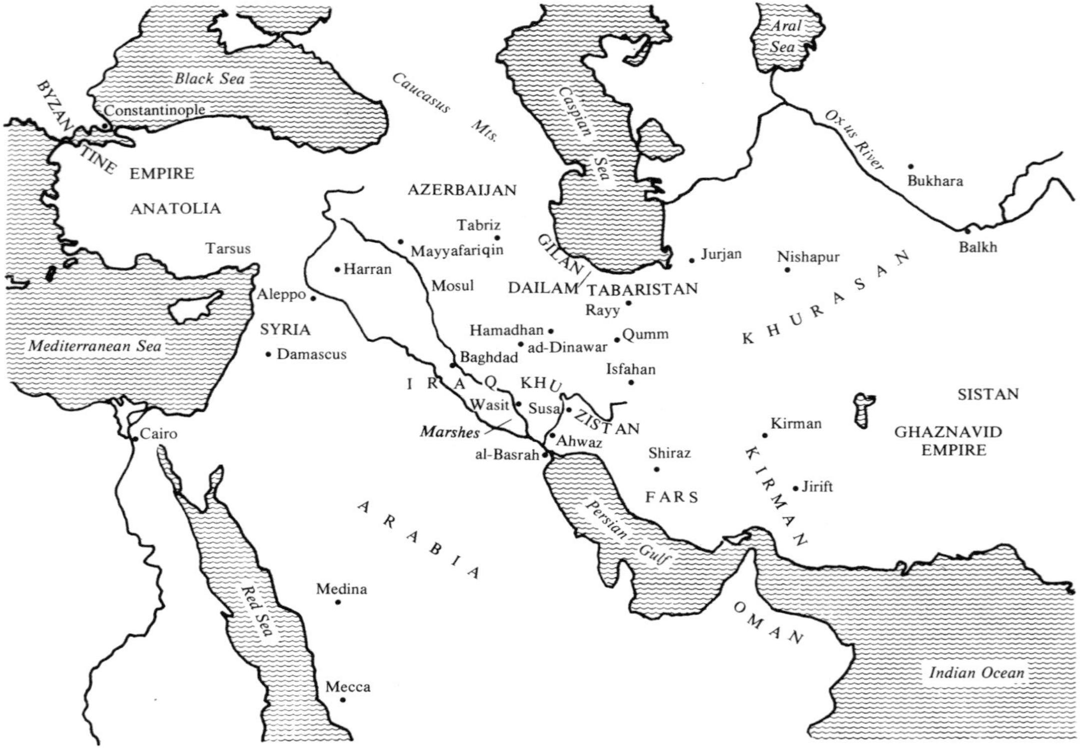
Black Sea
BYZANTINE EMPIRE
Constantinople
ANATOLIA
Tarsus
Caucasus Mts.
AZERBAIJAN
Caspian Sea
Aral Sea
Oxus River
Bukhara
Balkh
Tabriz
Mayyafariqin
Harran
Mosul
GILAN
DAILAM
TABARISTAN
Jurjan
Nishapur
KHURASAN
Aleppo
SYRIA
Damascus
Mediterranean Sea
Rayy
Hamadhan
ad-Dinawar
Qumm
Baghdad
Isfahan
IRAQ
KHUZISTAN
Wasit
Susa
Ahwaz
Marshes
al-Basrah
Cairo
SISTAN
Kirman
GHAZNAVID EMPIRE
Shiraz
KIRMAN
Jirift
FARS
ARABIA
Persian Gulf
Red Sea
Medina
Mecca
OMAN
Indian Ocean

CHAPTER I

Introduction

This book describes some of the manners that gave shape to the political life of a society that flourished a thousand years ago in the Near East. American readers will recall that de Tocqueville considered manners (*moeurs*), which he defined as "the sum of the moral and intellectual dispositions of men in society," to be the most important influence in maintaining American political institutions—more important than laws or physical circumstances. This "sum" is a figure too perfect for any observer of a contemporary society to obtain, even the brilliant de Tocqueville. It must remain still less obtainable for a society as long vanished as the society that is the subject of this book. Yet I feel confident that the manners discussed in this book were indeed important for the political life of that vanished society, important enough to be a significant part of the more nearly perfect sums that will be calculated by future historians.[1]

My first interest has been the manners of individuals rather than the manners of groups. I have tried to describe the ways in which the individuals in this society formed commitments to each other, and to suggest how the manners of these individuals can account for the shape of political life in this society as a whole. Individuals, not unexpectedly, formed such commitments in roughly similar ways for generation after generation; and it is this similarity, after all, that enables us to give general descriptions of their manners.

If the way in which commitments were formed remained roughly the same, the associations that were formed by these commitments seldom lasted more than a generation. The continuity in the way in which individual commitments were formed and the discontinuity of the associations formed through such commitments may, at first, appear puzzling. Some of the associations of Western life, such as the feudal manor and the craft guild, were so stable that social historians of premodern Western societies often begin with a description of these units, and from them build a composite picture of the social structure of the societies in which they existed. Social historians of the premodern Islamic Near East have followed this example, and have tried to identify fundamental social units in the societies they study. These historians have tried to define either the primary "networks" or, in the phrase of one excellent social historian, the "basic units" or building blocks of which these societies were composed.[2]

A few of the more stable associations of local life discussed in later chapters do in some ways resemble the basic units of premodern Western society. Yet in other ways they are strikingly different from their supposed counterparts in Western history. Most of these Near Eastern associations lacked formal internal structure, unless such structure was imposed by a central government. Their leaders were spokesmen, not directors. Entry into such groups was seldom marked by any formal observance, or datable from any specific moment. Men belonged to such groups because they identified themselves and others as belonging to certain accepted categories such as "merchant" or "scholar"; and, in general, they rallied to such groups only when the categories with which they identified were threatened. Even neighborhood factions, in which some historians have hoped to find the basic units of these societies, were only rarely a focus for positive loyalties, the means for sustained and predictable local cooperation. In most cases they were a focus for negative loyalties, a means for local defense. One can hardly say that men participated in society through their membership in such groups.

If, as will be argued below, men of the Buyid period did not participate in society primarily through their membership in basic building blocks, each of which could carry the allegiances of its members, how did the fears and inclinations of men work together to create the amazingly resilient social order of this period, a social order that not only survived the initial ignorance and violence of its conquerors, but succeeded in transforming those conquerors into participants? For, without guilds, church, gentry of official rank, caste, and the myriad other well-defined divisions and groups familiar from the study of other cultures, this society managed both to reproduce its forms from generation to generation, and to export these forms to new groups of people in lands farther to the east. It cannot even be said to owe its resilience to the stability of kin groups; for, among the settled people of this society, kinship seems to be a very unpredictable element in cooperation, and does not provide the model for cooperation among nonkin.

This book, in an attempt to answer the above question, makes the manners of individuals its central concern. Even if there had been formal and stable groups in this society comparable to the feudal manor and the medieval European trade guild, there would be a strong argument for describing the moral attitudes and customs that governed the entry and participation of individual men in such groups. Social networks are only knit together, and social building blocks are themselves only built, by the fears and inclinations of the individuals who form them. No society can hope to coerce all the people all the time; before the industrial revolution no extensive society could hope to coerce most of the people most of the time. Between coercion and chance lie the associations that are to some extent chosen. To understand these associations we should at the very least give an account of the moral world in terms of which men explained their choices.

It is, of course, possible to exaggerate the differences between the society considered in this book and other societies. For example, a good part of the second chapter is devoted to describing the importance of *ni'mah* or "benefit" in creating formal ties of obligation between men who lived in the Buyid period. *Ni'mah* is no stranger to us. Dr. Johnson in 1766 explained to Boswell that in courting great men, "you must not give a shilling's worth of court for sixpence worth of good. But if you can get a shilling's worth of good for sixpence worth of court, you are a fool if you do not pay court." But even this analysis of the mechanics of benefit sounds more appropriate to a Western than to a Middle Eastern context; for the ties are less formal and are seen more strictly in terms of turning a "profit." Furthermore, a few self-perpetuating groups comparable to the building blocks of Western history did exist in Buyid society. Already in the Buyid period there were forerunners of the mystical brotherhoods that would later become a significant feature of Near Eastern societies; and some of these early brotherhoods were well defined in membership and structure. Yet, in the Buyid period, these brotherhoods were still uncommon and had few analogues in the society around them. There is only a difference of emphasis and of style; but this difference is very evident, and forms part of the fascination of this subject for social historians.

Buyid society was characterized by the formality of certain ties between individuals, and the informality of ties within groups that are not composites of ties between individuals. The moral world in which such ties could sustain a resilient and self-renewing social order are described below in terms of loyalty, obligation, and leadership. The second and third chapters consider the forms of loyalty and obligation which, in the moral world as understood by the men of the Buyid period, made this resilient social order possible. The second chapter discusses acquired loyalties, forms of obligation that men acquired by deliberate acts and not through the ascription of those men to a category. Such acquired loyalties formed associations that were not intended to outlive the people who participated in them; and, in fact, acquired loyalties in the great majority of cases died with the people who acquired them. The third chapter discusses loyalties of category, loyalties that men felt they owed each other because of their common participation in categories that existed before they were born and would exist after they died. This chapter also considers the varieties and functions of leadership in such categories. The last chapter deals with a different sort of leader, the king; and suggests why kings, although standing largely outside the categories discussed earlier, may have been necessary to the social order as a whole. The remainder of the present chapter attempts to give an idea of the historical context in which the examples of later chapters should be understood.

Roughly two years before his death in 11/632, the Prophet Muḥammad made his last pilgrimage to Mecca. On this occasion he gave a moving (and often quoted) address to his followers, in the course of which he said, according to one source, "God has given two safeguards to the world: His Book [the Koran] and the *sunnah* [that is, example] of His Prophet [Muḥammad]." According to another source, Muḥammad said: "God has given two safeguards to the world: His Book and the family of His Prophet." Taken together, these two statements contain all the basic ingredients of Muḥammad's legacy for the future political life of his community: the Koran, the family of Muḥammad, and the example of Muḥammad. Yet the correct mix of these ingredients remained a subject of active (and sometimes bitter) disagreement among Muslims. Disputes over their relative importance reflected the variety of political positions among Muslims that developed in the three hundred years between the death of Muḥammad and the rise of the Buyid dynasty.[3]

Even before he led a political community, it had been clear to Muḥammad that the moral vision of Islam had political implications. Islam was a religion in which public life was very much a collective responsibility of the community, and the Koran provided regulations according to which the community should discharge the responsibility. When, for the last twelve years of his life, Muḥammad was the actual leader of a political community, the political aspect of Islamic belief was confirmed and extensively elaborated.

When Muḥammad died, the Islamic community no longer had a divinely inspired leader, and quarrels over choosing a new leader immediately broke out. These quarrels have so preoccupied most historians (Eastern and Western) that they have neglected the gradual emergence of a remarkable unanimity among Muslims on an issue even more fundamental than the choice of a successor to Muḥammad: the consensus of Muslims in the original centers of Islam in Arabia that the community should have a single leader. They agreed that the community of believers should neither be divided into separate Muslim political communities (like the separate Christian and Jewish political communities), nor accept some form of collective leadership, such as a governing council. In the decade after Muḥammad's death, the Muslims of the Ḥijāz thoroughly defeated separatist movements in Arabia, after which the great majority of Muslims everywhere and for centuries after accepted the idea that the Muslim community (*ummah*) should be politically unified under a single leader. This unity of the *ummah* and of its leadership was in perfect agreement with the character of the Islamic revelation. In the view of Muslims, God had revealed in Islam a moral law intended for all mankind, and the vehicle of this revelation was a single man (Muḥammad) who lived a life of exemplary obedience to that law. Muḥammad, the single vehicle of revelation and perfect example, had maintained a unified community under his sole leadership. After his death, Muslims quite naturally felt that his example of single leadership should be followed.

The Muslim community also agreed on the status of the Koran, the first "safeguard" that Muḥammad had left for his community. The Koran is, in the belief of Muslims, the infallible word of God. The earlier revelations that are described in Jewish and Christian scripture have been distorted through time, and were never intended to have the completeness of Islam. The Koran is the undistorted revelation in which, as God tells the believers in the Koran itself, "I have perfected your religion for you and completed My favor (or 'benefit,' *ni'mah*) to you" (5:3). But the Koran discussed leadership in general terms. It gave no direct indication as to how a new leader should be chosen, although later commentators constructed many and conflicting interpretations of the implications of Koranic verses for this question.

If the agreement of the Islamic community on the status of the Koran did not solve the constitutional problem of succession to leadership, it did guarantee the central importance of the Koran for Islamic culture. The most complete revelation must have implicit in it something of relevance for every human situation; and most Muslim thinkers sought to make some connection between their ideas and the contents of the Koran. It is also important for the purposes of this book to notice the linguistic formalism that can be built on a scripturalist tradition in which an immutable text lies at the heart of religious study. In the society discussed in this book, the formalism of the language in which personal ties were contracted and subsequently described was in conscious agreement with the universal desire to refer moral questions to the words of the Koran.

The second safeguard left for the Muslim community was the *sunnah* of the Prophet. If there was widespread agreement as to the importance of the *sunnah*, there was equally widespread disagreement as to its contents. The word *sunnah* means customary practice; and in the context of Muḥammad's speech quoted above, it means the practice established by the example of Muḥammad (and, to a lesser extent, by his closest companions, who were presumed to be most deeply influenced by him). The Koran may have been comparable to the Christian Logos in its role and its preternatural perfection; but the Koran did not directly legislate for all circumstances, and the Koran was a book, not a person. Muḥammad was the perfect example of a Muslim; and his example, therefore, was a nearly indispensable guide to living the life of a Muslim and to making the implicit concepts of the Koran explicit.

This example was known to later generations through *ḥadīth*. The word *ḥadīth* is often translated "tradition," and is explained as a report of a saying or action of Muḥammad. But *ḥadīth* is more than this; it is the body of accounts of what Muḥammad said and did, what was done in his presence and not forbidden by him, and even includes some of the sayings and doings of his close companions. It is, in effect, all the historical material available to establish the *sunnah*. To draw another analogy with Christianity, from the point of view of many Muslims the Gospels are a form of Christian *ḥadīth* about Jesus.[4]

The *sunnah*, therefore, was very much a "safeguard" to the community. It gave the Islamic community a means for extending the teachings of Islam, and it assumed an underlying unity in these teachings. It assumed this unity not only because an extensive spiritual and ethical system needs some degree of harmony between its parts, but also because reverence for the *sunnah* meant that such extensions would, if at all possible, be traced to a single historical source, the life of the Prophet and his closest companions. The study of the Koran had primacy over the study of *ḥadīth*; but anyone who has looked at the earliest extant Koran commentaries knows that in the first two Islamic centuries the greater part of such commentary consisted of *ḥadīth*. Together, the study of Koran and *ḥadīth* gave a further unity of focus for future Islamic cultures, because Arabic philology developed in large part out of a desire to understand the sometimes difficult and often elliptical language of Koran and *ḥadīth*. As a result, wherever there were Muslim men of learning they cultivated the so-called "Arabic sciences" as an integral part of religious learning.

A body of material so important and so lacking in boundaries could not pass through history unmolested. *Ḥadīth* appeared that were generally thought to be forgeries; and the "science" or "knowledge" (*'ilm*) of *ḥadīth*, which studied the validity of *ḥadīths*, developed gradually but with ever growing elaboration over the first four centuries of the Islamic era. *Ḥadīth* was the central ingredient of religious "knowledge" (*'ilm*) and, consequently, ulema (Arabic *'ulamā'*, "knowers" of religious knowledge, from the root *'ilm*) were above all knowers of Koran and *ḥadīth*. The knowledge or science of *ḥadīth* involved a careful study of the chain or *isnād* of transmitters through which a *ḥadīth* had been handed down from a companion of Muḥammad to the generation of the scholar; and gatherings to transmit *ḥadīth* were probably the most common occasions on which ulema met together in formal meetings. Only in the fifth Islamic century does the study of *ḥadīth* seem to have decreased in its importance among the religious sciences. By this time, *isnāds* were becoming impossibly long, and there was increasing consensus as to which written *ḥadīth* collections were reliable. Moreover, other religious sciences had been more fully elaborated. For example, the implications, or pseudo implications, of *ḥadīth* for law had been distilled into law books, and however much early law and *ḥadīth* may have been intertwined, scholars—especially if they wanted a career involving law—could hardly study their subject without making the law books their principal concern.

The third "safeguard" was the family of Muḥammad. Neither of the other two safeguards was the cause of so much disagreement as was this one. Some believed that Muḥammad intended his family to succeed him in leadership of the community, and saw in this safeguard the only correct understanding of Koran and *sunnah*; for how could there be agreement in interpreting the Koran and the *sunnah* without the (possibly infallible) leadership of a member of this family? Others saw in this legitimist attitude a denial of the whole rationale of the *sunnah*. If the *sunnah* was the example of Muḥammad as reported by his close companions and confirmed by the subsequent actions of these companions, how could anyone claim that the reports and actions of these companions should be radically discounted unless confirmed by the interpretation and example of leaders from Muḥammad's family?

At the death of Muḥammad, the family-centered theory of leadership looked to 'Alī, Muḥammad's cousin and son-in-law, as the obvious successor (*khalīfah* or caliph) to the Prophet. 'Alī had been one of the very earliest (possibly the earliest male) to accept Muḥammad's message. He was, moreover, the adopted son of Muḥammad and, through his marriage to Fāṭimah, he was father of Muḥammad's only grandsons to grow to maturity, al-Ḥasan and al-Ḥusain. However, at the death of Muḥammad, the majority of Muslims did not accept the family-centered theory. The advocates of the family said that because the other companions of Muḥammad wanted the leadership, these companions chose to disregard the obvious claims of 'Alī and the expressed intention of Muḥammad that the descendants of 'Alī themselves should take over the leadership.

In contrast, the majority of Muslims did not believe that Muḥammad had clearly designated 'Alī as his successor, or that 'Alī was a choice clearly superior to other close companions of Muḥammad. 'Alī did not press his claims, but after the third caliph or "successor" was killed, many Muslims accepted 'Alī as the new caliph. The death of 'Alī's predecessor, however, had marked the beginning of the first civil war in Islam; and 'Alī was swept into this civil war without being able to bring it to an end. 'Alī, in turn, was killed in 41/661, and the successorship or caliphate passed away from his branch of Muḥammad's family.

The descendants of 'Alī, or 'Alids, as they will be called below, continued to play an important role in the Islamic world. Even those who rejected 'Alī's claim to be the appointed successor of Muḥammad revered the 'Alids for the family ties that had distinguished their ancestors. In fact, because most of them were descended from al-Ḥasan and al-Ḥusain, the sons of 'Alī and Fāṭimah, they were through their mother lineal descendants of Muḥammad himself. Most Muslims considered it a religious duty to show the 'Alids signs of their great respect, signs that sometimes included gifts of money. Therefore, even 'Alids who did not claim any special right to the caliphate had a certain advantage in seeking political power; and there have been many 'Alid kings in Islamic history, including the present King Hasan of Morocco and King Husain of Jordan. A *ḥadīth* of the Prophet says: "Every bond of relationship and consanguinity will be severed on the day of resurrection except mine." We will discuss this bond again in the chapter on loyalties of category.[5]

There were always 'Alids, however, who regarded the honor of their ancestry not as a possible focus for the reverence of other Muslims, but as a positive claim for their political allegiance. The supporters of these 'Alid claimants were called *shī'atu 'Alī* or "the party of 'Alī"; hence they became known to Muslims as Shī'īs. Shī'ism was in the first instance based on a political claim; and for one branch of Shī'īs, the Zaidīs, the political claim continues to be the most important element of belief that distinguishes them from non-Shī'īs. The Zaidīs believe that any 'Alid who personally and militarily seeks the leadership of the Islamic community, and has the religious learning necessary for leadership, can be the caliph. The recent rulers of the northern Yemen, the Imams, are such leaders. The Zaidī theory recognizes that two or more 'Alids may make such a claim to leadership simultaneously. But the principle of unified rule is preserved in that, if the territories of two Zaidī 'Alid leaders come close enough to be in effective contact, one of them must resign (or be forced to resign) leadership in favor of the other.

In the earliest Islamic period these political claims seem to have been the most important element in Shī'ism; but claims to spiritual leadership soon came to be of central importance to a large group of Shī'īs. As was discussed above, such claims allowed the Shī'īs to maintain a unified view of religious life by making a single 'Alid leader the authoritative standard for the interpretation of legal, political, metaphysical, and all other matters. It was also natural that some branches of Shī'ism should emphasize the spiritual leadership of their leaders because, in most cases, real political leadership remained in the hands of non-Shī'īs. Many Shī'īs, therefore, came to distinguish between caliphate—actual political leadership—and imamate—the theoretical right to leadership. Muslims in their collective daily prayer stand behind an imam who leads them and is the model for their movements; and where an imam is not officially appointed by the government, any group of Muslims is supposed to defer to the "best" among them as imam. The overall leader of authority and model for the Islamic community was, in the view of the Shī'īs, an 'Alid, who was also called "imam" in this more particular sense. The Shī'īs held that the imam should also be caliph, though circumstances might prevent him from attaining this office. Even if he passed his life in unrelieved obscurity, the one God-given imam for any period was, in the view of his followers, the only real authority for the spiritual and political life of his age.

After a few generations, there were hundreds of descendants of 'Alī. If only one of them could be the imam (and, it was hoped, the caliph), which one should it be? As we have seen, the Zaidī answer was both clear and confusing—the imam was any learned 'Alid who was militarily successful in claiming leadership. But other Shī'īs laid much more emphasis than the Zaidīs on the imam's role as authoritative interpreter, and they therefore sought to explain the presence of this authority as the result of something more than individual initiative. Most Shī'īs other than Zaidīs felt that the 'Alid imam could be identified because he had directly inherited his station and/or had been specifically designated by his predecessor.

Neither of these principles, however, could induce agreement among the non-Zaidī Shī'īs. Inheritance was essential to the overall claim of the 'Alids, and the line of imams most widely recognized by present-day Shī'īs is a line in which the imamate usually passed to the eldest son. Yet the principle of primogeniture was never very strong in the Islamic Near East; and even in this widely recognized line, the imamate passed from al-Ḥasan ('Alī's eldest son by Fāṭimah, Muḥammad's daughter) to al-Ḥusain (the second eldest son by this mother). Specific designation proved just as unreliable a means of guaranteeing an undisputed succession. Most non-Zaidī 'Alid claimants to the imamate kept such claims secret or, at least, were wise enough not to discuss them publicly, for these claims implied a challenge to the existing non-Shī'ī leadership, especially to the non-'Alid caliphs. Therefore, specific designation was almost never performed publicly, and the claims of any supposed designee were hard to establish. As most such designations seem to have been made orally by the dying imam in his last hours, their authenticity was almost inevitably suspect to some of the followers who had not been present.

It is not surprising, then, that Shī'īs often disagreed as to which 'Alid was the imam. It is also not surprising that frequently, after the apparent death of an imam, some of his followers held either that he had not really died, or that his successor was living in such perfect secrecy that even those close to him did not know of his station. 'Alid pretenders had been repeatedly defeated, and God had allowed their opponents to continue in power. Therefore, some Shī'īs were not at all astonished to hear that their imam had not died, but disappeared, and would reappear in the fullness of time to become, with divine aid, the actual ruler of the Islamic community.

The most important instance of such an interruption to a line of visible imams took place in 260/873, when the eleventh imam in succession from 'Alī through al-Ḥusain died in Iraq. Some of his followers held that he was succeeded by his infant son, the twelfth imam, who had disappeared to return as a messianic figure. The Shī'īs who awaited the return of this twelfth imam were called "Twelvers." The "Twelvers" changed their allegiance from a visible to an unseen imam at a juncture in Islamic history when, as we shall see, divisions had forever destroyed the political unity of the Islamic *ummah*, and the caliphs who still ruled the core of the former empire, Iraq and surrounding territories, were being murdered periodically by their Turkish palace guard. It was a good moment for the Twelvers to put aside their aspirations for worldly power. Moreover, non-Shī'ī Muslims were willing to tolerate the Twelvers more than they did most other Shī'ī groups, especially if the Twelvers had no immediately present candidate for the caliphate. At present the majority of the inhabitants of Iran and southern Iraq are Twelvers.

While Shī'īs, deprived of power, were evolving a variety of political theories, historical events were hammering out the political theory of the non-Shī'īs. Later Muslims would look back and call these early non-Shī'ī Muslims Sunnīs or *ahl as-sunnah*, as most non-Shī'īs came to be called in a later period. In the early Muslim world, however, there were two groups of Muslims, the Shī'īs and the Khārijīs (or Khawārij), who had strongly held definite positions on succession to the caliphate. For the other Muslims, events moved faster than theory, and their theory was to a large extent an explanation of events and a reaction to the more exclusive political theories of the Shī'īs and Khārijīs. Only later did this initially less well-defined theory become the basis of conscious sectarian self-definition. Sunnism, the sect of Islam espoused by the great majority of present-day Muslims, was the historicist solution to the problems presented by Muḥammad's death; and the shape of this historicist solution only emerged when the Islamic community had lived through a sufficiently long historical experience.

On the day of Muḥammad's death, after heated discussion, a large meeting in Muḥammad's capital city of Medina chose Abū Bakr as his successor; and in token of their choice, each of them swore a *bai'ah*, an oath of allegiance to Abū Bakr.

Abū Bakr had a measure of authority among Muslims because of his very long and close association with Muḥammad. He was, for example, Muḥammad's father-in-law, and had been appointed by the Prophet to be the prayer leader (imam) in his place during his illness. Just as important was Abū Bakr's membership in the tribe of Quraish, the tribe that ruled the nearby city of Mecca. Mecca was the most important city of the region; it had only recently been won to Islam, and had traditionally exercised leadership among the tribes of the region. The next day, when the Meccans heard that a fellow Meccan of Quraish had been chosen as caliph, they accepted the choice. These historical events were later to become fundamental points of reference for *sunnī* political theory.

In Medina, several further choices of caliph by discussion and/or acclamation followed; it was a procedure familiar from the practice of Arab tribes in Islam, and sanctioned by a verse in the Koran that said, "[Better and more enduring is the reward of God] to those who obey their Lord, attend to their prayers, and conduct their affairs by consultation" (40:38). No clear precedent for the method of consultation emerged in these early choices of caliph, and the Islamic world was soon plunged into a civil war that ended, after the murder of 'Alī, with the victory of the Umayyads, a clan of Muḥammad's tribe, the Quraish. The Umayyads set up the first successful hereditary succession to the caliphate, though their right to this succession was not uncontested.

Finally, in the 130s of the Islamic era, another family of the tribe of Quraish, the descendants of Muḥammad's uncle al-'Abbās, defeated the Umayyads and assumed the dignity of the caliphate. From their capital in Baghdad, they ruled virtually all of the Islamic world except Spain, which passed into the hands of a descendant of the Umayyads. The 'Abbāsids tried to win the support of the ulema by their extensive patronage of religious learning. Even if they did not claim the infallibility that was attributed to various 'Alid leaders, the

'Abbāsids hoped to be accepted as the spiritual guides of the Islamic community. Despite the caliphs' vacillating support of conflicting views of orthodoxy, however, the great majority of Muslims refused to concede to the 'Abbāsid caliphs any special authority to regulate such matters. Yet their patronage of learning and their ostentatious use of religious symbols made the 'Abbāsid caliphate itself a religious symbol. Therefore, as we will see, Muslims who had lost any desire to obey the 'Abbāsids nevertheless defended the principle that the 'Abbāsid caliphs should, even if deprived of executive power, be maintained as a symbol of legitimate government and of unity among Muslims.

That the 'Abbāsids should lose actual control of an empire stretching from the Atlantic to Central Asia was hardly surprising. More surprising is the frequency with which both the 'Abbāsids and their usurpers agreed to cover each loss with the fiction that the caliph had kept full theoretical sovereignty over the province while granting actual control to the usurper. In token of this sovereignty, the actual ruler (often called an emir or "commander") had the name of the reigning 'Abbāsid caliph mentioned in the Friday congregational prayer and on the coinage. By the fourth/tenth century, these rulers (including the *Buyids*) called themselves "kings" (singular: *mālik*), a title that had been used in the pre-Islamic period. Because of the pagan associations of kingship, the caliphs had always sought to disassociate themselves from this title, and kingship and caliphate continued to have separate existences. In exchange for the recognition offered by an emir, the 'Abbāsid caliph often (but not invariably) sent a diploma investing the emir with the right to rule his territories. Among the many advantages offered by this exchange of formalities was that it recognized the continuing agreement of most Muslims to the principles that had prevailed after the selection of the first caliph Abū Bakr, namely, an agreement that there was not nor could there be a plurality of Islamic communities. There was one Islamic community, by definition a unity of all

Muslims; and the symbol of its unity was the single leader, the "successor" or caliph of the Prophet.

If the ruler was the personal symbol of the unity of the Islamic community, the principle that symbolized the will to unity was *ijmāʿ*, which means "consensus" or agreement. Both Shīʿīs and those groups who later came to be called Sunnīs accepted the validity of the famous *ḥadīth* that "my community (*ummah*) will never agree upon an error." The theory of most Shīʿī groups in some sense anticipated the basic political needs of the Islamic community, and provided a precise means for their complete fulfillment: the community needed an ʿAlid leader chosen according to a definite principle, and considered this leader to be the most authoritative interpreter of Islam for his age. Most non-Shīʿīs believed that God had intended that the leader of the Islamic community be chosen by some sort of consultative process. Beyond that, they did not agree as to the procedure to be used in this consultative process, or the scope of the authority of a leader so chosen. They believed in the historical mission of the community, which in the long term would not "agree upon an error."

Early Muslims realized that the military achievement of the Islamic community was little short of miraculous. For some, the "miracle" of these successes must have been proof of the correctness of their leadership in this period. Even if it were not accepted as confirmation of this leadership, the military achievement seemed to many Muslims too valuable a gain to risk in uncertain struggles for new leadership. Therefore, both for practical reasons and to live within the religious injunction to consensus, they accepted leadership that was not necessarily the "best" that the Islamic community could provide. They felt that unity was more important than purity, and that no leader or other individual could by himself establish the norms for the Islamic community, since they were an extension of the norms of all of the close companions of Muḥammad. It cannot have been clear to Muslims in the period immediately after Muḥammad's death how Muslims should treat variations in these extensions of the *sunnah*. Gradually, however, it became clear that *ijmā'* was one way of judging such variation. Interpretations of Islam that did not allow themselves to be judged by *ijmā'* could not, of course, be accepted within this framework.

In general, consensus-minded Muslims were more prone to inclusion than exclusion, to postponement rather than haste, and remained close to the spirit of the famous saying of St. Thomas à Kempis that "man proposes but God disposes." In areas not unambiguously discussed in the Koran, men would act and suggest how other men should act according to their understanding of Islam; and the long-term judgment of the Islamic community would judge whether their actions and injunctions were appropriate models for future Muslims. The reception of moral principle was similar to the reception of *ḥadīth*: anyone could elaborate the norms of Islam or transmit *ḥadīth*, but only the collective judgment of the Islamic community could accept a *ḥadīth* as genuine or accept that a principle was truly in the spirit of Islam.

For a long time, this attitude of consensus-minded Muslims corresponded with the shared political and economic interests of Muslims. For over two centuries, Muslims were a minority in their new empire. At first, their law and theology were far from being fully elaborated. More particularly, they had, as we have seen, only very general principles to guide them in developing a constitutional theory. Various legal and theological positions did, of course, appear in these early centuries. If factions had succeeded in persuading the majority of Muslims that they must choose a position and fight to impose this position on other Muslims, the Islamic empire might well have shrunk back to the wastes of Arabia from which it had sprung. The privileged Muslim minority did recognize its shared interests well enough to stay and prosper.

Moreover, Islam, in the view of most of its followers, was more a religion of orthopraxis than of orthodoxy. Four of the five "pillars" of Islam, often listed as the fundamental principles of the Islamic faith, are things one should do, not ideas one should believe. To preserve a unified Islamic community, consensus-minded Muslims demanded considerable uniformity in the public acts demanded of Muslims in the Koran, and avoidance of open contradiction to the explicit teachings of the Koran. For the rest, they usually allowed variation and did not seek to anticipate the judgment of history.

Through the collective judgment of the Islamic community, and especially of the ulema, history did slowly but ineluctably render its judgment. There was not then, nor has there ever since been, a consensus even on the method for consensus. Was the *ijmāʿ* the consensus among the people of Medina, or among the ulema, or among all Muslims? The emergence of widely accepted views, in spite of the vagueness and variableness in the definition of *ijmāʿ*, shows how strongly Muslims were determined to maintain some degree of unity. Often this consensus was achieved by virtue of allowing that a limited variety of positions was acceptable on certain questions. Accordingly, differing schools of law arose that came (sometimes reluctantly) to accept each other.

The consensus-minded scholars were able to preserve the sense that they were working within a shared tradition only by continual backward glances at the particular strand of that tradition which they were elaborating. Hence the strong piety of each school of elaboration toward its founders (often *ḥadīth* scholars), and toward the companions of Muḥammad whose practice became a common reference point for these schools. This piety had actually increased as the period of the companions receded into the remote past, and as the study of *ḥadīth* became more elaborately scientific in its attempts to link each *ḥadīth* with a known companion.

Only after considerable historical experience could *ijmāʿ* create distinctive positions for the consensus-minded Muslims. Agreement as to the canonical body of *ḥadīth*, the *sunnah* in its strictest sense, was an essential element in the evolution of a defined Sunnism; but such agreement was slow in coming. For example, of the six books of *ḥadīth* that are supposedly canonical to Sunnīs, the *Sunan* of Ibn Mājah (d. A.H. 209) began to be accepted as canonical only in the fifth century A.H. North African Muslims seem never to have accepted it as canonical, yet they remained Sunnīs both in their own view and in the view of Near Eastern Muslims. In its treatment of *ḥadīth*, as in so many other respects, the more clearly defined and sectarian Sunnism of later generations emerged only gradually, and was far from being fully developed in the period discussed in this book.[6]

Another supposed mark of a defined Sunnism is the doctrine that there were four and only four schools of law acceptable to Sunnīs. This doctrine is based on the contention that the individual right to bring new ideas into Islamic law by interpreting Koran and *ḥadīth* ceased in the late third century, when the founders of the four schools and a handful of their most important followers had died. In the classic phrase of the Muslim lawyers, the "gate" of individual interpretation had closed. While it is true that Muslim lawyers of the late third/ninth century were increasingly persuaded that there was no more room for individual reasoning on the law, it is also true that they were not agreed as to which of the existing schools were "canonical," and would not agree for centuries. In Syria, the law school of al-Auzāʿī was predominant until the end of the fourth century A.H., and still existed in the fifth century. Its followers no doubt regarded themselves, and were widely accepted, as *ahl as-sunnah*, even though their school disappeared so that it could not be included in the canonical four. The school of Dā'ūd b. ʿAlī b. Khalaf (d. A.H. 270) or Ẓāhirīs and the school of aṭ-Ṭabarī (d. A.H. 310) were founded during or shortly after the period in which the "gate" of individual interpretation was closed. Both schools found influential supporters in the fourth century, and the followers of both schools regarded themselves and were often accepted as *ahl as-sunnah*. By the sixth century, these three schools of law were virtually dead. As with the six books of *ḥadīth*, the definition of legal Sunnī orthodoxy reflects a body of opinion which, growing in the fourth and fifth centuries A.H., solidified in the sixth century A.H.

In becoming more rigid, Sunnism retrospectively established an early date in the Islamic period as the end of the period in which certain kinds of creative speculation were permissible to qualified scholars. We should not confuse the time in which the view was adapted with the dates that were subsequently chosen to mark the end of a classical age. Many of the Muslims who lived in the fourth and early fifth centuries A.H., the period discussed in this book, believed that they lived in a period in which the canon of acceptable law schools and *ḥadīth* was not closed. It was, in other words, a period in which Sunnism was still loosely defined, and tended to be more inclusive than it became in later periods.

There were, however, many reasons why there should be a constant movement toward tighter definition of what was or was not acceptable to the *ahl as-sunnah*. With the passage of time, Sunnism became rigid simply because the collective judgment of the Muslim community had established positions on a great number of issues. But the historical circumstances of the Muslim community were an even greater incentive to delimit a Sunnī form of Islam. When the ʿAbbāsid caliphs lost actual control of vast provinces of the Islamic empire, it became clear that the Muslims could not rely on a central government to preserve a community of belief among Muslims. To confuse matters further, most of the new regimes of the fourth century were *Shīʿī*. And most of them were founded by men from peripheral areas of the Near East, nomads or mountain dwellers, who had little interest in the fine points of the religion of their city-dwelling subjects. The *ahl as-sunnah* saw that in the presence of alien and occasionally hostile governments they had to rely largely on themselves to preserve the achievement of earlier consensus-minded Muslims, and to prevent deviant speculation from pulling the community in so many directions that it would be irretrievably rent. An increasing number of scholars therefore sought to find an inclusive but clear definition of the boundaries of Sunnism.

They were spurred on in this effort by the activities of the Ismā'īlī Shī'īs and the Ḥanbalī Sunnīs. Other forms of Shī'ism were, compared to Ismā'īlism, ideologically benign. Zaidī Shī'ism was in most respects similar to Sunni Islam, except that it reserved the imamate-caliphate for descendants of 'Alī. By claiming that its leader had disappeared, Twelver Shī'ism left the confused and dangerous field of late third-century caliphal politics. The Ismā'īlī branch of the Shī'īs, however, refused to bury their claim. A successful Ismā'īlī rebellion in Tunisia gave a living 'Alid control of an important segment of the Islamic world. In 358 his descendants conquered Egypt, where the Fāṭimids, as this 'Alid dynasty came to be known, ruled until the middle of the sixth century A.H.

The Fāṭimids assumed the title of caliph, and claimed the doctrinal authority granted to the 'Alid Imam by most forms of Shī'ism. For the first time, this kind of Shī'ism had the support of a government; and law codes, works of theology, and other expressions of this interpretation of Islam poured forth from the pens of Fāṭimid supporters in Cairo. The Ismā'īlī Fāṭimids also had a carefully organized propaganda service; and their agents were amazingly successful in establishing clandestine groups of Ismā'īlīs throughout the Islamic Near East. The elaborate definition of this form of Shī'ism; the direct challenge of its leader's assumption of the title caliph, in open opposition to the 'Abbāsid caliphate, the symbol of consensus-minded Islam; and its successful missionary activity—all these things forced the non-Shī'īs to define their attitude toward the Shī'īs, and so to become, in their own turn, more sectarian.

The Ḥanbalīs were ready to answer this challenge even before the Fāṭimids appeared. Ḥanbalism is a school of law and of theology. The Ḥanbalīs insisted on finding *ḥadīth* solutions to questions whenever possible. Correspondingly, they insisted that the close companions of Muḥammad were all to be respected, and Ḥanbalīs were horrified that the Shī'īs should denounce some of the companions while venerating 'Alī in what was, to their mind, a pagan spirit. In the seat of the caliphate, Baghdad, Ḥanbalism became a genuinely popular movement, in part because it seemed to offer a remedy for the decline of the Sunnī caliphate and the related fortunes of its capital. Ḥanbalīs felt that Muslims should take individual action to combat innovations introduced into the Islamic community since the time of the Companions. In early fourth-century Baghdad, the Ḥanbalīs were the most active of all religious groups in mounting popular demonstrations which, since they were often directed against other religious groups (the followers of Ṭabarī, Shī'īs, and so on), did a great deal to sharpen the boundaries between religious groups.[7]

Fear of sharpened boundaries and annoyance at Ḥanbalī agitation drove the 'Abbāsid caliph himself to compromise the inclusive spirit of consensus-minded Islam. In A.H. 322, because of "their imposing conditions on people" and causing unrest, the caliph issued a rescript (*tauqī'*) declaring that if the Ḥanbalīs persisted, he would use fire and sword against them. Significantly, the decree accuses them of "ascribing unbelief and error to the party (*shī'ah*) of the Prophet's family." The decree implicitly contrasts the Ḥanbalīs with the great majority of Muslims, who only called each other unbelievers in extraordinary circumstances. Ḥanbalī thinkers would probably have rejected the charge that they called Shī'īs unbelievers; but their attitude to anything that they regarded as deviation from Islam was so severe that it may well have seemed to their victims as if they had been treated as unbelievers.[8]

Ismā'īlism and Ḥanbalism, therefore, had a definite role in creating the more sharply defined Sunnism of later centuries; but such definition was slow in coming, and did not fully arrive until the Saljūqs conquered the kingdoms of the Buyids. The period discussed in this book was a century and a half of flux between two relatively clear and, in the view of later

Muslims, classical Sunnī views on the relation of government and society. As we have seen, the Buyid kings were preceded by the 'Abbāsid caliphs, whose empire at one time encompassed almost the whole Islamic world, and who claimed a degree of religious authority over all Muslims. The Buyids were followed by the Saljūq dynasty of the late fifth/eleventh and sixth/twelfth centuries, whose government reunited western Asia in an empire over which, however, the Saljūqs exercised a looser authority than the 'Abbāsids.

Government and society may have changed as rapidly and as significantly in the late 'Abbāsid and early Saljūq periods as they did in the Buyid period. In both the 'Abbāsid and the Saljūq periods, however, scholars of Islamic law and experts in administration wrote accounts of the government of those periods that were considered classical points of reference for many later generations in the Islamic Near East. Since the rulers of both governments were *ahl as-sunnah*, both the 'Abbāsid and Saljūq views on the relation of government and society were classical to Sunnīs, and had an important influence on Shī'ī political theory, as well. The Buyid period stood between these two classical points of reference, and never achieved the prestige of either its successor or predecessor. It was subsequently seen, and is still seen, as a period of transition.

We have already described the 'Abbāsid definition of a world of political and social ideas guided by an imam-caliph, an ideal that had been most fully elaborated in the third century, and then disappeared with the failure of 'Abbāsid government in the early fourth century. By the last half of the fifth century, a period often called the Sunnī revival, a new definition was emerging to suit the new Saljūq rulers of western Asia. In this new definition, the ruler was called by a new title, sultan. While the sultan was the protector of Islam both as an orthodoxy and as a territorial entity, he could not claim that he was delegating power to his inferiors, as the imam-caliph had claimed. For example, the men whom the sultan appointed as judges were often, in name, not the delegates of the sultan but of the 'Abbāsid caliph, who was maintained partly to lend his name to such appointments by the sultan. The sultan was in this sense an arbiter and not a guide for the society he ruled.

There was another sense in which the Saljūq sultan was more of an arbiter than a guide: he was less able than the caliph to decree a change in anyone's social position. The 'Abbāsid ruler, as imam-caliph, could in theory raise men to honored positions and strip them of these honors, according to his wish. By the Saljūq period, people were less dependent on recognition from the ruler for their social position, and the ruler was consequently more restricted in the number of possible candidates for any appointive position. This difference, of course, is only relative; inherited distinctions of position and honor were far more numerous in 'Abbāsid society than in American society today, and there was far more social mobility among the subjects of the Saljūqs than would have been allowable in the system prescribed by the Brahman lawgiver, Manu. The change was, nevertheless, discernible in several areas of life.

We have said that Buyid society was characterized by the formality of ties between individuals, and the informality of ties within groups that were not mere chains of such individual ties. In this respect, as well, the Buyid period saw a transition in the spheres in which formality or informality was thought to be appropriate. We have already given a brief sketch of the first three hundred years of Islamic political theory, and an even briefer sketch of the actual evolution of central government in the same period. As we have seen, theory sometimes tried to justify historical experience, but was made less flexible by the weight of these justifications. The evolution of actual governmental practices continued at a more rapid pace. There was an increasing rigidity in many of the religiously sanctioned forms of proper public and private behavior. In private life, these forms continued to be widely used for their original purposes. But in public life, they were increasingly used not for their original purposes, but to indicate the continued respect by the user for the private application of Islamic forms. It was partly for this reason that Buyid society showed a formality of ties between individuals and an informality of ties within groups.

In the Buyid period, the collapse of many Islamic public institutions in their original sense was clear; but it was not immediately clear what the Islamic community would do in the face of this collapse. The 'Abbāsid caliphate was the most important of these public forms that ceased to have their original meaning. Should it be replaced by an existing counter-caliphate like that of the Fāṭimids, in which the caliph was an effective ruler? Should an 'Alid be given the military support that would create an effective Zaidī imamate in the central Islamic lands? Or was there a way in which the seeming rigidity of the law could become less rigid, or the letter of the law be preserved, while adapting its prescriptions to new circumstances?

These and many more solutions were advocated, but their advocates were treated with indifference by many of the Buyid rulers, who allowed a variety of constitutional theories to exist as long as no one attempted to put in practice any theory that would directly threaten Buyid rule. The Buyids, as we shall discuss below, were in some vague sense Shī'īs, but they preserved the 'Abbāsid caliphate in Baghdad for its value as a public symbol. Cynicism on such issues, which was shown not only by the Buyids but also by many Islamic dynasties that were their contemporaries, may have lost these rulers the respect of some of their morally punctilious subjects. But, in return, it allowed these subjects a latitude of patronage that few periods of the Islamic Near East could match. No single standard of religious orthodoxy, or even of taste, was imposed by these courts for the patronage that flowed to theologians, philosophers, astronomers, and men of every kind of written learning admired in this period. It is not surprising that Ibn Sīnā (Avicenna), whose impact on philosophy and medicine would be felt for centuries after his death in 428/1037, fled from eastern Iran when it was conquered by Maḥmūd the Ghaznavid, one of a new breed of sternly Sunnī rulers who appeared at the end of this period. Predictably, Ibn Sīnā sought refuge in the more tolerant courts of the Buyids and a like-minded dynasty in western Iran.

The tolerance of the Buyid courts was well suited to the broadmindedness characteristic of much of the intellectual life of this period. Numerous Arabic translations from classical philosophers had been made in a somewhat earlier period; and by the Buyid period, the Islamic philosophers (and some Arabic-speaking Christian and Jewish philosophers of the Near East) were fully at home in their own use of the analytical and speculative style that they found in these translations. Yet the works written by Muslim philosophers and theologians stood in uncertain relation to the central beliefs of most Muslims; Islamic speculative thought had not yet found those points of agreement that would give a common character to its later history.

It is often stated that this common character came at the beginning of the fourth century. A. J. Wensinck, for example, wrote that the theologian al-Ash'arī, who died in A.H. 324 at the very beginning of our period, "enjoys the credit of having overcome the antipathy of the older Muslim scholars to dialectic in articles of faith by his successful utilisation of it to combat the Mu'tazilites and the chiefs of other sects who were suspected of heresy. He is, therefore, the founder of orthodox scholasticism (*kalām*)." In his lifetime and in the century following, however, al-Ash'arī's right to this credit was very hotly disputed, and the antipathy of Muslim scholars to dialectic far from overcome. The leading, though never overwhelming, position of Ash'arism was the achievement of early Saljūq thinkers such as al-Juwainī (d. A.H. 478) and al-Ghazālī (d. A.H. 505). In the intervening century and a half, the "other sects," including Mu'tazilism, thrived and prospered; and systematic expositions of Islamic thought showed a variety that was seldom matched in subsequent periods.[9]

This wider, freer, and less directed discussion of theology and philosophy produced expressions of religious uncertainty that would also rarely be matched in subsequent periods. The polymath Abū Ḥaiyān at-Tauḥīdī makes Abū Sulaimān, one of the most influential thinkers of his period, express this uncertainty in a dialogue that is supposed to have taken place in the presence of Ibn Sa'dān, a vizier of the Buyid king of Iraq. When Abū Sulaimān was asked why he believed in Islam when he claimed that religious groups were all equal in their ability to defend their positions, he answered, "Because it has a veneration that belongs to no other [religion]. That is, [I feel this veneration because] I was born into it, raised in it, was nurtured on its sweetness, and have become accustomed to the practice of its followers. I am in the situation of a man who has entered the courtyard of a caravansary by day to seek a moment's shade, at a time when the sky was cloudless. The keeper of the caravansary brought him to an apartment without asking about his condition or health. In this situation he suddenly found that a cloud had blown up and released a downpour. The apartment leaked, so the occupant looked at the other apartments in the inn, and saw that they too were leaking. He saw mud in the courtyard of the building, and considered staying where he was and not moving to another apartment; [for, by remaining,] he could enjoy his ease and avoid getting his legs splattered by the thick mud and slime of the courtyard. [So] he was inclined to wait patiently in his apartment and stay in the situation in which he found himself. This man is like me: at the time of my birth I could not reason; then my parents brought me into this religion without my prior experience of it. Then, when I examined it closely, I found its ways to be like the ways of other religions. [However] I considered my staying in it patiently to be a more inviting course than my abandoning it, since I could leave it and become inclined to another [religion] only if I had some clear preference of choice for that [religion], and predilection for it over [my present religion]. Yet I have not found any proof in its favor without finding a like proof of another religion against it." No wonder this was the age of Abu 'l-'Alā al-Ma'arrī, the greatest skeptical poet of the Arab tradition, and of al-Bīrunī, the most impartial observer of non-Muslim societies in the pre-modern Islamic Near Eastern tradition.[10]

The vigor and variety of the cultural life of this century and a half caused Adam Mez, one of the most perceptive European historians of the pre-modern Islamic Near East, to call this period "the renaissance of Islam." If this description does not quite fit (what is being reborn?), no one would deny the great flowering of culture of his period, a flowering that produced not only Avicenna and al-Bīrūnī, but many of the other men known even to European medieval learning. Buyid rule did not produce these men, and it is unlikely that most Buyid rulers had any understanding of the works that they or their high officials patronized. Nevertheless, a writer of this period had a better chance of patronage because of the competition of many small courts that now offered patronage, in place of a single imperial court. Since no single standard of taste or religious orthodoxy could be imposed as the price of patronage, even if a ruler were not broad-minded, a writer who found that his views began to offend had only to travel a hundred miles or so to find a ruler whom his views might please. Furthermore, as we have seen, it was an age in which a man's standing was not as dependent on the recognition of the central government as it had been in the 'Abbāsid period, nor as inheritable as it would become in the Saljūq period. It was, therefore, an age in which men were presented with a somewhat wider variety of paths to recognition and patronage; and their great achievement shows the eagerness with which they pursued these paths.

Some historians would deny that the society of southern Iraq and western Iran flourished in the fourth and fifth centuries; they would maintain that it languished. And they would find support in the statements of many of the writers who lived in this period and thought themselves to be in a period of decline. For two hundred years after the collapse of the 'Abbāsids, Baghdad remained the most important center of Islamic religious thought. But this was a Baghdad severed from the prestige of imperial government, and from the vast territories whose revenues had sustained its luxuries and large population. Not only were imperial revenues lost, but so were the profits of the carrying trade from the countries bordering the Indian Ocean to the Mediterranean world; for this trade began to shift from the Persian Gulf route, which benefited Iraq, to the Red Sea route, which benefited Egypt. As we have discussed, implicit in the Islamic belief in the perfect example of Muḥammad's life and the very high example of the lives of his companions was a doctrine that the farther one moved away historically from the time of Muḥammad, the more diluted the influence of Muḥammad's example was likely to become. The scholars of Baghdad, sitting in view of the decayed palaces of the 'Abbāsids and the nearly empty quarters of their city, claimed that they saw the physical evidence that this doctrine was true. The still influential Iraqis had both regional and theological reasons to believe that the disappearance of actual government by an imam-caliph was yet another evidence of *fasād az-zamān*, "the [ever-growing] corruption brought by time"; and they reinforced the general tendency among Islamic religious scholars to accept this doctrine.

If the general Muslim community needed any confirmation of this corruption, the military successes of the Christian Byzantines against the Muslims seemed to offer such confirmation in the most dramatic form. The Byzantines had been on the defensive for so many generations that it was hard for Muslims to understand that the Islamic governments of northern Syria and northern Iraq were no match for their Christian opponents. For much of the tenth and early eleventh centuries, the Muslims of these areas were fighting desperate wars to prevent the ever-deeper penetration of Byzantine armies, one of which was reported to have gone as far as the outskirts of Palestine.

Western historians, impressed by the great interest of the Crusading movement to the European world, have often remarked on the comparatively subdued reaction of the Islamic sources to the arrival of the first Crusade in Palestine in A.D. 1096. When the Muslim chronicles for the preceding century are read, this subdued reaction can be easily understood: the violent shock had taken place a hundred and thirty years before the arrival of the Western European Crusaders. For the Byzantines, their wars against the Muslims were already a kind of Crusade, and the Western Crusaders believed that they came at the explicit invitation of the Byzantines, who had long claimed some special right to protect the Christians and Christian holy places of the Near East. The Muslim belief in the continuity of these wars with the Crusades was not, therefore, so very different from the Christian understanding of these events.

Many Muslims were probably first aware of the dramatic change in the fortunes of warfare with Byzantium in 351/962, when Aleppo was temporarily captured by the Byzantine emperor who, after nine days of pillaging, led ten thousand Muslim children into captivity. When the people of Baghdad heard what had happened in Aleppo, they went to the caliph's gates, raised a tumult, and demanded that the caliph write to all regions and gather armies. The powerless caliph could do little, of course, except appeal to the Buyid king, who was the actual ruler of Iraq. Alarm spread through the Islamic world, and in 352/963, six hundred Muslim volunteer fighters from Khurasan appeared in Mosul, which was also under threat of Byzantine attack.[11]

Worse was to come: in A.H. 354, the Byzantines permanently recaptured Tarsus, which had been in Muslim hands for over three hundred years, and turned the mosque into a stable. The following year an estimated twenty thousand Muslim volunteer warriors started on the twelve hundred-mile road from Khurasan to the Byzantine frontier, and rather unrealistically tried to bring along a number of elephants. The seriousness with which the Muslim volunteer warriors viewed the Byzantine advance is shown in their address to Rukn ad-Daulah, the Buyid ruler of Rayy, through whose territory they passed. They demanded the entire income from land tax of his kingdom, which, they said, had been collected only "for the treasury of the Muslims to be used if a disaster occurs; and there is no greater disaster than the ambition of the Byzantines and Armenians toward us, their conquest of our border strong points, and the inability of the Muslims to resist them." Not surprisingly, Rukn ad-Daulah refused to comply.[12]

Byzantines continued to make successful raids into Islamic territory for over a century, and their more successful campaigns were followed by violent riots in Baghdad, where the populace expressed the general indignation of Muslims that nothing was being done to restore to Islamic armies the advantage they had held in previous centuries. But no concerted Muslim reaction was forthcoming, and Muslim rulers near the border had to fend for themselves against their powerful Christian neighbor. The slender economic and military resources of more distant Muslim governments, such as the Buyids of Iraq and Iran, prevented them from taking over any of these border states; and all the governments of the period were too jealous of each other to cooperate effectively in a military effort against the Byzantines.

For many, these reverses were positive proof of the corruption brought by time, and they strengthened the resolve of most religious men to preserve the integrity of Islam and its intellectual unity in the face of divided government that was so ineffective against external enemies, as well as indifferent to them. Then, in the early fifth/eleventh century, the ardent Sunnī, Maḥmūd of Ghaznah, began his victorious campaigns from southeastern Iran into India. Maḥmūd's success at expanding the eastern boundaries of the Islamic world seemed to more partisan Sunnīs to be a confirmation that the corruption brought by time might to some degree be arrested if Shī'ī kings like the Buyids disappeared.[13]

The resolution sought by these more partisan Sunnīs was achieved in two senses by the Sunnī Saljūq Turks. First, the Saljūqs removed the remaining Buyid rulers in the mid-fifth/eleventh century. Next, the Central Asian Turkish warriors who formed the army of the Saljūqs defeated the Byzantines at Manzikert in 463/1071, a victory that put the Byzantines on the defensive and opened the center of Anatolia to Islamic conquest. As we have said, the resolution of the struggle on the Anatolian frontiers was only one chapter in the long struggle between Muslim and Christian powers in the Levant. A generation after Manzikert, Western Europeans came to the aid of the Byzantines; and after this event, Western Europe, Byzantium, and the Islamic powers were entangled in a seesaw of warfare in the Levant that was only ended by the Muslim conquests of Acre in 1291 and of Constantinople in 1453.

It was not only in military affairs that Buyid society appeared to languish in the fourth and fifth centuries; it also seemed to be reduced from the comparative prosperity of the preceding period to a hand-to-mouth existence. Again, the decline of Iraq makes this change seem disproportionately sharp. The Iraqis, as we have said, were harder hit than most areas by the collapse of empire and the change in trade routes. Yet the Iraqis were still the intellectual leaders in several fields of Islamic learning, and their complaints at the impoverishment of their province therefore occupy a disproportionately large portion of the literature that has survived from this period. They also felt more keenly than others that their poverty did not have the compensation of supporting an august and imposing government. Many Iraqis preferred to see an 'Abbāsid caliph squander their money in shows of imperial grandeur than to have a Buyid king squander it in endless and usually indecisive warfare against his relatives and equally petty neighbors.

Yet the change in the economic life of the whole area, including the still prosperous regions of western Iran, was not merely a projection of the Iraqi scholars. The Islamic caliphal empire had united gold- and silver-producing areas for a long period, which allowed the extensive use of a bimetallic currency of fixed standards of purity. With the loss of provinces, this union ceased, and the currency of the area went haywire. The political confusion of the late 'Abbāsid period had sufficiently disrupted supply routes to make prices fluctuate violently. As gold and silver began to fluctuate equally violently in their supply, in their comparative value, and in the standard of purity at which they were struck into coins, Buyid governments had to find a way to buy services that would not financially harm the government or cause the seller of such services to flee from fear of an exaggerated loss.

Their solution was to make extensive use of the *iqṭā'* (plural: *iqṭā'āt*), a financial arrangement in which government revenues were assigned to specific employees or pensioners of the government. Since the largest part of the government's revenues came from taxes on agriculture, assignments of income from the *kharāj* or land tax made up the largest category of *iqṭā'āt*. However, virtually any governmental source of income could be assigned as an *iqṭā'āt*, even water rights or rights of access. Through these assignments, the government was freed from the burden of anticipating fluctuations in currency. These assignments were for a short period, usually a year, so that some degree of government control was preserved. The Buyids made extensive use of *iqṭā'āt* before any other Near Eastern Islamic regime, partly because they were in an area very severely affected by the monetary crisis of the fourth/tenth century. The system may have had its origins in this monetary crisis, but it was so well suited to the post-'Abbāsid style of decentralized government, and to the aspirations of military regimes, that it continued to exist in the Near East in various forms for nearly a millennium after the Buyids came to power. Regimes founded by military leaders were, of course, pleased to put soldiers more directly in charge of the revenue of the state.

Economic life in the nongovernmental sphere in this period showed a somewhat different pattern of formality and informality from the one discussed above. Open-ended formal commitments were rare; in general, businesses did not have employees, and landlords did not have serfs. Long-term informal commitment, however, was common. If a business contracted with a porter or broker to do a specific job, that business would be likely to use that porter or broker whenever the need arose, often without looking for a cheaper source of services. More permanent ties of subordination would probably have required a stable hierarchy of individuals and groups; but, as will be discussed in the next two chapters, a very different system of hierarchy existed. These informal but long-term forms of subordination were sometimes reinforced by the enchainment of debt; not only did the farmer owe the landowner and the retailer owe the wholesaler, but the ordinary man made many of his purchases on credit, and settled up only periodically.

If the fourth/tenth and early fifth/eleventh century was one of the great creative periods of Near Eastern intellectual history, no people seem less likely candidates to preside over this cultural efflorescence than the Dailamīs, the people from whom the Buyid dynasty and their original armies were drawn. Dailam was a region of the rugged mountains that surrounds the southern coast of the Caspian Sea. It had been conquered by Muslim armies about a century after the rest of Iran; and it soon slipped out of the control of the caliphal government. Its subjects showed their hostility to ʿAbbāsid central control by becoming Shīʿīs. At first, as they conquered areas beyond their mountain homelands, non-Shīʿī Muslims feared that if the Dailamīs conquered the heartlands of the caliphate, they would replace the 'Abbāsid caliph with an 'Alid.

After many rapid changes of fortune among the leaders of these Dailamīs, three brothers emerged as their leaders. They were rough soldiers, the sons of a fisherman, Būyah, who gave his name to their dynasty. After the two elder brothers had conquered most of western Iran in the 320s and 330s A.H., the youngest brother conquered Iraq and took possession of the 'Abbāsid caliph himself in 334/945. The Buyids preserved the 'Abbāsid caliphate, as they had every reason to do. The majority of their subjects were non-Shī'īs, and respected the 'Abbāsid caliphate as an institution (while being indifferent to which 'Abbāsid held the office). The 'Abbāsid caliph obligingly granted the Buyids titles like Mu'izz ad-Daulah, "Strengthener of the ['Abbāsid] Dynasty," and diplomas authorizing the Buyids to rule in the name of the 'Abbāsids. In any case, the Buyids were Shī'īs of a very vague cast, and felt no specific obligation to hand the caliphate over to any 'Alid. They also realized that, had they done so, they would have created someone whom they could not treat with the cynicism that governed their treatment of the 'Abbāsid caliphs, whom the earlier Buyids deposed at will.

The three Buyid brothers maintained three courts: one in Baghdad, one in Rayy (near modern Tehran), and one in Shiraz in southwestern Iran. For forty years the separate kingdoms of Buyid rulers cooperated. Then this family system broke down, and the remainder of Buyid dynastic history is a sad story of recurrent quarrels between the different Buyid kingdoms. The Buyids were further weakened by the internal division in their armies; for, like the 'Abbāsids before them, they bought Turkish slave boys and raised them to be the elite cavalry of their army. The bad feeling between the Dailamīs and the Turkish slave soldiers allowed the Buyids to play these elements off against each other, however, and no rebellion in any of their armies ever succeeded in permanently replacing a Buyid by a member of another family. External powers capable of displacing the Buyids eventually appeared. Maḥmūd of Ghaznah, a staunch Sunnī and the conqueror of northern India for Islam, put an end to the Buyid kingdom of Rayy in 420/1022, and the Saljūqs conquered the Buyid kingdoms of Iraq and Fars in the 440s/1050s.[14]

The comparative weakness of the Buyids and their somewhat makeshift attempts to validate their rule by use of caliphal diplomas, claims of descent from the pre-Islamic Iranian kings, and the like, have in the end deprived this period of the share of attention that it deserves. The very weakness and makeshift character of government encouraged experimentation in administration, and some of the fruits of this experimentation, like the *iqṭā'*, were imitated by governments for centuries afterwards. We have also argued that the decentralization of government encouraged intellectual life. But most importantly, from the point of view of the social historian, the weakness of government threw society back on its own resources. Society proved able to generate self-renewing patterns of loyalty and of leadership, while accepting and even expecting a different role to be played by government. These patterns of loyalty and leadership are the subject of the following chapters.

CHAPTER II

Acquired Loyalties

In the Near East of the tenth and eleventh centuries, deliberately acquired obligations created the positive and predictable loyalties that shaped society. Such loyalties were not "positive" because they were good, or "predictable" because men always lived up to them. Acquired loyalties were "positive" in that they were used as a basis for cooperation even when group self-interest was not threatened. And they were "predictable" because, thanks to their somewhat formal nature, men who accepted them knew in considerable detail just what commitments such loyalties were believed to imply.

These acquired loyalties are best seen in times of stress, when men were trying to make effective their demands on others by explicitly referring to the validity of such loyalties. The rebellion of the caliphal army in 317/929 provided such a moment. In a letter written by the caliph al-Muqtadir in these circumstances to his troops, we have a striking and unusually clear example of the explicit evocation of the basic varieties of such loyalties and obligations. The caliph, faced with deposition, presented his troops with a statement of the most important motives that, in his opinion, ought to impel them to support his rule. In the first section of the letter, the caliph tries to placate the troops; then he says, "most of your benefits (singular: *ni'mah*) are from me, but it would not be my way to reproach you with any favor that I have conferred, and that I regarded at the time—and still regard—as small compared with your merits; rather, it suits me to fertilize and increase them . . . [and] I long to bring you to the utmost limit of your aspirations. . . . I claim from you that oath of allegiance (*bai'ah*) which you have affirmed time after time. Whoever has sworn allegiance to me has sworn allegiance to God, so that whosoever violates that oath, violates the covenant with God (*'ahd Allāh*). I also claim gratitude for benefits and favors you enjoy, benefits and gifts from me that I hope you will acknowledge and consider binding."[1]

Even though the troops had strong grievances against the caliph al-Muqtadir, the rebellion collapsed, largely because al-Mu'nis, the leading general to whom the letter was addressed, disappointed the rebels, who had expected his open support. There is no reason to believe that the letter changed his mind. Yet the arguments used in the letter are characteristic of all discussions of loyalty in this period. We have every reason to think that al-Muqtadir wrote in the belief that if *any* arguments could change the mind of al-Mu'nis and his troops, they would be arguments of the kind quoted above.

The two bases of loyalty mentioned in the letter of al-Muqtadir are oath and benefit. The first part of this chapter discusses oath-bound loyalties in general, and their relations to the covenant between man and God that forms a fundamental feature of Islamic belief. Then several specific categories of oath are described, such as oaths between caliphs and emirs. The following section of this chapter deals with the vow, a close cousin of the oath. Vows are "personal" in the sense that they are an oath between a person and God. But since others could be the beneficiaries of vows, they were frequently used to express a formal commitment to others.

The second part of the chapter is concerned with benefit, or *ni'mah*, as it is called in the above letter and in many other contexts. The formal ties created by giving and accepting benefit are a persistent, if disregarded, subject in the literature of this period; and patronage, particularly of the variety called *iṣṭinā'*, is an outgrowth of the idea of formal exchange of benefit. A more elusive extension of the formal ties of exchanged benefit can be seen in the loyalty of men who rose together. The chapter concludes with a discussion of the general character of acquired loyalties, and the distinction between them and the loyalties based on category, which are discussed in the next chapter.

Oaths

Not only in the caliph's letter, but in the great majority of discussions of political loyalty, oaths are regarded as the explicit and formal vehicle by which one man committed himself to another. There were other equally formal vehicles, and many vehicles less formal and less explicit. Since, however, oaths are the best attested of all these vehicles, it is appropriate that this discussion of acquired loyalties begin with oaths. Oaths are also a vehicle of commitment that appear prominently in the formal discussions of morality written in this period. And, to some extent, men regarded oaths as prototypes of other forms of commitment. They did so in part because, as I try to show in later sections of this chapter, oaths were typical of all of these vehicles of commitment.

The *bai'ah* mentioned in the letter was an oath of allegiance taken in God's name between the caliph and any Muslim. Quite naturally, in his letter the caliph al-Muqtadir sought to bring home forcibly to the rebels that to break such an oath was to perjure oneself before God. Yet for men of the fourth/tenth century, al-Muqtadir's reference to covenants—and even to ties of gratitude—had a less obvious but profoundly important point of reference in the compactual relations that existed between man and God. In the Koran, a whole series of covenants between man and his Creator, starting with the primal covenant of Adam, stand as the archetype and the ultimate guarantee for all solemn and weighty undertakings between one man and another. The Koran directly addressed the perennial religious questions of the origin of man's responsibility to God; and it is of great significance that, in the Koran, the proof of man's responsibility is a solemn covenant between man and God made at the beginning of time.

In a sense, man is depicted as having full moral responsibility only because of this covenant. All men were brought forth *in posse*: "And when your Lord drew the descendants of Adam from the loins of the sons of Adam, and called on them to bear witness: 'Am I not your Lord?' They answered, 'Yes, truly; we bear witness to this.' [We called on them to bear witness] lest you should say, on the day of Resurrection, 'We have been unmindful (*ghāfilīn*) of this,' or lest you should say: 'Our ancestors before us have given partners [to God]. We are their descendants after them; will you then destroy us for what was done by upholders of falsehood?' " (7:171-172/172-173). According to these verses, it is no excuse for a man to claim that he is "unmindful" (whether this means, as some commentators believe, that men pretend they have forgotten, or—as others believe—that men pretend never to have been told of this covenant). It is not even an excuse that a man is born to parents who have turned from God, and who might therefore be held responsible for the heedlessness of their children. All future men were in some sense present at this primal compact, and they have individually "borne witness" and thereby entered into an agreement with God that makes them responsible to God. Some Muslim thinkers have said that God could hold men responsible even if there had been no compact, and that this compact merely confirmed a responsibility inherent in man's situation. For our purposes, it is only important to notice that the Islamic tradition considered this solemn primal covenant between man and God to be a powerful argument for the fundamental moral responsibility of every human being.

The force of this argument came from—and was borne out by—the respect with which the Islamic tradition in its early centuries regarded oaths, compacts, and covenants. In the time of the Buyids, formal oaths were the most prominent feature of all discussions about duties and obligations that could be enforced without coercion. Undoubtedly, oaths carried only a comparatively small part of the weight of that sense of obligation and loyalty which held society together;

but because oaths were formal statements of obligation, they make explicit some of the presuppositions that underlay other forms of social obligation. And because oaths were universally acceptable, other forms of social obligation were to some extent adapted to the pattern of oaths.

The Islamic tradition did not give such a central position to oaths on the basis of a single passage in the Koran. It did so because the system of oaths was well suited to contemporary Near Eastern society, and because the Koran and the example of Muḥammad offered many precedents in which oaths had precisely this central importance. In the following paragraphs I discuss a few of these Koranic passages, and attempt to show their central importance to the moral view that the Koran prescribes for mankind.

As we have seen above, in the Koranic view man accepted moral responsibility in a kind of oath, a primal compact with God. Three verses before describing this compact, the Koran mentions a more restricted kind of oath which, nevertheless, remained a classical point of reference: God's covenant with Israel. The ancient Israelites thought that everything would be forgiven them; yet, says the Koran, "Was not the covenant (*mīthāq*) of the Book taken from them, that they would not ascribe to God anything but the truth?" (7:168/169). One reason that this covenant is mentioned a few verses before the primal compact is that the word here used for covenant, *mīthāq*, also means the confirmation of the compactual agreement between man and God which every believer makes: "Those who violate the compact with God (*'ahd Allāh*), after its confirmation (*mīthāq*), and who cut the ties which God has ordered to be joined, and do evil in the earth, those will truly lose" (2:25/27; compare 13:25). The more restricted covenant of God and Israel, and by extension any oath-bound agreement, can be seen as confirmations or ratifications of the fundamental oath by which men accepted moral responsibility. As the caliph al-Muqtadir said to the rebels, "Whoever has sworn allegiance to me has sworn allegiance to

God; so that whoever violates that oath, violates the compact with God (*'ahd Allāh*)."

The degree to which violators "will truly lose" is described in many passages in the Koran. For example, in one such passage the Koran says, "He who fulfills his compact (*'ahd*) and is righteous [will be rewarded], for God loves the righteous. Those, however, who sell the compact with God (*'ahd Allāh*) and their oaths (singular: *yamīn*) for [what must in exchange be] a paltry price, they have no portion in the Hereafter; nor will God speak to them, and theirs will be a painful torment" (3:70-71/76-77). The Koran repeatedly emphasizes the severity with which such perjurers will be punished.

In another Koranic passage, the sanctity of oaths and importance of gratitude to one's benefactor are linked together in much the same way as in the caliph's letter. This passage seems to refer both to the so-called "constitution of Medina," an oath-bound agreement that was the foundation of Muḥammad's authority when he moved to Medina and established a state, and to the primal compact between man and God: "Be mindful of the favor (*ni'mah*) of God to you, and His covenant (*mīthāq*), which He confirmed (*wāthaqa*) with you when you said 'We hear and obey.' Be righteous before God; God knows the secrets of your hearts" (5:8/11).

God, therefore, is "our Lord" to whose moral law we owe obedience through a primal compact. This compact overshadows any later oaths we take; we cannot, for example, in any valid sense, swear to commit a sin. We cannot do so, moreover, because God is a party to all valid oaths. Sometimes an oath "by Muḥammad" or "by the Koran" is recognized as valid, but only because an oath by the vehicle or concrete form of God's revelation recognizes both the Lordship of God and the original covenant to obey the moral law, which the Islamic revelation brings in its most perfect form. God is an active and not just a passive witness to a valid oath; for, when we swear by God, we are in effect invoking God's curse if we do not live up to the oath. This reasoning seems to have been accepted by the great majoriy of Muslims both in the time of the Buyids and in the centuries immediately before and after the Buyids. The very widespread use of the oath in this period to create or confirm obligations shows that it was a line of reasoning that men took very much to heart.[2]

The seriousness of oaths is shown most dramatically by the shock and horror with which the medieval Islamic historians discuss those occasions when men openly perjured themselves. Every age knows hardy villains who boldly, and sometimes successfully, disregard its central moral principles. The reaction to such men, however, tells us something about the strength with which other men claimed to support these principles. Twenty pages of any chronicle (Buyid, medieval European, or of any people or time) will offer a variety of acts that might offend a tender conscience. Yet few of the acts described in the chronicles of our period could so arouse the moral outrage of the Near Eastern chroniclers as could acts of perjury.

The drama of such an act to contemporaries is well represented by the accounts of Tūzūn's arrest of the caliph in 333/944, shortly before the Buyids occupied Baghdad. Tūzūn was the most successful of the several generals who, for ten years before the Buyids took Baghdad, controlled the caliph's affairs, much as the Buyids would subsequently control them. The caliph in whose name he served was al-Muttaqī; and al-Muttaqī, in violation of agreements with Tūzūn, had run away from Tūzūn's control in Baghdad and openly flirted with independent dynasties that ruled nearby kingdoms: the Ḥamdānids of Mosul and the Ikhshīdids of Egypt. The caliph had thereby shown his desire to break permanently with Tūzūn, and to replace him with a new mayor of the palace or *amīr al-'umarā*. Nonetheless, when intermediaries obtained from Tūzūn the most solemn oaths of good conduct toward al-Muttaqī, witnessed before judges, notaries, the leading members of the 'Alid and 'Abbāsid families, and clerks, all of whom gave their attestation to this effect, al-Muttaqī started back toward Baghdad; and on the way, an envoy of Tūzūn renewed the oaths. On 28 Ṣafar 333, Tūzūn met al-Muttaqī north of Baghdad and kissed the ground before al-Muttaqī, then kissed his hand and leg. After this, he arrested and blinded him. As the fourth/tenth century history of Miskawaih tells us, "the world trembled with shock (*irtajjat*)."[3]

A more circumstantial account in an eleventh-century chronicle describes even more vividly the extreme seriousness of this act of perjury to contemporaries. This version of al-Muttaqī's arrest may be based on the account of a court chamberlain of the time of Tūzūn; in any case it reflects the kind of emotions that perjury could evoke. According to this account, when someone first suggested to Tūzūn that he arrest al-Muttaqī, he said, "how could I do such a thing when he has made an agreement (*'āqada*) with us, and I have had all the people of the court (*nās*) testify to my compliance, and this matter is well known in other regions?" The advisor said to Tūzūn: "Master, these 'Abbāsids are men with little fidelity." Then, according to this account, Tūzūn and the future al-Mustakfī, Tūzūn's candidate to replace al-Muttaqī, exchanged oaths (*yataḥālafūna*) in secret before the arrest. Clearly, Tūzūn still believed in the utility of oaths, even if he was about to break an oath publicly.

"When," the chronicle continues, "in this manner Tūzūn blinded al-Muttaqī and betrayed him, broke his oath to him (*ḥanitha aimānahū*), and violated the covenants (*'uhūd*) which he had taken before God to support and obey him, [this act] deeply troubled men both high and low, and they thought it a momentous event. Everyone who has believed and had faith in His promise and warning [knew] that God—He is powerful and glorious—would grant him no respite or enjoyment of life hereafter." The chronicle then quotes from a source clearly identified as a contemporary of Tūzūn: "When Tūzūn betrayed and blinded al-Muttaqī, he bitterly regretted what he had done. He sat on one of the boxes [in his tent] and asked for wine to drink; and when the wine came, he had a stroke.

He fell from the top of the box to the ground stricken, and remained in this state for the rest of his life; [that is] from the time he did this act until he died. His sight went before he died. This is God's way with such people." The theologian Ibn al-Jauzī in his later chronicle mentions that Tūzūn died in 334, "not a year having passed since his foul (*qabīh*) act and his disregard of the oaths he had taken."[4]

The seriousness of oaths is confirmed by other men's efforts to avoid oaths that they knew they might have to repudiate. Few men wanted to risk the infamy (and, perhaps, the distress of conscience) experienced by perjurers like Tūzūn. When the Buyid Sharaf ad-Daulah was advancing on Iraq in 375 to free his full brother from his half brother Ṣamṣām ad-Daulah, cities fell into Sharaf ad-Daulah's hands without a struggle. Ṣamṣām ad-Daulah was soon willing to meet all of the demands of Sharaf ad-Daulah, and swore to this effect before intermediaries. They returned to the advancing army, and found that the lack of resistance had changed Sharaf ad-Daulah's mind: he had decided to take Baghdad as well as gain his brother's release, and so "did not swear to his [half] brother." Similarly, the great conqueror of northern India, Maḥmūd of Ghaznah (d. 421/1030), is supposed to have asked his son Mas'ūd to swear that he would not fight Muḥammad, his brother, after the death of their father Maḥmūd. Mas'ūd said, "I will do so as soon as our master [Maḥmūd] swears that I am not his son." "How could that be?" asked Maḥmūd. "Because," said Mas'ūd, "if I were his son, I would have a claim (*ḥaqq*) to Khurāsān and to the wealth [which has been assigned to Muḥammad]." After a long dispute, Maḥmūd said, "swear to me that you will never marry with the Dailam," and to this [less confining oath] Mas'ūd agreed.[5]

The system of oaths was so universally accepted and so essential to many forms of political action that no leader could afford to disregard it for long. The Buyid ruler Bahā' ad-Daulah (d. 403/1012), known to have broken his oath on several occasions, was a man with no morals but with some practical sense. It is not surprising, therefore, to see him in the following anecdote bow to the general expectations of society and pretend to treat with great seriousness the oaths that others imposed on him. Abū 'Alī b. Ismā'īl, the talented minister of Bahā' ad-Daulah whom that king had disgraced, escaped from prison in 392/1002 and then, after a while on the run, wanted to return to the capital city of Shiraz in safety. He therefore sent an emissary to ask that Bahā' ad-Daulah grant him a guarantee of safety attested by a leading 'Alid, Abū Aḥmad al-Mūsawī. Bahā' ad-Daulah agreed, though he requested that the document not be "exhaustive." The emissary, however, turned up with a long written oath (*yamīn*), and Bahā' ad-Daulah immediately noticed that it was, in fact, intended to be exhaustive. He started to read it out loud, then stopped in the middle to ask a question. The emissary kissed the ground before the king and asked his gracious favor in reading straight through from the beginning again without interruption. Bahā' ad-Daulah was angry but did reread the document without interruption, and at the end of the document, he wrote: "I have sworn to this oath (*yamīn*) and undertake to observe its stipulations."[6]

This story illustrates the seriousness with which people of this period took even the oath of a comparatively immoral ruler like Bahā' ad-Daulah. Abū 'Alī's emissary doubtless knew that the king was treacherous, but still thought it worth risking the king's anger to make sure that the oath was technically sound because read without interruption. He also knew the seriousness with which Abū Aḥmad al-Mūsawī would take the oath, and that Bahā' ad-Daulah might be restrained from treachery by fear of future embarrassment before this revered leader of the family of 'Alī. It was precisely the grave importance of oaths to such prestigious men that allowed the oath to remain a central form of political action, in spite of dishonorable kings like Bahā' ad-Daulah.

When Muḥammad b. 'Umar, a rich and highly political,

but less revered, descendant of 'Alī returned in 388 from the "Marsh" in southern Iraq, where he had sought refuge during a period of disfavor, he secured his safety by getting an oath (*yamīn*) in Bahā' ad-Daulah's own handwriting, and had the ruler of the Marsh, Muhadhdhib ad-Daulah, write at the end of the document, "Good faith toward the *sharīf* [Muḥammad b. 'Umar] is bound up with good faith to me, and treachery to him. If he should deviate from the compacts [here] undertaken (*al-'uhūd al-ma'khūdhah*), then Bahā' ad-Daulah has no further claim on me (*lā 'ahda li Bahā' ad-Daulah fī 'unqī*) or my allegiance." Even men who did not fear God had reason to fear an attestation like this.[7]

The Bai'ah *or Oath of Allegiance*

If some men foreswore themselves, or avoided oaths, or feared only oaths laced with fearful threats, most men seem to have shown their unambiguous respect for oaths by honoring them. One form of oath we have briefly described is the *bai'ah*, the oath of allegiance that the caliph al-Muqtadir refers to in his letter to his army. The *bai'ah* was used to swear allegiance to kings as well as caliphs; it was an oath notorious for the completeness of its sanctions; and so we sometimes read of a personal oath taken "with the oaths of the *bai'ah*" (*bi-aimān al-bai'ah*).[8] In its usual sense, however, the *bai'ah* was the oath of allegiance, and was not confused with other oaths. For example, the officers who killed al-Muqtadir chose the future al-Qāhir to be his successor; "and when they had made sure of him by oaths and compacts (*al-aimān wa'l-'uhūd*) they took the oath of allegiance (*al-mubāya'ah*) to him"—eloquent testimony, by the way, that there existed no better method of making sure of men than the formal oath.[9]

The *bai'ah* had become by tradition distinct from a mere private compact. From the time of the *bai'ah* rendered to the first caliph at the death of Muḥammad, the *bai'ah* was a voluntary offering of allegiance to a ruler. Later theory, bowing to almost universal later practice, made the *bai'ah* to the caliph more a public recognition of an established rule, a sort of "homage." It was claimed that a dangerous interruption to the sequence of caliphs would be avoided if the *bai'ah* were given by a few men immediately around the dead caliph to an heir apparent. The rest of the Muslim community therefore swore the *bai'ah* as an oath of public acceptance of the succession by this heir apparent. Yet it was hard to argue that such a justification could be extended to the swearing of *bai'ahs* to emirs, who often owed their rule to conquest, and created a confusion as bad as any interregnum by their military ambitions. The first time any person took such an oath to a ruler or pretender, therefore, his *bai'ah* to the emir was usually considered to be something more than homage to an established succession.[10]

To receive the *bai'ah* continued to be a sign that one claimed military authority, and not just "deputized" rule—within, of course, the system by which the caliph authorized emirs to assume such authority. In the period in which the caliph gave independent authority to the *amīr al-'umarā'* in his capital of Baghdad, the vizier Ibn Shīrzād tried, during a brief vacuum of power after the death of Tūzūn in 324/935, to establish himself as the equivalent of an emir. He was already head of the civil administration, but he published and tried to make effective his new claim by taking the *bai'ah* from the entire army in Baghdad by himself. He had been "vizier" before the event, but the title of vizier did not in practice convey any claim to an independent military following; to take the *bai'ah* to oneself clearly did make such a claim. The semi-independent dynasties of the 'Abbāsid period had, of course, already imported the *bai'ah* from the political world of the caliphate to the world of kingship. The Sāmānids, for example, took the *bai'ah* not only to themselves, but even to their heirs apparent, as the caliphs had done.

The Buyids continued this practice, and considered the *bai'ah* as a powerful means to ensure the loyalty of their active supporters. When 'Aḍud ad-Daulah died, his attendants hid his death, and told his son Sharaf ad-Daulah that he had been appointed heir apparent (*walī 'ahd*), while his brother was to be deputy ruler of Fārs; then letters to this effect were written in 'Aḍud ad-Daulah's name to all regions, and with each letter was a copy of an oath (*yamīn*) of the *bai'ah* to be taken by commanders, officers, and their men. Only after such preparation did the attendants and Sharaf ad-Daulah announce 'Aḍud ad-Daulah's death.[11]

New dynasties in some circumstances took the *bai'ah* from a town. To do so meant, of course, to take the *bai'ah* from leading men and volunteer soldiers of the town, since there were no municipalities that could swear on behalf of their members. Generally, however, the *bai'ah* was taken from the *awliyā'*, those actually employed as agents of the dynasty: the high officials and, above all, the soldiers. The *bai'ah* conveyed a real commitment, and soldiers gave the *bai'ah* only with deliberation. Officers might signal their intention to cast off allegiance and seek independent military authority by suddenly taking the *bai'ah* to themselves, as did Mardāwīj when he lured the army from loyalty to Asfār. If, however, a commander intended, as was far more often the case, to enter the service of a new monarchy, he openly took the *bai'ah* from his soldiers in order to commit the soldiers individually to his new policy. Thus, when Ibn Muḥtāj in exile in Buyid territory decided in 334 to support a fellow exile, the Sāmānid pretender Ibrāhīm, he took the *bai'ah* to Ibrāhīm from his fellow soldiers in exile, even though Ibrāhīm had not yet joined him.

Since the *bai'ah* conveyed a real obligation, soldiers were not willing to concede it cheaply. In the time of the 'Abbāsids, the army usually demanded from the caliph "the customary payment for the oath of allegiance" or *rasm al-bai'ah* in exchange for the formal oath, and the troops took the same toll for their first oath of allegiance to any Buyid king. Without a satisfactory payment, the troops would sometimes refuse even a temporary and informal commitment. For example, when Jalāl ad-Daulah died in 435/1043, his son al-Malik al-'Azīz was nearby in Wāsiṭ, but was unable to satisfy the Baghdad garrison as to what would be paid for their *bai'ah*; he was therefore unable to occupy Baghdad, and unable to consolidate his position against a richer Buyid, Abū Kālījār, to whom the troops eventually offered their loyalty.[12]

It is not surprising, therefore, that oaths were a necessary part of political conspiracies. Oaths were, of course, essential to any plot because the sanctions of the oath were the only device for ensuring loyalty when all other sanctions belonged to the established government. But oaths were also the basic means of expressing political loyalty, and it was natural that men should swear an oath to their future leader which would be renewed with the public *bai'ah* when the plot succeeded. In a typical conspiracy of this sort, 'Abd al-'Azīz b. Yūsuf, disgusted with his joint vizierate with Ibn Barmūyah to Ṣamṣām ad-Daulah, plotted in 375 with a leading general to have Abū Manṣūr (the future Bahā' ad-Daulah) rule Iraq as the deputy of his brother, Sharaf ad-Daulah, in place of Ṣamṣām ad-Daulah. To get the conspiracy under way, the leading general obtained from his soldiers "the assurances of oaths" (*mawāthīq al-aimān*) to support his policy. This conspiracy failed, though only when the general and his followers were defeated. In a more successful conspiracy, the vizier Ibn 'Abbād arranged during Mu'ayyid ad-Daulah's illness for the succession of Fakhr ad-Daulah, in spite of the contrary instructions in the will and testament of Mu'ayyid ad-Daulah. In this case, the vizier sent some of his "reliable men" (*thiqāt*) to get Fakhr ad-Daulah's oath (*yamīm*) of fidelity to the compact (*'ahd*) that regulated the new succession.[13]

Even when the ruler was not chosen in secret, and the soldiers, as the sources often say, gathered openly "to choose an emir," that choice was most probably confirmed in every case by some form of oath. We read, for example, that when, in the middle of the tenth century, a provincial Sāmānid army in Ghaznah found themselves without a leader, they gathered and compared their options, and at first disagreed. Eventually they agreed to put Sabuktakīn in charge of themselves, and "swore to him (*ḥalafū lahū*)." By this act they inaugurated the Ghaznavid dynasty, which would last over two hundred years.[14]

Oath between Caliphs and Emirs

Of the oaths between men who already held some established authority, none are better documented than the complex chain of oaths that bound the Buyid emir and the 'Abbāsid caliph together. Relations between the first Buyid emir of Baghdad, Mu'izz ad-Daulah, and the 'Abbāsids, were at first clouded with suspicion. When Mu'izz ad-Daulah arrived in Baghdad he took the *bai'ah* to al-Mustakfī in the caliph's presence, and swore "with the most solemn of oaths" (*bi-aghlaẓ al-aimān*) to him; the caliph in return swore (*ḥalafa*) to 'Alī b. Būyah (the eldest Buyid) and his two brothers, and a document containing their oaths was attested.

It may seem strange that Mu'izz ad-Daulah does not receive the opprobrium that covers the name of Tūzūn, since he deposed al-Mustakfī a few months later. But it was widely known that Mu'izz ad-Daulah believed that al-Mustakfī was plotting against Buyid rule and therefore felt released from his oath. Al-Mustakfī, moreover, had come to the caliphate by participating in Tūzūn's crime against al-Muttaqī, proving himself to be, like the other 'Abbāsids, "a man of little fidelity." In any case, successful treachery to a caliph always carried a built-in pardon; the next caliph always obliged by publicly blessing the act that had brought him to the throne. Even so, in 355 Mu'izz ad-Daulah, who was still on principle suspicious of any 'Abbāsid, decided to make even more sure of (*tawaththaqa*) his candidate, al-Muṭī' lillāh. He took the caliph into custody, and made him swear great oaths not to separate himself from the Buyid emir, or to side with his enemies, or to harbor evil designs; only then was al-Muṭī' let go. Obviously, whatever he had done to al-Mustakfī, Mu'izz ad-Daulah still believed in oaths.[15]

From this time on, caliphs and Buyid emirs regularly exchanged mighty oaths of sincere good faith and good intentions, both at accessions and at bestowals of patents of investiture. They also exchanged such oaths at threatening moments, when the caliph and emir felt obliged to reassure each other, as when Musharrif ad-Daulah found out that the caliph suspected (without cause) that the Buyid emir intended to depose him in 415/1024. It was in the reign of Musharrif ad-Daulah's successor, the long-suffering Jalāl ad-Daulah (416–435), that we find the most fulsome and florid oaths sworn between caliph and emir. The caliph by now had regained a certain amount of authority, yet neither caliph nor emir could live without the support of the other. As happened so often in the Buyid period when there was dependence and suspicion between near equals, a complex set of oaths was employed to give form to, and make enforceable, the appropriate kinds of obligation. The caliph al-Qādir recognized the weight of these obligations, and probably also recognized that although the caliph had become almost as powerful as the Buyid emir who ruled alongside him in Baghdad, it was too soon for the caliph to try to exercise independent military authority in defiance of the neighboring Buyid kingdoms.

When in 418/1027 the Turkish soldiers went to the caliphal palace in Baghdad and offered the caliph their direct allegiance, the caliph, therefore, did not accept. The caliph's answer was that "you are the children of our regime (*abnā' daulatinā*) . . . [and] you have entered a formal agreement (*'aqadtum 'aqdan*) with Abu Kālījar which it would be improper to dissolve (*ḥall*) casually. The Buyids have compacts (*'uhūd*) incumbent on us (*fī riqābinā*), which it is not permissible [for us] to disregard." The caliph probably refused their offer both for genuine reasons of conscience, and also because he was reluctant to become part of a political game in which he had more to lose than gain. Nevertheless, he did quietly strengthen his position by reminding the soldiers that they might some day be solely devoted to the caliph's interests like the first 'Abbāsid army, the original *abnā' ad-daulah*, and by offering to write on their behalf to Abū Kālījār, which reaffirmed the impression that the caliph was an honest broker in a world of unscrupulous men.[16]

After Abū Kālījār's repeated hesitations, Jalāl ad-Daulah finally came to Baghdad, where he tried continually and never quite succeeded in evoking an effective loyalty in this same group of Turkish soldiers. The soldiers had turned to the caliph more than once; for this and other reasons, in those periods in which he had the upper hand, Jalāl ad-Daulah made the caliph swear elaborate and exhaustive statements of fidelity. In 423/1031, Jalāl ad-Daulah and the caliph al-Qā'im exchanged oaths, and we are fortunate enough to have the text of most of the caliph's oath: "al-Qā'im bi Amr Allāh, Commander of the Faithful, has sworn and said: 'by God . . . and by the claim (*ḥaqq*) [owed to] his messenger Muḥammad . . . I will most certainly continue in [my] loyalty of intention (*ikhlāṣ an-niyah*) and sincerity of friendship (*aṣ-ṣafā*) to Rukn ad-Dīn Jalāl ad-Daulah Abū Ṭahir b. Bahā' ad-Daulah Abū Naṣr, and will most certainly comply with the requirements (*shurūṭ*) of support and fidelity, without failing in anything which might be beneficial to his situation and might preserve his condition; and that I will most certainly be vigilant as he would desire in protecting him in his person and whatever is associated with it, and I will do so for the *wazīr al-wuzarā'* Abū al-Qāsim [b. Mākūlā] and his retinue; and I will do so in maintaining him in his station (*rutbah*). A compact before God (*'ahd Allāh*) toward him in this manner is [hereby] imposed on me, as well as His covenant (*mīthāq*) and whatever [covenants] He has assumed to His Angels who are drawn near to Him, and to His Prophets, whom He has sent as Messengers. God is a witness. . . .' " Here, as in several other cases, the oath derives some of its force by directly stating that it was part of the universal system of covenants between

God, men, and the angels that maintained the moral order of the universe.[17]

It is also significant that, in the anarchic world of late Buyid Iraq, the number of participants named in oaths was growing, along with the chain of people tied by oaths. But Jalāl ad-Daulah found that, much as he needed such oaths, their entanglements could even deprive him of what little authority he had left. In 420, when Jalāl ad-Daulah arrested his vizier ʿAmīd ad-Daulah, the caliph and the Turkish soldiers refused to condone this act on the basis of oaths they themselves had sworn, and that Jalāl ad-Daulah had sworn, to the vizier; the vizier was therefore restored to office. The caliph was even faithful to his oaths to the last Buyid, al-Malik ar-Raḥīm, and sent his agent to Ṭughril Beg before he entered Baghdad to have the Saljūq conqueror swear to both the caliph and ar-Raḥīm. The caliph need not have included the Buyid, whose resources to resist the Saljūq were laughable; and Ṭughril, who wanted to pose as champion of the caliph's interest against the Buyids, had no reason to admire the caliph's fidelity to this ancient alliance. In any case Ṭughril, like the other early Ghuzz leaders, respected the caliph's position, but had scant respect for oaths; after entering Baghdad he arrested ar-Raḥīm, apparently without any qualms.[18]

Oaths between the Emir and His Officials

These vast conjurations that appear at the end of the Buyid period are only the culmination of the long-standing practice whereby members of the administration made sure of each others' loyalty and avoided the effects of an unrestrained competition. Very occasionally, when viziers were unusually powerful, emirs and viziers exchanged vows, as did Jalāl ad-Daulah. Fakhr ad-Daulah, as related above, exchanged oaths with his vizier when Ibn ʿAbbād brought him to the throne. ʿIzz ad-Daulah, who ruled in the early Buyid period, had no similar reason to become formally beholden to his vizier. Nevertheless, through his incompetence 'Izz ad-Daulah was obliged to exchange oaths with several of his officials, since they feared what he might do, yet recognized how much they in turn depended on him. In 360, his vizier ash-Shīrāzī asked for and got "an inviolable oath" (*yamīn ghamūs*) with all the oaths of the *bai'ah* sworn before army officers, judges, and other leading men, that 'Izz ad-Daulah would never again appoint a certain rival of the vizier to any post unless this official came out of concealment within a month. In 362, 'Izz ad-Daulah and his commander-in-chief swore a "binding oath" (*yamīn mu'akkadah*) to be friends. After 'Izz ad-Daulah was restored to power his vizier Ibn Baqīyah, who was much the more strong-minded of the two, exchanged oaths of good will with the king in 364.[19]

Although we hear more about oaths that involved the king himself, we have evidence that oaths were a major feature of life in other levels of the administration. Officials who had quarreled with each other made the sincerity of their reconciliation clear by exchanging oaths; and such oaths were even more frequently exchanged when an official arranged for the release of a general or another official who might harbor a grudge against the administration that had imprisoned him. Oaths between officials without quarrels, who nonetheless wanted to rely on each other's help through the future windings of public life, were probably just as common, although they are far less often attested. We know that when two officials, al-Ḥasan b. Hārūn and al-Muhallabī, were among the strongest candidates to succeed aṣ-Ṣaimarī as vizier in 339, they swore (*taḥālafā*) that they would help each other no matter which of them might get the job; and, as far as we know, they lived up to these oaths. Similar oaths must have cemented together the inner cores of the powerful factions of officials from the time of the 'Abbāsids through the Buyid period, and after. The officials had no reason to reveal such agreements and every reason to hide them from the king, who preferred to pretend that he could elevate or disgrace an official without dragging along the secret allies of that official. It is not surprising, then, that these oaths are almost never mentioned in the sources.[20]

Factions in the army may also have thrived on secret oaths. We do know that soldiers were often involved in public ceremonies in which very large numbers of officers (and, possibly, soldiers of all ranks) swore friendship to each other. One such conjuration took place at the end of the 'Abbāsid period, when the Sājī regiment in 332 feared that their commander would be arrested by the caliph; their officers met with the leaders of the Ḥujarī regiment, who were the potential ally of the caliph, and the officers of the two regiments swore (*taḥālafa*) to act in common, "after which [the officers] took an oath from the rest of both regiments to do the same." Presumably, other extensive conjurations among soldiers followed the same patterns; they were still, basically, oaths between individuals, but were taken between a large number of individuals to ensure that they could count on each other's help. 'Izz ad-Daulah made the personal nature of these extensive oaths apparent when he used them to end hostilities between his Turkish and Dailamī soldiers in 360; he arranged marriage alliances between the two parties, and had the soldiers from each party involved in each alliance swear to officers of the other party. Similarly, when fighting started between Turks and Dailamīs in 379, and Bahā' ad-Daulah joined the Turks as the stronger side, both parties saw that they had more to lose than gain in such fighting. They agreed to make peace, and "they swore oaths to one another." Such oaths, as we have seen, could be sworn during an interregnum, and could—as in the case of the Ghaznavids—become the first formal agreement from which a new dynasty might grow.[21]

Oaths extended even further down the hierarchy of government, and were used in some instances to ensure the compliance of local leaders. When 'Aḍud ad-Daulah's soldiers marched from Jirift in Kirmān to the Persian Gulf, they passed through areas that had hardly ever seen an army of Muslims. The people of the conquered area offered their submission and agreed to adopt Islam, and they gave oaths to this effect. Not long after, however, the Bālūṣ (Baluchee) of the area, the most courageous "and most pagan (*kāfir*)" of the local tribes, threw off their submission, "and violated the compacts (*'uhūd*) which they had undertaken." When they did so, 'Aḍud ad-Daulah became convinced that there was no means to reform them. At this point he personally undertook a more systematic reduction of the Baluchees, and transported the survivors to a new area.

Populations better integrated into the political system of this period took their oaths more seriously, and thereby showed themselves to be more "civilized" than faithless pagans like the Baluchees. When Hibat Allāh, a Ḥamdānid prince, killed an important officer of his uncle, Saif ad-Daulah, he fled to the town of Ḥarrān in Mesopotamia. He falsely told the townspeople that Saif ad-Daulah was dead, and asked them to swear to fight with him against those who might fight him, and to make peace with whomever he made peace. They swore (*ḥalafū*) to do so with the reservation in their oath (*yamīn*) that they would not fight Saif ad-Daulah, since they did not wholly believe the prince's story. In spite of their doubts, they stuck by their oath at great risk, and locked out an officer of Saif ad-Daulah who came to their gates. Subsequently, when Hibat Allāh realized that they would soon hear that his uncle was still alive, he fled and left the townspeople to their fate. They suffered a heavy fine for their generosity and their fidelity to this oath.[22]

Oaths of Treaty

Oaths of treaty constituted another category of formal oath that played an extremely prominent role in the political style of this period. If two rulers did not swear oaths to each other, there was no treaty between two kingdoms, only a state of "nonbelligerency." To some extent, of course, by their oaths of loyalty to the caliph who gave them patents (*'uhūd*) for their provinces, rulers of this period were limited to these territories and not supposed to attack a neighbor who held an equally valid patent. While the 'Abbāsids still exercised some independent military power, this argument was used by semi-independent rulers in their quarrels. But even in this period, the 'Abbāsid caliph was not above granting patents for the same province simultaneously to two rulers; and after the 'Abbāsids lost military power, everyone recognized that such patents were simply acknowledgments of the fact of conquest (or of the intentions of the Buyid emir of Baghdad).

Oaths of treaty were sometimes between equals, and sometimes they implied suzerainty. They were almost always publicly witnessed by such important dignitaries as the caliph, the *qāḍīs*, witness-notaries, and notables. In this way both parties to a treaty had full assurance that their remote neighbor had actually sworn to the agreement. Moreover, both parties recognized that the shame of public exposure as a perjurer added considerable strength to the treaty-oath.

The importance of public witnessing to treaty-oaths is shown by the instruction given by the ever-astute 'Aḍud ad-Daulah to the three judges whom he sent as envoys to the Sāmānids in 371. He told them that if they succeeded in making peace with the Sāmānid general in Nīshāpūr, they should then go to Bukhārā, the Sāmānid capital, and conclude the agreement with a deposition (*maḥḍar*) from the *qāḍīs*, witness-notaries, leading courtiers, officers, *ghāzīs* (volunteer fighters against non-Muslim governments), and great men of the region witnessing that the Sāmānid ruler had actually agreed to the peace. When such agreements were prepared, apparently two copies of them were made, each of which concluded with the oath by one of the rulers, contingent on the taking of a similar oath by the other ruler.[23]

All the oaths described above were between real persons. They were, moreover, between real persons present in this world (including, of course, God). None of these oaths was sworn, for example, between two men on behalf of their descendants; and none of them was between a man and an artificial person like a municipality or clan or school. When people expected a city to be carried along by the oaths of its notables, it was not because those notables could legally obligate their followers by their oaths, but because these notables could deliver the cooperation of their followers, who were bound to them by other loyalties. The oaths that the notables took were not oaths to the "state"—no such artificial person existed with whom one might exchange oaths. Even the first generation of men, the sons of Adam, in the primal oath that was the example and guarantee that overshadowed all later oaths, could not swear on behalf of all his descendants to recognize God's eternal sovereignty; all future men had to be brought forth in the form of seed so that they could individually swear.

The Vow

The vow is, by its nature, a close kin to the oath. Oaths, as we have seen, were almost the only manner in which Muslims of this period formally accepted new obligations to each other; and in the eyes of the law, most formal obligations were newly contracted by each individual, and not transferred to him by virtue of inheritance, or some status not wilfully acquired by that individual. The vow had a related function. The vow follows the style of the oath, except that it is unilateral swearing by one man to God, instead of a swearing between two men with God as a witness. We have abundant evidence of the importance of oaths to political action, but somewhat less evidence for the vow. This is not surprising, since a vow, by its nature, is a more private affair.

What evidence we have does show that the vow must have been an extremely common manner of stating an obligation, and was perhaps even more important than the formal oath.

Certainly the "private" vow, in which the pledge to act in a certain way does not importantly affect anyone except the taker of the vow, still forms a basic part of the spiritual life of very many people in the Near East. Such "private" vows cannot directly affect social and political life, and so are not directly relevant to this book. Nevertheless, we can gauge the seriousness with which men regarded public vows, which had the added sanction of shame, by the seriousness with which they regarded vows to which God alone was the witness, and for which a sense of guilt was the only sanction.

There are many examples of this sort of "private" vow. One occurs in a story told by the ex-vizier al-Khaṣībī; and since al-Khaṣībī paints himself in such a bad light, the story may well be true. Ibn Muqlah, on becoming vizier in 322, exiled al-Khaṣībī and Sulaimān b. al-Ḥaṣan to Oman; on the way, when he almost drowned in a storm, al-Khaṣībī repented of his sins and vowed to God never to pay back those who had done him harm, with the exception of Ibn Muqlah. " 'If I am given power over [Ibn Muqlah, he said] I will repay him for this night and what has happened to me in it, and go to the utmost extremities in mistreating him.' Sulaimān said, 'in circumstances like these, when face to face with death, you talk in this manner?' 'I was not,' said al-Khaṣībī, 'going to deceive my Lord.' " God saved al-Khaṣībī, and—good to his vow—he seems not to have taken revenge on his enemies when he again received high office. But al-Khaṣībī had shrewdly saved himself the satisfaction of mistreating Ibn Muqlah, whom he cheerfully handed over to a torturer.[24]

The "public" vow was useful not only as a spiritual tool, but also as a political instrument; it was the most solemn way that one man could unilaterally assure another that he was in earnest. Like the oath, but probably even more commonly than the oath, it was strengthened by the offer to give up things vitally important to the swearer if he did not fulfill the vow. When in 328 Abū 'Abd Allāh al-Barīdī wanted the envoy to the *amīr al-umarā*, Bajkam, to return to Baghdad, and to assure Bajkam that he had no reason to be suspicious of the Barīdīs, who controlled al-Baṣrah, Abū 'Abd Allāh said to the envoy: " 'Give me your hand.' I [the envoy] held it out and he put it on his ear and said: 'Take me to the slave traders and sell me [if I let you down]; but just take care of this matter for me and don't ask how.' " The envoy knew that Abū 'Abd Allāh's limitless ambitions made him a fountain of lies. All the same, he was impressed with the seriousness of Abū 'Abd Allāh's vow to be sold as a slave (with a ring in his ear, the mark of servitude) if he were not in this instance sincere. The envoy kissed Abū 'Abd Allāh's hand and agreed.

Such vows were so serious that men often organized elaborate forms of symbolic action so that the maker of a vow could carry out the letter if not the spirit of his vow. For example, when the Kurdish Ḥasanwaihid ruler, Badr, assigned to his son Hilāl a district too insignificant for Hilāl's dignity, Hilāl vowed to conquer the more important neighboring district of Shahrazūr, which was ruled by a close and obedient friend of Badr. Badr wrote instructing Hilāl to leave Shahrazūr alone; but Hilāl replied, " 'I have sworn not to stop in this matter and not to turn back until I have entered his city.' So Badr said, 'go to his city with a few men and I will order him to open the gate and you will enter and be freed (*tabarra'a*) from your oath (*yamīn*).' " Hilāl, incidentally, refused to settle for this symbolic resolution of his vow; instead, in about 401, he conquered Shahrazūr.[25]

Vows and oaths are usually treated together in works of Islamic law; the *amān*, or guarantee of safe conduct, is, however, often treated in chapters on the ethics of war. The *amān* is essentially akin to the vow, because it is a unilateral swearing before God to adhere to some future course of action. Consequently the *amān*, the oath, and the vow very often overlapped in actual practice. When, in 392/1002, Abū 'Alī Ismā'il, as discussed above, asked for an *amān* from Bahā' ad-Daulah, the king, after he had read it through, wrote on it, "I have sworn (*ḥalaftu*) to this oath (*yamīn*) and undertake to observe it with fidelity (*wafā'*)." Rebellious military officials, disgraced officials, and even tributary kings often requested and received *amāns*; and they usually acted as if they could give full trust to these guarantees. Such guarantees were, of all formally sworn oaths and vows, the most tempting to break, since reasons of state argued so strongly for disarming a rebel by any means, even by perjury. When al-Manṣūr, the second 'Abbāsid caliph, offered an *amān* to the 'Alid Muḥammad an-Nafs az-Zakīyah, who had started a militarily weak (if morally threatening) rebellion in the Ḥijāz in 145, Muḥammad replied "which of [your] *amāns* are you offering us [the 'Alids], that of Ibn Hubairah, or your uncle 'Abd Allāh b. 'Alī, or of Abū Muslim?" Each of these important men had received an *amān* from al-Manṣūr or from his brother, and each one had been betrayed; in the short run, the 'Abbāsids had prospered through their bad faith.[26]

Vows had a more basic political function than just indicating the earnest seriousness of the swearer, or his intention to guarantee someone's safety; but to understand this function, we must describe the larger importance of *nīyah*, intention, in contemporary Islamic ethics. Oaths, *amāns*, and vows respecting future conduct toward others very often included a declaration of good *nīyah* or intention; and "intention" was one of the bridges that joined oath-bound loyalties to other loyalties in Buyid society. There is a famous *ḥadith* that states, "works are really according to intention"; that is, that the value of a man's works will be reckoned by God only according to what a man intended, and not according to what a man actually did. This concept of *nīyah* forms a central axis around which all Islamic discussions of morality revolve, both in this period and in most other periods. When Rukn ad-Daulah's vizier Abū 'l-Faḍl b. al-'Amīd said that Rukn ad-Daulah had defeated the Khurasanian *ghāzīs* in 355 because of "his good intention (*ḥusn nīyatihī*) and the prayers of his subjects (*ra'īyah*) on his behalf, and Almighty God's concern for men," the vizier was speaking both of the good "intention" made explicit in certain of the king's vows, and of the intention implicit in his many cognate acts of solicitude for his subjects. This "good intention" was understood to cause God to support his rule. It was assumed that if the consequence of the king's good intention was both the support of God and the gratitude of his subjects, this good intention would so inspire his subjects that they would pray to God on the king's behalf.[27]

Sovereignty and the Vow

It could be said that in some respects both a ruler and his dynasty believed themselves to hold their position through a special compact, resembling a vow, which the ruler and the dynasty had contracted with God. This compact did not amount to a "social contract," of course, since the subject population were not parties to the compact. Subjects were, nevertheless, the beneficiaries of the compact; and it was therefore in the interest of the dynasty to encourage the population to believe that the compact was still in force, and was still acting to the advantage of its beneficiaries. A striking example of this kind of compact is offered by the story that Abū 'l-Faḍl b. al-'Amīd himself told to explain the unexpected success of Rukn ad-Daulah when heavily pressed by the Sāmānid army near Isfahan in 340. Rukn ad-Daulah, short of supplies and outnumbered, told his vizier, Ibn al-'Amīd, that he wanted to flee. " 'A week ago,' Ibn al-'Amid replied, 'you were respected by kings throughout the Islamic world; now you only rule a small encampment. There is no refuge' " he continued, " 'except in God Almighty. So purify your intention toward Him (*ukhluṣṣ nīyataka lahū*), and make a resolution (*i'qid 'azīmataka*) privately between yourself and Him, the sincerity and earnestness of which He may know; and determine henceforth to do good to the Muslim community and to all mankind. Make vows to Him (*'āhiduhū*), which you will perform and fulfill, to do good works (*al-a'māl aṣ-ṣāliḥah*), and to show kindness (*iḥsān*) to all those over whom you may come to rule; for all human expedients are exhausted.' He smiled [related Ibn al-'Amid], and said to me, 'Abu 'l-Faḍl [Ibn al-'Amīd], I had resorted to those expedients before you spoke. I have already made my intention correct (*ṣidq an-nīyah*) and formed vows appropriate for such a case.' " Later that night, Rukn ad-Daulah summoned Ibn al-'Amīd, and said that in a dream, " 'I seemed to be on my horse Fīrūz and our enemy had fled; and you were riding at my side and reminding me of God's favor (*ni'mah*) in this matter, and how a victory had come that we had not expected. We were talking of this and of similar things until my eye reached through the dust of the cavalcade to the ground and I saw the glint of a signet (*khātam*) on the ground where it had fallen from its owner into the dirt. I said to my *rikābī*, "*ghulām*, bring me that signet." He bent and raised it to me, and it proved to be a *khātam* of turquoise (*fīrūzaj*). I took it and put it on my index finger and considered myself blessed through it (*tabarraktu bihī*).' " Since *fīrūz* meant "victory" and *fīrūzaj* meant "victorious" in Persian, Rukn ad-Daulah took their appearance in his dream to be an omen. At dawn the next day the king and his followers found that the Sāmānid army, unable to endure hunger with the fortitude of the Dailamīs, had given up and deserted their camp; and when they rode into their camp, Rukn ad-Daulah, according to Ibn al-'Amīd's story, found a signet of turquoise (*fīrūzaj*).[28]

The night before this unexpected victory, the vizier may actually have said, "better to die on a throne than in a stable," or, "the Sāmānids are more desperate than we; tomorrow, when they have fled, let us represent the victory as God's work." It is even possible that the vizier said the words he quoted himself as saying. For us, all that matters is that Ibn al-'Amīd thought it worth telling a story that represented God as saving the rule of Rukn ad-Daulah because the ruler had formed an "intention" that was "correct" for a king, and because the king had made the appropriate vows. As we have seen, Ibn al-'Amīd also told people that Rukn ad-Daulah had defeated the Khurasanian *ghāzīs* because of his "goodness of intention, and the prayers of his subjects on his behalf, and Almighty God's concern for men." The vizier was clearly trying to establish for his employer an image consonant with the social style and the self-interest of his subjects—the image of a king confirmed in his rule by a compact with God.

Exactly because such vows and the support or sanction that God gave them were so well understood, we know of many rulers and dynasties who were represented as ruling in the shadow of the divine grace that such compacts granted to them. The caliph ar-Rāḍī (ruled 322/329/940-944) told his courtiers that when the soldiers of the previous caliph, al-Qāhir, who meant him great harm, were searching the house in which he was hiding, " 'I made a compact before God [that is, obligated myself before God (*'āhadtu Allāh*)] that if he saved me from the hand of al-Qāhir, I would refrain from many sinful things; and that I would, if invested with the caliphate, grant amnesty to those who went into hiding, release the estates of those disgraced, and give pious endowments for the support of the Ṭālibids [the clan of 'Alī]. I had hardly finished my vow (*nadhr*) when the people [searching for me] left."[29] He fulfilled his vows on acceding to the throne. In a larger sense, when Abū 'l-'Abbās said in the inaugural speech of the 'Abbāsid dynasty in 149, "you have the guarantee of God (*dhimmah Allāh*), of his Prophet, and of al-'Abbās that we will govern you in accord with what God has revealed . . . and will behave toward both high and low among you according to the example of the Messenger of God," he was stating the original compact under which his dynasty would claim to rule; for *dhimmah Allāh*, like *'ahd Allāh*, is one of the basic forms of stating a pledge to God.[30]

It is important to realize how often public works were represented as fulfillments of vows, and therefore served to confirm that the basic contractual relation of the ruler and God was in force and was working, as God wished, to benefit the subjects of such a ruler. The great vizier 'Alī b. 'Īsā was the exemplar in the late ʿAbbāsid period of the tradition of ethical administration as scrupulous custodianship. When the Buyid Muʿizz ad-Daulah conquered Iraq, ʿAlī, although an old man, came to pay his respects. He said to the young king, " 'one of the matters most worthy of receiving the attention of the emir and of priority in his regard is the repair of these breaches [in the irrigation canals of central Iraq], which are the root of the ruin and devastation of the Sawād.' Muʿizz ad-Daulah said, 'I take a vow to God (*nadhartu li-llāh*) in the presence of those here that I will give nothing precedence over this matter, even if I must spend all I possess on it.' "

His subjects knew that Muʿizz ad-Daulah was sincere in his vow, and his efforts to fulfill this vow evoked the kind of nonmilitary loyalty that helped the Buyid regime consolidate its rule. When Muʿizz ad-Daulah reentered Baghdad after defeating the rebellious Dailamī general Rūzbahān in 345/957, "the people gathered on the banks and invoked blessings (*dāʿū*) on him, and curses on Rūzbahān. For indeed the populace (*ʿāmmah*) were attached to the reign (*muḥibbīn li-ayyām*) of Muʿizz ad-Daulah because of what he had done to repair the breach of the Nahr Rūfīl and that of Bādūriyā. For he had himself gone out to repair this breach and himself carried earth in the bosom of his cloak, to set an example to his whole army. . . . When he had repaired the breaches, Baghdad became prosperous, fine bread being sold at twenty *raṭls* the *dirham*. Hence the populace were attached to his reign and loved him." No doubt, for such benefits they would have loved him without any vow. It is significant, however, to find that here, as in so many other places, at an important psychological moment in his regime, the ruler signals his intentions toward his subjects by publicly forming a covenant with God. ʿAlī b. ʿĪsā, as a "grand old man" of the previous regime, had taught the young king a political as well as a moral lesson.[31]

The "dream of sovereignty" as a form of the compactual basis for rule is closely similar to the vow. Such dreams are a common theme in Near Eastern literature, but little attention has been paid to the compact between the ruler and God that these dreams imply. It is not surprising that the dream is used to express a compact of sovereignty, since dreams were commonly taken as omens that predicted political events. For example, the Buyid king 'Aḍud ad-Daulah told his courtiers that his mother, when she was pregnant with him, saw the revered 'Alī in a dream and asked 'Alī to pray to God for her. 'Alī promised her a son, whose brilliant future he predicted, with suspiciously accurate detail; and 'Alī also predicted the future of his grandsons descended through 'Aḍud ad-Daulah. It cost the great king nothing to tell such a story, which may have had a kernel of truth; in fact, a similar story was apparently told by the first three Buyids about a dream of their father, Būyah. Doubtless all these stories confirmed that the achievements of the Buyids were divinely ordained, and that they were men of destiny.

The dream of sovereignty is found in its full form in the history of the Ṭāhirids, the dynasty that ruled Khurasan from 205/820 to 259/872. In a dream, Ṭāhir, the founder of the dynasty, had been promised worldly greatness if he protected the Prophet's descendants. Then, when Ṭāhir's grandson killed the 'Alid Yaḥyā b. 'Umar in 250, the Prophet Muḥammad told the grandson in a dream that "you have violated your oath (*nakathtum*)"; and, of course, this grandson was the last king of his line. The story may well have been fabricated by descendants of 'Alī; but none of its traits seemed improbable to its audience. A story told on more certain authority concerns the dream that the future caliph al-Qādir had when he was a refugee in the Marsh. He claimed that he dreamed that 'Alī helped him cross a body of water, then told him that sovereignty would come to him, and instructed him to treat the 'Alids and their partisans well. Al-Qādir (ruled 381/991–422/1030), according to his own account, acceded to the caliphate almost immediately after this event. Other dynasties and rulers probably used such dreams to express the divine compact that had conferred rule upon them, or so they wished their subjects to believe. Unfortunately, we only rarely hear a full account of the conditions, if any, joined by God to the promises of sovereignty that are given in such dreams.[32]

All of these vows and vow-like promises share certain general characteristics. They are all, like oaths, compacts involving two persons, God and a man. While God is merely the divine witness to an oath, He is one of the two principal parties in the making and accepting of a vow. Since God has no need for the benefits that men can exchange by oaths, the principal object of vows is some form of conduct by the human party to the vow. The human party may form a vow that involves only himself. But vows often include a resolution to act toward certain groups of people, or toward every one in the future, in a certain fashion: one may vow, for example, to treat one's subjects with justice and generosity, or the like. Oaths between two humans do at times contain such clauses concerning other parties, but the treatment of third parties is usually incidental to the main purpose of the oath.

In the case of vows, the treatment of third parties is very often the main purpose of the vow, since God, the owner of the world and of the day of judgment, can hardly be said to need the promise of good treatment from men who contract a vow with Him. Vows, therefore, come closest to formal open-ended commitments to groups of people, even to people one has not yet met, and even to those unborn. In the absence of artificial or juridical persons like the corporation and the municipality to which, in contemporary law, one can undertake certain obligations, the vow was as near as anyone came in the Buyid Near East to undertaking a personal and formal commitment to a group. There is still a very great distance between the vow and our contemporary understanding of such a personal and formal commitment. Almost no group in the Buyid period could be committed *de jure* by the oaths or vows of its leaders, since capacity, the legal right to contract, still remained individual; and the vow was a form of unilateral contract between God and a single man. Western societies are familiar not only with commitments by individuals to groups, but also by groups to an individual and by groups to each other. The vow cannot admit these other categories; and, in fact, in the Near Eastern context of the fourth/tenth and fifth/eleventh centuries, commitments of these varieties were virtually all informal.

Gratitude for Benefit

We have seen how some form of loyalty was inspired in the subject population when the ruler was believed to carry out good works in fulfillment of his vow. In consequence, his subjects invoked God's blessings on the ruler, and offered cooperation with the processes of government. Yet even when a king or caliph performed good works to the benefit of his subordinates outside of the context of a vow, these good works were understood to carry some kind of obligation. It is this obligation to which al-Muqtadir referred when he said in his letter to his rebellious troops, "I claim gratitude for benefits and favors; you enjoy benefits and gifts from me which I hope you will acknowledge and consider binding." The ties created by "benefit" were obviously not contracted in the ceremonious fashion in which men made oaths; these ties could, nevertheless, be formal and were often considered binding.

Again, the moral relation that was created by benefit had been prefigured by the relation between man and God as Muslims understood it to be described in the Koran. In the Koran, benefits that God has granted to men, for which men are repeatedly urged to be "grateful," extend from the very substances of life and the beauty of creation to the blessing of revelation and the Koran itself. Collectively, these benefits are beyond counting (16:18), yet God holds men accountable for the acceptance or rejection of any specific benefit; speaking of the signs of the truth of revelation, the Koran says, "if any one, after God's benefit (*ni'mah*) has come to him, substitutes [something else], God is strict in punishment" (2:211).

The Koran repeatedly emphasizes that the Believer is "thankful" (*shākir*) for these countless benefits; and that gratitude is one of the basic spiritual qualities that accompanies true belief. Man should be like Abraham, who was "a model," "showing gratitude for His benefits (*shākiran li-an'umihī*)" (16:121). The opposite of *shukr an-ni'mah*, "gratitude for benefit," with its implications of the appreciation and recognition of God's lordship and generosity with a responsive heart, is *kufr an-ni'mah*, "ingratitude for benefit," with its implication of rejection, resistance, and denial. Hence, of course, the disbeliever is called in the Koran, and in the Islamic tradition in general, *al-kāfir*, the "ingrate." Speaking of the ancient Israelites, the Koran says, "And remember, your Lord caused it to be proclaimed, 'If you are grateful, I will add more [benefits]; but if you show ingratitude, my punishment is terrible indeed' " (14:7).

It is not surprising, therefore, that when subjects received any sort of bounty from their ruler, he should describe the loyalty and obligation created as *shukr an-ni'mah*, "gratitude for benefit." For those immediately associated with the regime, the benefits were so obvious that the ruler regarded his *ni'mah* as tying them to a very self-evident obligation. Correspondingly, ambitious men asked for open benefit if they wished to be associated with the regime. The venomous and ill-tempered Abū Ḥaiyān at-Tauḥīdī, who spent much of his life wandering from court to court hoping to be benefited in the extravagant fashion that he felt he deserved, expressed this idea very succinctly when he said, "the exclusion of an aspirant by a leader (*ra'īs*) is like the ingratitude of a follower for a benefit (*ni'mah*)."[34]

The obligations imposed by *ni'mah* were so openly acknowledged that we find rulers and subjects continually involved in a calculus of their mutual liability. ʿAḍud ad-Daulah said that if troops were paid a day before their pay was actually due, "the difference (*al-faḍl*) weighs on them in our favor." But if paid late, they would complain to the paymaster and "the gratitude arising from generosity (*al-minnah*) is lost," and the government, ʿAḍud ad-Daulah concluded, thereby loses far more than it could profit from delay. A letter written to congratulate the Ḥamdānid Abū Taghlib for his victory over his brothers in 360/971 tells us that his expedition has returned "with the people's gratitude (*shukr ar-raʿīyah*) and their blessings . . . [since] God has realized the thoughts (*ẓunūn*) of his friends and subjects (*ahl ṭāʿatihī*) concerning him, and has confirmed . . . the suppositions of his servants, and of the slaves of his benefits (*ʿabīd niʿamihī*)."

If the loyalty of the general population is described in terms of the collective *niʿmah* received by the population, the far more direct loyalty of servants of the government to the ruler is often described in terms of the specific benefits these servants enjoy. In 315, at the end of the Abbasid period, when ʿAlī b. ʿĪsā was interrogating the ex-vizier al-Khaṣībī on his handling of the government's finances, ʿAlī explained that he did not dispute the right of officials to become wealthy through legal salaries assigned to them. "How [he said], shall we challenge you in this respect when we, like all clerks (*kuttāb*) of the Commander of the Faithful, have our livelihood only through his bounty (*niʿmah*) and beneficence (*iḥsān*), and possess estates we have earned in his service and the service of his ancestor?"[35]

The obligation imposed by God's *niʿmah* found its nearest analogy in the *niʿmah* of the king to his subject; but the obligations that existed between near equals and even the obligations of superiors to inferiors are also often described in terms of *niʿmah*. The Ḥamdānid Nāṣir ad-Daulah had let his sons attack Baghdad in 346, while the Buyids were challenged by the rebellion of one of their officers, Rūzbahān. After his forces defeated both the attacking Ḥamdānids and the rebel Rūzbahān, the Buyid king Mu'izz ad-Daulah wrote Nāṣir ad-Daulah to remind him that Nāṣir ad-Daulah should have controlled his sons, and that he owed his Buyid neighbor better treatment. After all, Mu'izz ad-Daulah had restored Nāṣir ad-Daulah when Takīn ash-Shīrzādī had rebelled against the Ḥamdānids; and, said Mu'izz ad-Daulah, "I thought that you [Nāṣir ad-Daulah] would recognize my claim for this benefit (*haqq hādhihī an-ni'mah*), and that, as a result, your soul would move you to repay it (*al-mujāzāt*)." Instead, said Mu'izz ad-Daulah, he had been greeted with "betrayal" (*ghadr*). Nāṣir ad-Daulah in his answer acknowledged that Mu'izz ad-Daulah was right to reprove him, and said his sons had acted on their own initiative.[36]

In one remarkable conversation, we even hear the possible beneficiary of a political plot tell his chief supporter that the expected benefit would oblige him, the beneficiary, as deeply as would an oath sworn to the supporter. During the final illness of the caliph al-Muktafī (d. 289/902), the vizier al-'Abbās considered possible candidates for the succession in the 'Abbāsid family. For this purpose he secretly interviewed Muḥammad, the son of the former caliph al-Mu'tamid: " '[The vizier said to him,] what will I get if I hand this government over to you?' Muḥammad, son of al-Mu'tamid, said to him, 'You will get the reward, esteem, and favored position that you deserve.' Al-'Abbās said to him, 'I want you to swear to me that you will not abandon me in either of two situations: if you wish my services, I will advise you sincerely and exert every effort in obedience to your wishes and in collecting money for you, as I have done for others; and if you favor someone else, then treat me with honor and preserve me, not laying a hand on my person or wealth, nor on any one of my dependents.' Muḥammad, son of al-Mu'tamid, who had a good mind and excellent principles, said, 'If you do not hand this authority to me, I will not have the means to reward you justly and appropriately; [otherwise] how could I [fail to do so] when you have been the cause and means [of my access] to such [authority]?' " Al-'Abbās again asked him to swear, and he said, " 'If I do not fulfill what you desire without an oath, I will not fulfill it with an oath.' The judge Muḥammad [who was probably the only other person present] said to al-'Abbās, 'Be pleased with this much from him—it is better than an oath.' " The implication is that for a truly honorable man, acknowledgment of *ni'mah* is as sacred as the tie of an oath; by extension, of course, we see that the oath seemed a safer way to guarantee a specific course of conduct in the future. Muḥammad b. al-Mu'tamid, incidentally, never became caliph.[37]

The reverse of this explicit identification of loyalty and gratitude was, of course, the association of ingratitude and disloyalty. As the Koranic analogy implied, ingratitude was morally reprehensible between man and man, as well as between man and God. Men were sincerely troubled to think that they might be considered "ingrates." When the caliphal general Yāqūt was in southern Iraq in the 320s, he hesitated to fight a hostile army because, he said, "it will be thought that I was ungrateful to my benefactor (*kafartu ni'mata maulāya*), and so people will curse me." Eventually this hesitation cost Yāqūt his life. Doubtless Yāqūt feared not only what his contemporaries would think of him, but also the disgrace to his name after his death. When the severed head of Abū 'l-Haijā' b. Ḥamdān, the ancestor of the Ḥamdānids, was paraded through Baghdad in 317 (after the collapse of the rebellion in favor of the caliph al-Qāhir), it was accompanied by a crier who called out, "this is the recompense of one who rebels against his master and is ungrateful for his benefits." The opinion of one's contemporaries and post-mortem disgrace were not, however, the only sanctions against ingratitude; God, it was said, would even seal the fate of a dynasty for its ingratitude. When the last of the semi-independent Sīmjūrid governors of Khurasan was defeated in 385/995, it was "the end of the importance of the house of Sīmjūr, as a retribution for their ingratitude to the kindness of their master (*jazā'an li-kufrān iḥsān maulāhum*)."[38]

Since one acknowledged ties by accepting *ni'mah*, a man could cast off ties, and in particular could cast off his allegiance, by claiming that no *ni'mah* had been given by the other party. Men even extended this argument to their relations with God; and in spite of the horrifying blasphemy of disclaiming God's bounty, at least two authors of the fourth/tenth century ask why a man owes anything to God if he gets almost nothing in return. An author living in Bukhārā in the early tenth century writes, "as a pauper I do not pray to God; to Him pray the powerful and wealthy. . . . Of course Nūḥ [the Sāmānid ruler] prays, since the East bends before his power; but why should I pray? Where is my power, my house, my horse, my bridle, my fine belt? . . . Were I to pray when my right hand does not possess an inch of earth, I would be a hypocrite. Yes, if God creates prosperity for me, then I will not stop praying as long as lightning flashes in the heavens; but the prayer of one in evil condition is a fraud."[39]

Ni'mah, then, like the oath, was a means to establish important new ties in society; and like the oath, it remained largely concerned with ties between individuals. A vizier, according to the Buyid official and historian Miskawaih, should beware lest the soldiers attribute what they receive to him "rather than to their master and the [real] author of their benefits (*walī ni'amihim*)," since the king will resent their forming gratitude to anyone but himself. No abstract gratitude to the state is imaginable. Some forms of *ni'mah*, like public works, resembled the vow in that they were transactions between a single man and an abstractly defined category of men; but those men were presumed to be grateful individually, and "to invoke God's blessing" on the donor rather than to be grateful in any corporate fashion. They were in many ways like those who benefited from a vow.

Nevertheless, *ni'mah* differed from the oath and the vow in that benefaction and gratitude were less definable commitments, and commitments that could be retracted; in contrast, an oath or vow was a clear commitment that could be retracted only in extraordinary circumstances. The commercial analogy fitted the continuing barter of *ni'mah* and gratitude, while it was appropriate only for the final and irrevocable "sale" that took place at the origin of a course of action dependent on an oath or vow. This commercial analogy was therefore frequently and self-consciously used; but it was an analogy appropriate to a commerce of long-standing patterns of trade, in which, for all the calculus of benefit, neither seller nor customer wanted a final "reckoning" of accounts between them, since such a reckoning would sever the bonds of loyalty that the exchange had created.

Al-Ḥasan b. 'Alī b. Zaid al-Munajjim, long employed as tax collector for Wāsiṭ under the Buyid Mu'izz ad-Daulah, used to be praised for establishing pious endowments in his district, for repairing the local irrigation system, and for giving alms to the appropriate people. Privately, al-Munajjim said that he did these things for God; but, he added, if he had done them for appearances, that would be good too, and why shouldn't the local population keep up appearances (*riyā'an*) by a matching hypocritical pretense that they believed in the high-minded motives of the benefactor? Nowadays, he complained, if a man is munificent (*jawād*) they say he is "making commerce with his munificence" (*mutājirun bi-jūdihī*) and consider him a miser. We can discount the claim in this anecdote that men were so much more pious in a period before al-Munajjim's governorship; al-Munajjim wants the exchange of gratitude and benefit to continue, since he believes men should continue to praise him to his face, and he only hopes they will practice similar hypocrisy behind his back.[40]

Royal Generosity and Ties of Benefit

To establish a loyalty based on such an open-ended barter in benefits and gratitude took time, especially when several benefactors were competing for the loyalty of the same beneficiaries. Contemporary observers clearly understood that the Buyids—and their competitors—were struggling to establish these ties with their troops, and that the consolidation of their power was a direct reflection of their success in doing so. The series of events by which the Buyids came to control their fellow countrymen, the Dailamīs, show their gradual success in establishing these ties. When the Shī'ī Dailamīs invaded the Iranian plateau, they entered regions in which the majority of the population in some sense or other recognized the 'Abbāsid claim, a claim in which most of the Dailamīs had never believed. Even the traditional "kings" of the Dailamīs, who had once exercised relatively weak and localized authority over them, had been cast aside. No traditional source of authority seemed capable of restraining them, and in the first instance, before they adopted the views of the other inhabitants of western Iran and Iraq, the obligation of *ni'mah* proved to be the most powerful means to persuade the Dailamīs to adhere to any fixed loyalty.

The rulers of the early fourth/tenth century who accepted Dailamī mercenaries into their armies recognized the urgency of creating such ties even if they were, at first, a very fragile basis for loyalty. In order to frighten the caliph and extort money from him, Abū 'Abd Allāh al-Barīdī sent him a message when he occupied Baghdad in 329/941 that the Dailamī soldiers of fortune in the army of the Barīdīs "do not recognize the *bai'ah* [to the 'Abbāsids], and no acts of generosity from you have laid them under any obligation (*lā minan laka fī riqābihim*)." The Dailamīs at this period were not greatly restrained by short-lived ties of *ni'mah*; they were ready to bolt from one leader to another in search of enormous and immediate grants of money. Al-Barīdī was not the only political leader who feared them; the Dailamī leaders themselves faced this problem. When Mardāwīj, for example, revolted against the freebooting Dailamī general Asfār b. Shīrawaih, the latter decided to give up the struggle, in spite of his considerable prestige among the Dailamīs, because he found he had too little money to lure back his troops.

The only resource open to these condottieri was an unstinting generosity and a frank avowal that self-interest argued for cooperation in plundering these new conquests, so that all—leaders and simple soldiers—might have a larger share. The independent Turkish general Tūzūn, after he defeated the Ḥamdānid Saif ad-Daulah in 332/943, distributed some of the stores captured in the battle, then gathered his men and said, "I am one of you, and it is your interest that I want." In this manner some leaders could buy time and nurture the sense of obligation that such benefaction might create; then, gradually, other arguments could be advanced to give leadership a dimension of royalty.

As we have seen, in western Iran and in Iraq, the Buyids eventually outstripped all other leaders in this effort; but the Ziyārids had already begun to succeed in this respect when the Buyids started their career, and their dynasty outlasted the Buyids. As the fortunes of the Ziyārid Mardāwīj improved, Dailamīs came to him from all sides because of his "generosity" to his army. The young sons of the fisherman Būyah, who were then officers in the service of Mākān, felt the attraction of Mardāwīj's success. When Mākān was defeated, 'Alī b. Būyah and his brother al-Ḥasan asked his permission to join Mardāwīj, adding with winning candor, "if you become powerful again, we will return to you." Permission was granted, and the Ziyārid immediately assigned the small town and district of al-Karaj in western Iran to 'Alī.

From this point on, all sources emphasize the role of generosity in 'Alī's success. "The cause of the rise of 'Alī b. Būyah," says Miskawaih, "and of his attaining what he did, was the great generosity (*samāḥah*) in his temperament, and his patience (*sa'ah aṣ-ṣadr*)." For over a decade, 'Alī gave away everything he got; he understood the soldiers' game of the mid-tenth century as few other leaders did, and ended as its most successful player. After he defeated the caliphal army under Yāqūt in 322, 'Alī was "generous" to the prisoners, and gave them the choice of staying with him or joining Yāqūt; naturally, most of them chose to stay. For the first generation of Buyid leaders there was no other policy; as Miskawaih points out, al-Ḥasan b. Būyah (Rukn ad-Daulah) "was the leader of the [Dailamīs] only by virtue of his great generosity (*samāḥah*) and his indulgence (*musāmaḥah*) in matters that [a genuine] ruler does not tolerate from those he rules." Yet, in the long run, these first Buyids also knew when to circumscribe their liberality, so that their generosity did not become an automatic and therefore worthless trait.[41]

The Buyids were also fortunate in their opponents. 'Abbāsid pretenders had always offered the central 'Abbāsid army generous rewards for support against the ruling member of the 'Abbāsid family, and the army of Baghdad had consequently become the most cynical and frankly mercenary army of the early fourth century. When Mu'nis was advancing on Baghdad in 320, the caliph's chief commander told his master that "the soldiers only fight for money; if it is produced, fighting will be unnecessary, for most of Mu'nis' men will desert." The caliph, however, was bankrupt, and was duly overthrown and replaced by a caliph chosen by Mu'nis. At least an 'Abbāsid, if not obeyed, would be replaced by another powerless 'Abbāsid; but many other opponents of the Buyids were not as fortunate as the 'Abbāsids, and lacked the awe of kingship created by a rule of even two generations. For example, when the first Barīdī ruler was killed in 332, he was succeeded by his brother and murderer Abū al-Ḥusain. But Abū al-Ḥusain did not give lavishly to the troops in a spirit of camaraderie, as his brother had done; instead, he treated the Turks and Dailamīs with haughty contempt. From this point on, the unexpected good fortune of this family of former clerks disappeared, and they were progressively deserted by their troops until their power disappeared about ten years later.[42]

Patronage

Gradually, the Buyids were able to transform their control of their army so that it was no longer based purely on transient moods of gratitude from the soldiers who received their largesse. The Buyids were able to establish a more permanent loyalty partly because soldiers became enmeshed in the calculus of *ni'mah*, partly because the Dailamīs came to believe that their own good fortune was tied to the success of the Buyids, and partly because the Buyids ruled long enough to foster a generation of soldiers who regarded themselves as the special protégés of the Buyids, for whom these kings were almost foster parents. The foster-parent relation was one of the most important ways in which new ties were established. This relation is described in the various forms of the word *ṣana'a*, which in its simplest sense means "to make," but also means "to do a kindness," "to tend well," and "to nourish, rear."

Moses, the classic foundling of fortune, is told by God in the Koran that when his mother put him in the Nile, "I cast [the garment of] loveableness from me over you, and did so that you might be reared (*tuṣna'a*) in my sight" (20:39/40). Moses therefore grew up with the education and experience that God had desired for him, at which point God said to him, "*Wa-ṣṭana'tu-ka li-nafsī*" (20:41/43), which Muslim commentators understood to mean, "I have chosen you for myself [to establish my proof and to serve as my spokesman]," or, "I have reared you for myself [for a special task]."

The form of the verb used in the last quotation, *iṣṭana'a* (infinitive *iṣṭinā'*), appears frequently in the texts of the fourth and fifth centuries in the sense "to foster someone's career."

Iṣṭināʿ is a surprisingly formal and serious relationship; a man expected from his protégé (*muṣṭanaʿ* or *ṣanīʿ* or *sanīʿah*) not an easy gratitude and affection, but a lifelong commitment of sizable dimensions. To say "he is my *ṣaniʿah*" meant "he is the person I have reared, educated, and trained well," and the obligation to such a patron was like the obligation to a parent, except that it was neither inherited nor transferable by legacy. It was, moreover, an obligation that could be made between men more nearly equal in age than father and son. It was an ideal way for political men to make formal ties out of the *niʿmah* that they bestowed on a few chosen subordinates.[43]

The most dangerous and unstable element in the state was the army; and the Buyids turned to *iṣṭināʿ* to control and make stable the loyalties that they could command at first only by lavish and necessarily short-lived displays of generosity. The Buyids were not the first Islamic regime to make extensive use of *iṣṭināʿ*. The ʿAbbāsids had rebuilt their army by combining slavery and *iṣṭināʿ* in a powerful new institution. This institution survived and became a central feature of most Near Eastern empires right up to the nineteenth century; since it is one of the best documented forms of *inṣṭināʿ*, it offers a convenient point to begin a discussion of loyalty acquired through patronage.

The ʿAbbāsids had originally built their empire with an army from the large northeastern Iranian province of Khurasan. But the disgrace of the Khurasanian officials of the Barmakid family, and the antagonism of the civil war against al-Amīn and al-Maʾmūn, destroyed the trust between Baghdad and Khurasan that had given the Khurasanians a reason to be actively loyal. Speaking on behalf of eastern Iranians, one poet who supported the Ṣaffārid rebellion against the ʿAbbāsids wrote, "our fathers gave you your sovereignty, but you showed no gratitude for our benefaction." When this poem was written, very few of their subjects seem to have felt that they had reason to stand up and fight for the ʿAbbāsids; the hopes raised by the ʿAbbāsid revolution had long since disappeared, and it was clear that no category of the 'Abbāsids' subjects or province of their empire felt they owed military support for the doubtful benefits that they could bestow. The 'Abbāsids reached beyond the borders of their state, and by purchase or gift acquired Turkish slave boys, *ghilmān* (singular *ghulām*), who were brought up as if they were foster children of the caliph.[44]

The Turkish "slave" soldier and his patron were bound together by the tie of *walā'* or clientship, as well as *iṣṭinā'*, though patrons in the fourth and fifth centuries seem to have very frequently reminded these soldiers of their obligations in terms of *iṣṭinā'*, and very seldom in terms of *walā'*. The military *ghulām* owed his training, his equipment, and above all his privileged place in society to the care and interest of his patron, who usually acted as the foster parent of the *ghulām* from adolescence. This training included continual efforts to inculcate obedience and gratitude to his patron. The gratitude of the *ghulām* for these benefits was strengthened by the general ethic of *ni'mah* and of filial duty. Even the teachings of Islamic law on the duty of the freed man to his former master supported this relationship, and scrupulous men did not set these teachings aside with indifference. When Yāqūt, the great *ghulām* commander referred to above, found that a lesser man had gained control of the caliph ar-Rāḍī in 324, and had, in the caliph's name, arrested Yāqūt's sons, this commander sought the opinions of the jurists (*fuqahā'*), who told him that they did not regard it as lawful for him to rebel against his master. Yāqūt, for this and other reasons, remained in Hamletic indecision in southern Iraq until he was destroyed.

The legal ties, however, were less important than the enduring ties of affection that often developed between a master and his *ghulām*, especially when the *ghulām* became an important military figure whom the law could not easily call to account. In 329, Bajkam, the Turkish *amīr al-umarā'*, heard that the patron who had raised and trained him, the fierce condottiere Mākān b. Kākī, had died. Bajkam had risen far higher in the world than Mākān, whom he had left years ago; nonetheless, he was deeply affected by news of Mākān's death, and sat to receive condolences. "He was my master (*maulāya*)," said Bajkam, "I have never seen a cavalier (*fāris*) like him."

When, as we have related above, in the reign of ar-Rāḍī the prominent general Yāqūt was squandering his resources in southern Iraq because of his reluctance to rebel against the caliph, who was then controlled by an *amīr al-umarā'* who had arrested Yāqūt's sons, one of Yāqūt's lieutenants decided to take the initiative. The lieutenant took three thousand of Yāqūt's troops and marched against the Barīdīs in al-Ahwāz so that Yāqūt might at least have a province to rule, after which he could either compromise with the *amīr al-umarā'* or go to Baghdad and himself become *amīr al-umarā'*. A messenger from Yāqūt overtook the lieutenant and foolishly dissuaded him from continuing his march. In his conversation with the messenger, the lieutenant graphically described his debt to Yāqūt. "I will not rebel against my master [Yāqūt]," he said, "for he bought me, raised me, and showed me favor (*iṣṭana'a-nī*)."[45]

According to the Islamic lawbooks, a patronage of clients was inheritable or transferable; but the more important personal tie of the *ghulām* to his foster parent was, by its nature, impossible to pass on. The *ghulām* sometimes extended his feelings of loyalty to his patron's children, whom he might have known since childhood; further extension of the tie between *ghulām* and patron was usually a formal working arrangement in which personal loyalty could only be created by a whole set of new acts of generosity to the *ghulām*: in effect, by a concerted effort of *iṣṭinā'* or patronage. After the defeat and death of the Buyid ruler of Iraq, 'Izz ad-Daulah, his family took refuge with Alftakīn in Damascus; for even though Alftakīn had led an unsuccessful rebellion against 'Izz ad-Daulah, he had originally been the client (*maulā*) of Mu'izz ad-Daulah, the father of 'Izz ad-Daulah. Alftakīn, hearing that the family of his patron was coming, "lived up to his duty by them" (*qaḍā ḥuqūqahum*). Together, they fought against al-'Azīz, who had determined to bring southern Syria permanently under Fatimid control. Al-'Azīz won, but was so impressed with his captured opponent that he purchased (presumably, from the family of 'Izz ad-Daulah) the right to be Alftakīn's patron (*ishtarā walā'ahū*), and Alftakīn became "like a slave" to al-'Azīz. Here, the transferrence of loyalty was accomplished by the marked favor of al-'Azīz, which soon made Alftakīn a major figure in the Fatimid state.[46]

In most cases, people expected the *ghulām* to have his strongest loyalty to his original patron. Since this patron might be the subject or even the *ghulām* of a king, the state was supported by a many-tiered loyalty that needed frequent adjustment. The landlords of Fārs had *ghulāms* (as very likely did large landholders elsewhere); and 'Alī b. Būyah had to fight some of them when he first entered Shiraz in 320/932. An argument appointing the tax-farmer Ḥāmid b. al-'Abbās as vizier in 306 was that he possessed four hundred personal *ghulāms*, each of whom possessed his own *ghulāms*. Ḥāmid's subsequent arrival in Baghdad, accompanied by the trumpet blasts of his personal army, caused a great sensation. Most often, however, we hear of the *ghulāms* who belonged to important *ghulām* commanders in government service. Mu'nis, when he quarreled with the caliph al-Qāhir in 320, left Baghdad accompanied by about two thousand *ghulāms*, including many blacks. This practice continued throughout the Būyid period; for example, in 363 the leading Turkish commander of the Buyid 'Izz ad-Daulah had four hundred "*mamlūk ghulāms*."[47]

Such regiments, founded on the patronage of a leading commander, lasted a generation or two after their founder's death. It is common in the later 'Abbāsid and Buyid periods to read of a group of soldiers named after their original but deceased patron, as, for example, we read of the Mu'nisīyah in 323/935, several years after the death of Mu'nis. If a *ghulām* died before his patron, the patron inherited his wealth and followers; in 332/944, for example, the Turkish *amīr al-umarā'* Tūzūn inherited from his *ghulām* commander Yanāl not only a considerable fortune, but also the *ghulāms* who belonged to Yanāl. In most cases, however, the patron was older and died first; and the subsequent transfer of the allegiance of the *ghulāms* was a sensitive matter. When Ya'nis al-Muwaffaqī (originally a *ghulām* of the 'Abbāsid al-Muwaffaq, as his name indicates), an excellent officer of the palace guard, died in 311, the caliph's chamberlain advised the caliph to have the heir apparent gather all of the soldiers, servants, and retinue of Ya'nis and say to them: "I now have Ya'nis's position with you and over you. Increasing magnanimity will be shown to you, and careful examination will be given to your circumstances." Instead, however, the caliph allowed himself to be persuaded by the vizier, Ibn al-Fūrāt, to plunder the dead man's estate. By failing to create an honorable transfer of the loyalties of the *ghulāms* from their former commander to a new commander, the caliph drove one more nail into the coffin of 'Abbāsid rule. In general, *ghulām* regiments, insofar as they preserved a separate identity without a formal transfer, eventually regrouped around one of their outstanding officers of the next generation, and were soon called after their new patron-commander.[48]

The *ghulām* was in general supposed to conduct his dealings with the ruler through his patron; to do otherwise would be to reject the primacy of his tie to that patron. Mu'nis, for example, had bought the clientship of a talented Turkish soldier, Shafī', after that soldier had been freed by the caliph al-Mu'taḍid. A decade or so later Mu'nis attached Shafī' to the service of the caliph al-Muqtadir, and Mu'nis soon grew furious with his "client" when Shafī' failed to support the policy of Mu'nis inside the government. The final straw, however, came in the reign of al-Qāhir, successor to al-Muqtadir. Under this caliph, Shafī' was in disfavor, but did not ask his legal patron, Mu'nis, to intervene with the new caliph for a guarantee of safety (*amān*); instead, Shafī' turned to al-

Kalwadhānī, the deputy vizier. Al-Mu'nis, in a rage, had Shafī' (who was by now a prominent general) brought and sold at auction in his presence; as a patron, Mu'nis had every right to do so. Al-Kalwadhānī bought Shafī' on behalf of the caliph for 70,000 *dinars*, and freed him. Eventually, Shafī' and Mu'nis were reconciled.[49]

Essential to the survival of each ruler was the corps of *ghulāms* whose training he had himself fostered, and who shared the strong affection that *ghulāms* usually felt only for patrons who had sustained their careers in this manner. These were the "king's men" in a very special way, and no one else was supposed to tamper with their affection for the king or call them to account; and outside parties seldom did so unless they intended conspiracy or open revolution. For example, when Abū 'Alī b. Ismā'īl's *ghulāms* were playing polo in Shiraz with the *ghulāms* of the Buyid king, Bahā' ad-Daulah, one of the brawls considered common to the game arose between the two sides. The vizier, Abū 'Alī, withdrew to his palace, refused to receive anyone from the other side, and sent a message suggesting that certain *ghulāms* on the other side be handed over to him. The king was angry at being addressed on the subject of his *ghulāms*, and even angrier at the suggestion that they be handed over. No one could call the king's men to account until he had shown the king that it was to the advantage of the regime. Abū 'Alī's mistake was considered one of the important reasons for his downfall.[50]

Ghulāms, as we have seen, could serve at many levels of government, and might be obliged by the death of their patron or by circumstances to have mixed loyalties. The attachment of *ghulāms* who had been acquired as children or young adolescents to their first master was, however, usually an emotional and direct loyalty that a generous master could count on. This is why they could become, in this special sense, "the king's men." On several occasions the deeply felt loyalties of the *ghulāms* were all that saved a Buyid ruler from defeat and death. The Dailamī general Rūzbahān led most of the army of Iraq into rebellion against Mu'izz ad-Daulah in 345/957; and in the final battle, when the Buyid king seemed near defeat, he addressed the *ghulāms* of his palace, those whom he had himself acquired and whose careers he had fostered: "My children, I have raised you as though you were my sons—now show me your worth." In fact, their final desperate charge carried all before it and crushed the rebellion. Similarly, in 419, when the Buyid Jalāl ad-Daulah was beseiged in his palace by the older *ghulāms* and was on the verge of leaving Baghdad, "the young *ghulāms*" (*aṣaghir al-ghilmān*), who must have been the *ghulāms* whom he had raised himself, rallied to his cause and made it possible for him to stay.

So strong was the tie of foster parenthood and patronage that even *ghulāms* in open rebellion were loath to press home an advantage over their former master. In 363, 'Izz ad-Daulah was in southern Iraq nearly defenseless in the face of the rebellion of his army under Sabuktakīn. Every time a Turkish soldier of the rebellious army would approach him in the thicket where he and a few followers were making a last stand, 'Izz ad-Daulah would remind the soldier of the "benefit" (*ni'mah*) he had received, and of God who, presumably, frowned on such ingratitude, and that the soldier was the "protégé" (*ṣanī'ah*) of himself and of his father; affected by his speech, the soldier would leave him.[51]

Iṣṭinā', or continued patronage, covered a wide variety of relations; and the relation of the freed *ghulām* to his master was only one form of *iṣṭinā'*. Ibn Khaldūn, the great Arab social thinker of the fourteenth century, describes the similarity of all *iṣṭinā'* in his *Muqaddimah*: "When people of group feeling (*'asabiyah*) take as followers (*iṣṭan'a*) people of another descent; or when they take slaves and clients (*mawālī*) into servitude and enter into close contact with them, as we have said, the clients and followers (*muṣṭana'ūn*) share in the group feeling of their masters and take it on as if it were their own group feeling." Sustained patronage was, therefore, an important means of creating new ties on all levels of life; and, undoubtedly, if we had more information on the lowest levels of life, we would see it at work in the relations of landlords to peasants and of grocers to sweepers.

Its importance to the cohesion and structure of the bureaucracy is, however, very well attested in our sources. The Christian clerk 'Īsā b. al-Ḥasan b. Abrūnā, who was private secretary to the Buyid vizier al-Muhallabī, was beaten after the vizier's death when he refused to reveal his patron's hidden wealth. His torturers then threatened him with death, and he said, "God be praised. Shall I be Ibn Abrūnā, the doctor and phlebotomist plying his trade on the street for a [measly fee] of one and a half *dāniqs*, whom the vizier Abū Muḥammad took and patronized (*iṣṭana'nī*), and made his private secretary, and who has become known as one in his service—and [yet] inform people of a treasure he has stored up for his son? By God, I would indeed not do so even if I were to perish." Ibn Fasānjas and al-'Abbās b. al-Ḥasan ash-Shīrāzī, the officials who had succeeded al-Muhallabī, thought so well of him for his loyalty to a deceased patron, that they freed him; and Ibn Abrūnā advanced in their service.[52]

Most professional government clerks, especially those who mastered the official styles of handwriting and composition, started as apprentice clerks at a comparatively young age, and were paid their salaries by the head of the department or section, who was apparently free to choose whichever young men he wanted as copyists and trainees. These heads of department or section were, therefore, in later life acknowledged by these trainees to be their original patrons, and this tie and the obligations it carried are frequently mentioned. Ibn al-Furāt, for example, rose to be the most powerful vizier of the late 'Abbāsid period, the model of the civilian minister who totally dominated the government. Yet he never forgot that Ibn Bisṭām had been his "chief" (*ra'īs*) at some early state in his career, and Ibn al-Furāt always acted toward him with great deference; for, he said, "one's obligation to his superior is not forgotten, and one's debt to him is not discharged." The histories sometimes note the calculated rudeness necessary to overlook such ties of patronage among bureaucrats. When in 333 the vizier Ibn Shīrzād began to fine prominent men arbitrarily in a desperate attempt to keep the government solvent, he included on the list of victims 'Alī b. 'Īsā, who "had fostered" (*iṣṭana'a*) Ibn Shīrzād's career. 'Alī b. 'Īsā came to visit him; Ibn Shīrzād, covered with embarrassment, refused to see him.[53]

A corollary of the important role of *iṣṭinā'* among the clerks was that a man who failed to "foster" protégés thereby failed to create the supporters (or even factions) necessary to monitor and manipulate the bureaucracy effectively when he achieved a position of authority. A man who did not give sustained patronage had, in fact, less chance of ending his career of governmental service alive. In 233/847, one of the former attendants of the ex-vizier Ibn az-Zayyāt said to his former master, as he was being tortured to death, "it was with a view to this or something like it that we used to urge you to act with kindness, to lay people under obligation by showing generosity (*imtinān*), and by doing favors (*ṣanā'i'*) while powerful so that you might reap the benefit when in need."[54]

In the Buyid period, sustained patronage or *iṣṭinā'* in the full sense seems to have been extended only by clerks to clerks and by soldiers to soldiers. The caliph was both a civilian and a soldier, and could claim that his civilian protégés were his "men," as were his *ghulāms*; but even in the 'Abbāsid period, this claim is seldom heard. In the post-'Abbāsid period, when the king was clearly a soldier, insofar as *iṣṭinā'* could cross the lines between the civil and military branches of the government, clerks do not seem to have become the protégés of rulers. In fact, had the ruler fostered the career of protégé clerks in the same way as the head of a department fostered the career of his apprentice clerk, he would have felt embarrassed to disgrace his ministers—an embarrassment no effective ruler would want. The clerks owed their resilience and survival to this distinction. The clerks could not throw their influence around as easily as the officers and generals who were so closely identified with their patron, the king. Yet the clerks, by not becoming "the king's men," were better able than the soldiers both to survive changes of dynasty and to enter the service of new masters.

There are some cases of *iṣṭinā'* patronage between adult men who were roughly equal in station or influence. Ibn Abi 's-Sāj, for example, fostered the Kurdish leader Daisam, who afterwards became ruler of Azerbaijan. The most elaborate example of a formal cultivation of *iṣṭinā'* between grown men appears in the relations of the Turkish *amīr al-umarā'* Bajkam and the caliph ar-Rāḍī. The caliph disliked Ibn Rā'iq, his first mayor of the palace, and secretly encouraged Bajkam to come to Baghdad and replace him as *amīr al-umarā'*. The caliph sent Bajkam his testament (*waṣīyah*) that he would be constantly faithful to Bajkam if Bajkam took over his affairs, while telling Bajkam that "it is incumbent on you to be faithful to the one who has fostered you (*iṣṭana'aka*) and been kind to you." Bajkam agreed to come, and accepted his role as the (pseudo) protégé of the caliph, even though the caliph was now powerless, and could give Bajkam nothing except honors. The caliph was grateful; he told his intimates that whereas Ibn Rā'iq would say, "I created you (*ṣana'tuka*)," or " 'I put you on the throne,' . . . on the contrary [in Bajkam's case] we took the step of making him a protégé (*iṣṭinā'*). If one of his subordinates acted wrongfully, we [said the caliph] found that [Bajkam] would be content with execution and the most severe punishments [for the wrongdoer]. . . . So I am pleased with him. . . . [Still, the caliph concluded,] it would be better if I had all the power, as those before me used to have; but destiny has not granted this to me." In a sense, these counterfeit forms of *iṣṭināʿ* pay tribute to the basic form of *iṣṭināʿ* that exists between superior and inferior. In many situations, when men wanted to portray their sustained affection for one another as something more than the result of an oath, they imitated a style of patronage whose effectiveness was to be seen all around them in society.[55]

The benefits of *iṣṭināʿ* for a protégé encouraged wide-scale imitation of the vocabulary of *iṣṭināʿ* by men who hoped by this means to curry favor with others. The vocabulary was initiated not only by men like Bajkam and the caliph, who wanted to give an honorable and recognizable name to their mutual respect, but also by men who had very casual and temporary ties. Bajkam himself, before he took Baghdad and found a patron worthy of his continued display of feigned humility, had tried to deceive a high secretary of Ibn Rā'iq and to win his confidence by saying, "I am your *ṣanīʿah* and the *ṣanīʿah* of [Ibn Rā'iq] and the seedling [planted] by the two of you."

Iṣṭināʿ even became a common word for favor, including the favor shown by a king to a courtier. After ʿAḍud ad-Daulah arrested the rich and powerful Muḥammad b. ʿUmar al-ʿAlawī in 369, he "showed favor" (*iṣṭanaʿa*) to his brother, who was doubtless supposed to give the king advice and support in the same way as Muḥammad had done. In 322, when the head of the Baghdad police found it impossible to control the famous robber chieftain Ibn Ḥamdī, the police tried to come to some agreement with him by showing him favor (*iṣṭināʿ*); fostering a criminal's career was a long way from the tie of master and apprentice clerk.

The most degenerate word of this family was *muṣānaʿah*, a relative of the words *iṣṭināʿ* and *ṣanīah*. It meant, in its simplest sense, "acting with favor toward a particular person," but was also a common word for bribe. These uses do not imply that the tie of the semiformal *iṣṭināʿ* was weak or weakening; by their flattery, they show its importance.[56]

The Loyalty of Men Who Rose Together

Akin to the sustained patronage of *iṣṭināʿ*, and derived in like manner from the ethic of *niʿmah*, was the loyalty to those who shared one's rise. Like *iṣṭināʿ*, this loyalty was often (though not exclusively) a tie between superior and inferior; and like *iṣṭināʿ*, it was an acquired tie that was often explained as approximating the inborn ties of common ancestry. Like *iṣṭināʿ*, however, it was strongly influenced by the belief in *daulah*, the "turn of good fortune" that was given by God to an individual, to a family, and even to a people.

This loyalty to those who shared one's rise is nowhere seen more vividly than in the ties between the rough soldiers who founded new states and their secretaries. ʿAlī b. Būyah ʿImād ad-Daulah felt that he received the blessing of fortune (*tabarraka*) through his first secretary, Abū Saʿd Isrāʾīl, and greatly favored him even after he founded a kingdom and had taken more technically competent men into royal service. When one of these more competent secretaries persistently attacked Abū Saʿd, the king said to him, "You so-and-so, this man was my companion when I was of humble station. Now I have achieved the position you see, and I cannot tell whether it is my good fortune (*daulatī*) or his that has brought me here. His position cannot be shaken; so beware of applying to me again on this matter." Similarly, when a high official urged Ibn Rāʾiq to dismiss his chief secretary in 325, he replied, "I have no intention of dismissing al-Ḥusain b. ʿAlī [an-Naubakhtī], whose advice to me has been sincere, and through whom I have the blessing of good fortune (*tabarrukī bihī*)." When an-Naubakhtī was ill and Ibn Rāʾiq was tricked into believing that he would die, the emir appointed another official in his place. Then, realizing he had been deceived, Ibn Rāʾiq considered reappointing an-Naubakhtī because of "his blessing for my turn of good fortune" (*barakatuhū ʿalā daulatī*).[57]

The ties of men who shared their rise probably existed on

many levels of life; and doubtless these ties reinforced the ties of men who, for example, left their village and went to Shiraz or Rayy, where at first their only friends were men from the same village. Ties of shared rise may have even helped to cement together the factions of clerks (or even the mixed civilian-military factions) in government that had been assembled in the first place for very different reasons. Once such a faction achieved a turn of good fortune, it had a metaphysical as well as strategic reason to hope that, if its composition remained stable, it might achieve good fortune again. But even shared experience of growing up, of having "seen life through together," which creates bonds in any culture, was said to create an explicit tie between two men. When a secretary under the Buyid vizier al-Muhallabī suddenly and tragically died, the vizier said he would attach the orphan son of the dead secretary to his own son of the same age; that way, he explained, "they will learn together and grow together, and [the orphaned child] will have a claim (*ḥaqq*) on him."[58]

The Character of Acquired Loyalties

All the ties described in this chapter were openly discussed and frequently invoked when men hoped to make effective demands on others. All of these ties were openly engaged, often with a ceremonial or semiformal undertaking between the two parties who claimed to accept these ties. Only the tie of clientship, which in this period meant the tie of the freed slave to his former master, could in turn be passed on legally to one's children. There are a few instances in which a former slave, or a protégé (*muṣṭana'*), actually felt some obligation to the children of his patron. For example, the vizier Ibn al-Furāt agreed that al-Muqtadir would be an acceptable choice as the successor of the caliph al-Muktafī, because al-Muqtadir was the son of an earlier caliph, al-Mu'taḍid, and "most of those we see around are protégés (*ṣanā'i'*) of al-Mu'taḍid." But it is doubtful that this sense of obligation would have been felt for the grandchildren of any patron. In most cases acquired ties died with the men who acquired them.[59]

All these ties are alike in that they are individual ties (again, with the possible exception of the freed slave who had some sort of attachment to the family of his former master). Men fostered the career of chosen individuals, not of predetermined groups. Behind all these acquired ties we see the individualistic presupposition that a man can accept or offer an obligation only on his own behalf, and not on behalf of a group. Spokesmen existed, of course; but, as we shall see in the next chapter, they were obliged to get the personal agreement of those for whom they spoke. As the Koran repeatedly says, "no man bears the burden of another."

Yet these ties also work within certain presuppositions about the categories and capacities of men. None of the ties we have discussed is in itself based on a tie of category: it is not stated that, for example, all men born in Isfahan owe obedience to the family of a certain lord because of oaths or any sort of contract engaged upon by their ancestors. Nevertheless, the presumptions of the likely capacities of different categories of men were always present; these acquired ties were not made at random, but they were repeatedly engaged upon by similar groups of men, generation after generation. It is to these less personal, less formal and usually inherited ties of category that we turn in the next chapter.

CHAPTER III

Loyalties of Category

Men of a common interest will, on some occasions, make common cause, whether their interest is the protection of their profession, their city, or their family. But such interests need to be self-conscious in order to produce self-conscious loyalties; and the purpose of this chapter is to describe some of the self-conscious interests that created loyalties in the society of western Iran and neighboring areas in the Buyid period. In order to give an account of these interests and loyalties, we will first describe how a man of this period believed that he had come to be included in a category that had such a common interest. In particular, we will discuss how, in the tenth and eleventh centuries, a man was presumed in the first instance to have or not to have the capacity to be a member of a certain profession, or to maintain a certain station in life. Then we will describe the vocabulary of "category," the abstract words that were used for an identifiable social group, as we now, for example, use the words "social class." Finally, we will deal with the loyalties that were produced by participation in these categories.

No sharp line can be drawn between these loyalties and the loyalties discussed in the last chapter. The loyalties shared by the Turkish *ghulāms*, for example, were the result both of certain contractual relations they had with their patrons, and of common membership in a special category to which even their patron, who was often himself a *ghulām*, might belong. Nevertheless, the ties of formally acquired loyalty and the ties of category were relatively distinct to men of the Buyid period, who generally did not use words like "station," "class," or "category" to describe a group united by such formally acquired ties. The two kinds of ties seem, moreover, to have been functionally different. For example, some sort of sanction against noncompliance was usually built into the formally acquired tie, while the informal tie of category was supported by informal and, in most cases, unspoken sanctions.

Estimating a Man's Worth

In the texts of the fourth century, the capacities of men are often described in terms of *ḥasab* and *nasab*. *Nasab* is genealogy, the influence of a man's pedigree on his condition. *Ḥasab* is the honor acquired through deeds. Sometimes a man's "worth" is also estimated in terms of a third category, *nashab*, or wealth. These terms were not synonymous to the men of the fourth/tenth and fifth/eleventh centuries; yet one contemporary author's definition of *ḥasab* will often overlap with another author's definition of *nasab*, and vice versa. Such overlapping does not imply that these terms were empty and unimportant; it reflects the confusion of any real society, where men have different ways of estimating each others' capacities, and—above all—of describing their own personal worth to their fellow men.

Of the two terms, *nasab* is the more easily defined, since it unambiguously designates a man's biological ancestry. But it is not so easy to describe what the importance was of a man's biological ancestry for an estimate of his capacity, or for a statement of his presumptive worth. Virtually everyone agreed that heredity had some influence on a man's capacity, and most men believed that it had a great influence. Groups of people presumed to have a common ancestry were believed to have special talents through the influence of their heredity.

The influence of heredity was not seen to be direct and invariable, however; as the third/ninth-century Arab essayist al-Jāḥiẓ said, not every Greek is a philosopher, nor every

Chinese a brilliant craftsman; but these talents are more generally and perfectly found among them than among other people. On this view, the same variation within an overall probability could be found if the effects of heredity were studied chronologically, as they could be studied synchronically among a group of common descent like the Greeks. The third/ninth-century writer, Ibn Qutaibah, explained that God had created Adam from a handful of material composed of bits of earth from all parts of the world and, therefore, with all of the great variety of human nature inherent in him. The influence of this heredity might skip a generation, so that "a man may be the opposite of his father in character (*akhlāq*) or in characteristics (*shamā'il*) and ambitions (*himam*) or in all these respects, because he has inherited [traits] from his ancestors that pull him from [the traits] of his father and mother." The implication of this statement is not that heredity should be disregarded; on the contrary, most authors felt that one should study heredity with the long view that allowed the identification of traits that might skip one or more generations, and then reappear.[1]

Everyone recognized that many genealogies were historicizing explanations of the adoption of one family or people by another. In formal terms, to accept someone as a client (*maulā*, pl. *mawālī*) meant to allow this person to claim the *nasab* of the patron; as al-Jāḥiẓ points out, the non-Arab *mawālī* can say that through clientship, "we have acquired a *nasab* that the Arab approves, and we have an origin (*aṣl*) in which the non-Arab takes pride." Yet it required generations before the transfer of *nasab* was so complete that a man could claim the same biological origin (*aṣl*) as the patrons of his ancestors. In the long run, therefore, clientship as described in the previous chapter contributed to an important loyalty of category—kinship—which is discussed in this chapter. But in the short run, at least in the period we are considering, self-conscious clientship was used only to express the ties of loyalty that a freedman was presumed to have to his former master, not to express any transfer of *nasab* that would imply a transfer of capacity.[2]

If one could estimate a man's capacity in part through his *nasab*, one could also estimate it in part through his *ḥasab*, the honor acquired through deeds. Yet *ḥasab* was not, as some modern scholars have mistakenly assumed, just the personal achievement of the possessor of *ḥasab*. According to most definitions, the majority of deeds that were calculated to form a man's *ḥasab* had been performed not by the possessor of *ḥasab* but by his ancestors. Al-Jāhiz plainly states that "the excellent deeds of the fathers (*ābā'*) and the former actions of ancestors (*ajdād*) are the *ḥasab* of the sons." Ibn Qutaibah gives a fuller description of the mechanics of *ḥasab*, which he derives from the verb *ḥasaba*, "to reckon something to someone's account." As he explains, "the noble man (*sharīf*) would reckon the accomplishments (*ma'āthir*) of his fathers (*ābā'*), and count them man by man. It would then be said, 'so and so has *ḥasab*,' that is, fathers who are counted and virtues that are reckoned."[3]

An alternate tradition existed, one that emphasized a man's personal achievement regardless of his inherited *ḥasab* and *nasab*. The Buyid judge at-Tanūkhī quotes the famous retort of an Arab who was taunted for his lowly origins: "My family line (*nasab*) begins with me; yours ends with you." At-Tanūkhī quotes a similar sentiment from his father, who said, "the poverty [of one's origins] is no disgrace, if a man is excellent (*fāḍil*) in himself; and men of religious learning in particular are not blamed for this [kind of background]. I think that he who has been humble and has risen in the world, or has been poor and become rich, is more excellent (*afḍal*) than the man born into wealth or into eminence (*jalālah*). For the man so born profits by someone else's efforts, and there is no specific thing for which he can be praised; while he who has achieved these things by his [own] striving and toil, is [in himself] more excellent." But this tradition, by the vigor with which it argues that we can consider the man of lowly background and great personal achievement even better than the man who has only an inherited nobility, pays tribute to the general assumption that the great majority of men took a man's genealogy, and the stockpile of honorable deeds that he inherited, into consideration both in estimating that man's capacities, and in assigning him a station in society.[4]

A man's heritage of *ḥasab* and *nasab* was significant not only because it permitted others to make a shrewd guess as to that man's capabilities, but also because it imposed on the heir of *ḥasab* and *nasab* the burden of living up to the tradition of his ancestors. A man whose ancestors had great talent and high estate would fear the loss of the collective "force" that his ancestors had bequeathed to him. In the opinions of men of the fourth and fifth centuries, this fear was more likely to compel him to live up to the level of his ancestors than was mere ambition likely to raise a man without such *ḥasab* and *nasab* to a comparable level of performance. Al-Mas'ūdī, who died in 335, wrote that "it is incumbent on a man of noble *nasab* and high glory that he not make this a stairway to relax from the performance of deeds appropriate to his *nasab*, and to rely on his fathers. Indeed, nobility (*sharaf*) of *nasab* spurs men to nobility in their actions, and such nobility [in actions] is more appropriate for a noble man. For nobility calls forth nobility instead of impeding it, just as goodness calls forth goodness, and one is aroused [by it to seek further goodness]."[5]

Men were therefore more likely to act like their ancestors both because of the obligation to live up to deeds and nobility of their ancestors, and because of the presumed biological force of their heredity. In these descriptions, *ḥasab* and *nasab* overlap, however different they may have been in original conception. In fact, although *ḥasab* and *nasab* are the terms most commonly used in theoretical discussions, in describing the suitability of specific men to their jobs or social position, we more commonly find the term *ubūwah*, or "paternity." The debasement of the judiciary began under the vizier Ibn al-Furāt, at-Tanūkhī tells us, because he had men "who had no knowledge and no *ubūwah*" appointed as judges. Ibn al-Jauzī tells us that the well-known litterateur and chess player, Muḥammad b. Yaḥyā al-Ṣūlī (d. 336), had excellent paternity (*ubūwah ḥasanah*), for his ancestor was a *ṣūl* (a Turkish word for leader), and his family were kings in Jurjān. Then the children of the *ṣūl* became leading secretaries (*kātibs*) and were assigned government posts.[6]

Some of these ideas can be seen at work in the recruitment of the personnel of the central administration. The continual prominence of secretarial families who had known disgrace in every generation must be, in large part, the result of the widespread belief in *ubūwah*. In choosing a vizier, the caliph did not restrict himself to choosing "the sons of viziers" (*awlād al-wuzarā'*). But it was so commonly assumed that such children were more likely than others to be appropriate for the vizierate that the caliphs in the 'Abbāsid period increasingly chose the "sons of viziers" in preference to others, and by the early fourth/tenth century there were virtual dynasties of viziers. The "sons of viziers" were by this period a recognizable category of men, and were collectively referred to by this name. Statistically, only a minority of them became viziers; yet they were considered to be the reservoir of talent on which the government could and should draw for high administrative responsibility.

When a government reached outside the circle of candidates defined by "paternity," a heavy burden of proof fell on the outsider; he had to show that in spite of his different paternity, he could live up to the highest standards for his post. In 442, for example, the Fāṭimid ruler of Egypt appointed as vizier a man who, in Ibn al-Athīr's words, was not "worthy of the vizierate (*ahl al-wizārah*); he was worthy of landholding (*tināyah*) and of farming." In the long run it seems that he failed to convince his contemporaries that he deserved his post, and was remembered as a man pushed beyond his proper station in life.[7]

Yet there *was* mobility in the society of the Islamic Near East in this period, and this mobility included the downward mobility by which sons of viziers and of leading generals became members of humbler professions. "Paternity" created a strong presumption as to a man's talents, and fathers usually created the environment and had the connections that made it easy for such talent, insofar as it existed, to display itself. Nevertheless, society would not support a man's claim to position and talent if he could not prove that he possessed such talent. In one of his poems, al-Babbaghā' (d. 398/1008), who spent a large part of his life in the court of Buyid kings, says, "he who does not attain mastery (*siyādah*) through his own effort, regardless of his paternity (*ubūwah*), will not be made a master (*musawwad*)." We read fairly frequently of men who, in spite of their *ubūwah*, when appointed to a post, proved incapable of it. In 301/914, for example, when an important general died, his son was immediately given his post as inspector-general (*'āriḍ*) of the caliphal army; the son, however, apparently had little in his favor except "paternity," since he was soon dismissed.

If paternity had been sufficient to guarantee each man his father's position, the government would have lost much of its power, and the king would have been reduced to orchestrating the succession of generations in their assigned castes. No such guarantee existed; and the government's continuing discretion over most appointments meant that the government could expect gratitude from most appointees. In 328/940, when an important judge in Baghdad died, the *amīr al-umarā'* Bajkam agreed (as was common) to have his son succeed him in his post; but he decided to impose the unusually heavy contribution of twenty thousand *dīnārs* on the son, who had to sell his goods in order to accept the role for which most men considered him destined. The ruler clearly could have appointed someone else, even if the judge's son had a uniquely suitable *ubūwah*. Society also reluctantly recognized the claim of those who thrust themselves forward and proved that even if they lacked appropriate *ubūwah*, they had talent; such talented men could say, with the Arab quoted above, that their *nasab* began with them. Most men, however, seem to have tried first to find their social role by trying to prove that they could, in fact, live up to their paternity.[8]

It will be noticed that in many of these examples (and in the theoretical discussion of *ḥasab* and *nasab*), honor, or the reverence shown to a man and his consequent rank, is often confused with capacity, or the ability a man shows to carry out his profession. If, as was the case in the Near East of the tenth and eleventh centuries, professions could be classified by common agreement according to their degree of honor, and if, as was the case in this period, it was generally agreed that a man needed to display certain general capacities to be worthy of a certain rank, then such confusion of honor and capacity was inevitable. In a poem of self-congratulation, the caliph ar-Rāḍī said, "were the men of *ḥasab* to obtain the very heavens by means of it, I have obtained the same without toil or weariness. The Prophet of God is one of us, with whom no one, either Arab or non-Arab, can be compared." The caliph rests his case entirely on *nasab*, but a *nasab* so distinguished that he does not need to wear himself out to prove that he actually possesses the ability or rank that men assumed he should have by inheritance. Since he is descended from the clan of Muḥammad, he has the primacy of honor and the associated ability to be caliph all in one stroke.[9]

The Vocabulary of Category

The words for social category reflect this mixed emphasis on honor and capacity. The distinction between the two was never lost, but it often became blurred. Such blurring increased in the century and a half of Buyid rule when, as we have seen, men came more and more to insist that they could keep the honorary rank conferred by a position even after they were discharged from that position. Nevertheless, there had been and, to some extent remained, a separate system of classification for categories of honor and categories of proven ability.

The word *ṭabaqah*, for example, in its original sense was much more a term for a category of honor than for a category defined by capacity; yet, as we shall see, in actual use it was often used for a professional category. *Ṭabaqah* in its most basic sense means "any one of two or more things that are placed or situated one above another; a state, story, or floor; a layer or stratum." The descriptions of the Abbasid court often say that at an audience the courtiers entered "according to their ranks" (*'alā ṭabaqātihim*). The metaphor of vertical arrangement, which is implied by the primitive meaning of *ṭabaqah*, was, therefore, itself directly translated into a scheme of protocol, an interpretation of rank according to honor. Such honor did derive in large part from the authority of the various categories of courtiers, but not exclusively so; for example, descendants of important early groups of Muslims such as the Anṣār had a rank in this hierarchy that did not correspond to any authority granted them by the government. The use of *ṭabaqah* for "category of courtier distinguished by protocol" continued throughout the Buyid period.[10]

Ṭabaqah was not used in this sense only for the courtiers of the king or caliph; in a more general sense, the whole population was conceived to be divided into layers (*ṭabaqāt*). 'Arīb writes that every *ṭabaqah* in Baghdad was distressed at the loss of life and property in the Qarmaṭī attack on the pilgrims in 312. Similarly, we read that the Buyid general al-Muṭahhar, on campaign in southern Iraq in 369/980, was greeted during an official appearance before his army by the officers, clerks (*kuttāb*), and *ṭabaqāt an-nās*, who may have been courtiers, but were, more probably, all the other ranks of people in or accompanying his army. Rukn ad-Daulah owed his security in office, Miskawaih tells us, to all categories (*aṣnāf*) and *ṭabaqāt* of the people.[11]

In this last passage, *ṭabaqāt* and *aṣnāf* are probably used as near synonyms, for *ṭabaqah* was also often used to mean "category" without regard to rank. The classical Arabic dictionary, *Lisān al-'Arab*, defines the *ṭabaqāt* of men as "the various categories" of mankind. *Ṣinf* (plural: *aṣnāf*) was a more neutral word for social category, which did not imply any hierarchy or arrangement of society into horizontal layers. *Ṣinf* was in its original sense neutral enough to be used, in Arabic logic, as a term for a set of objects distinguished from other sets by their accidents and not their essences; and the logicians give "Turk or Indian" as examples of *aṣnāf*.

We get a functional definition of *ṣinf* in the saying attributed to a man of the early Buyid period: "I saw three men each of whom led a different *ṣinf* of the sons of their species (*abnā' jinsihim*), and none vied with them [for that leadership]. Abū 'Abd Allāh al-Ḥusain b. Aḥmad al-Mūsāwī led (*yataqaddamu*) the Ṭālibids [descendants of the clan of 'Alī b. Abī Ṭālib] and no one vied with him. Abū 'Abd Allāh Muḥammad b. Abī Mūsā al-Hāshimī led the clan of the 'Abbāsids [as *naqīb* of the 'Abbāsids] and none vied with him; and Abū Bakr al-Akfanī led the witness-notaries (*shuhūd*) and none vied with him." In this quote, *ṣinf* clearly overlaps with *ṭabaqah*; the Ṭālibids, for example, constituted a *ṭabaqah*, or "rank," in court ceremonials. Yet a *ṣinf* seems to have more cohesion than a *ṭabaqah*, which—as we shall discuss below—is partly because a *ṭabaqah* is in itself graded into as many degrees as there are individuals. Men could vie with each other for leadership in the *ṣinf* to which they belonged because everyone thought it natural for a *ṣinf* to have leaders. All three of these leaders named above had certain responsibility as leaders, and the duty to perform these responsibilities was confirmed in at least two cases by government posts.[12]

In this quote the word *jins* has been translated "species," which may seem a rather strange term for a category like "witness-notaries." Yet the basic meaning of *jins* is quite close to the English words "species" and "race"; *jins*, for example, is the common word for a variety of bird or animal, such as camel or cow. In the usage of some medieval Arab biologists, it was a more general word than *ṣinf* (or than the nearly colorless word for category, *nau'*). *Jins* comes close to the modern word "race" if we remember that the characteristics by which men assigned people to "races" were not the same in medieval Islamic as in modern Western society. Ibn al-Athīr tells us that when the 'Uqailid leader, Qirwāsh, had a surprisingly complete victory in northern Iraq over a large party of Ghuzz Turcomans in 420, he sent a boatload of the heads of the defeated Ghuzz to Baghdad, where "the Turks took them and buried them as they associated [this event with their] pride and sense of protective honor for [their] *jins*." These Turks are not themselves Ghuzz; they are the Baghdadi Turks who had a separate shared "interest" and a separate leader, and would therefore be considered a *ṣinf*. Yet part of the shared distinction that made them a *ṣinf*—their unique qualities as mounted soldiers—came from their classification as part of the Turkish *jins*; and they therefore had reason to preserve the reputation of that *jins*.[13]

Ṭabaqah, *ṣinf*, and *jins* seem to be the most abstract words for social category, although a number of general terms like *ummah* and *ṭā'ifah* were used to cover categories that were more strictly defined. Some of these more specific words will be discussed later in this chapter; yet no study of the terminology for social division in the fourth and fifth centuries can convey the amazing variety of specific categories used in the contemporary sources for this period. Each of these categories was created by self-description and could, in the proper circumstances, create a consciousness of a shared interest. Such consciously shared interests inevitably produced a shared loyalty to guard or promote that interest. Nevertheless, many of these loyalties remained dormant either because the interest they represented was not threatened, or because the members of these categories had more pressing reasons to look after other interests (and therefore to cultivate other loyalties of category) first.

The remainder of this chapter will be devoted to a description of the principal categories mentioned in the sources for the Buyid period, and of the loyalties that they invoked. This catalogue should be read with the understanding that many important categories are omitted because of the prejudice of our sources, which distort any description of loyalties of category by their disproportionate interest in the activities and loyalties of men like the authors. For there were probably as many or more loyalties of category that the sources do not mention, either because they were dormant loyalties, or because they were loyalties between men too lowly to be—in the view of the scholarly historians—worthy of description.

The Clerks

There was a relatively clear-cut and persistent division between the two most important *ṣinfs* among the servants of the ruler: the *ṣinf* of the clerks and that of the soldiers. We are better informed about these two *ṣinfs* than about any similar categories of society, for many of our sources were written by clerks, and most of the dynasties they described were founded by soldiers. The common interest of the clerks appears even in the period of their worst factionalism, when two prominent families of bureaucrats, the Jarrāḥids and Furātids, struggled for control of the ʿAbbāsid government in the early fourth/tenth century, shortly before the Buyid conquest of Baghdad. One example of the way in which common interest overrode this factionalism is provided by an anecdote about Ibn al-Furāt, the leader of the Furātid faction. After the rebellion for Ibn al-Muʿtazz had failed in 296, Ibn al-Furāt ordered that all the lists of the supporters of the pretender, among whom were many Jarrāḥids, be thrown in the Tigris to conceal their identity. He even tried to save his archrival, the Jarrāḥid instigator and leader of the rebellion, Muḥammad b. Dāwūd, by warning him to change hiding places when an informer came to tell high officials where the unsuccessful ex-clerk was concealed.

The courtesy was repaid the Furātids by the other faction. The Jarrāḥid ʿAlī b. ʿĪsā, on his appointment as vizier to replace al-Khāqānī in 301/914, was in his usual manner moderate in his demands on clerks of the outgoing administration; but he singled out one clerk of the preceding administration, Ibn Thawābah, for harsh treatment. He probably allowed Ibn Thawābah to be badly treated because this clerk had, himself, treated the Furātids badly in the administration of al-Khāqānī; and ʿAlī resented such treatment of his fellow clerks even if the victims were his rivals. Ibn al-Furāt never forgot that the consideration which clerks showed each other when in and out of power had allowed his faction to survive the many disgraces they had suffered. During his administration of 311, when he heard that his half-crazed son al-Muḥassin had struck the Jarrāḥid ʿAlī b. ʿĪsā, Ibn al-Furāt was extremely alarmed, and wrote apologetically to the caliph to assure him that he thought ʿAlī to be "one of the most distinguished of the clerks." In fact, if the caliph had not condoned the violence of al-Muḥassin toward his fellow clerks, a violence which temporarily destroyed the sense of mutual interest among ʿAbbāsid officials, Ibn al-Furāt would have curbed his son's wildly destructive behavior. Thanks to the caliph's support, al-Muḥassin initiated a cycle of torture and murder that resulted in his own death and the death of his father, and his actions discredited the clerks for over a generation.[14]

The mutual interest of the Jarrāḥids and Furātids (before these insane acts of al-Muḥassin) is seen most clearly in the efforts of both the Furātids and Jarrāḥids to help their disgraced rivals pay the fines levied on them by the faction in favor. In 306, when ʿAlī b. ʿĪsā was deputy vizier to Ḥāmid b. al-ʿAbbās, he offered to contribute fifty thousand *dīnārs* to the fine of a half a million *dīnārs* that had been imposed on Ibn al-Furāt. Similarly, in 311, when Ibn al-Furāt was vizier, he offered 'Alī b. 'Īsā, who had just been discharged and fined, a contribution toward his fine. In fact, many clerks offered to help 'Alī at this point; 'Alī refused all offers except those from his leading opponents, the family of Ibn al-Furāt, and from Ibn Farajawaih, a close associate of Ibn al-Furāt. He probably refused the other offers in order to avoid ties of obligation that might encumber him if he were reappointed to high office. But he did not want to refuse help from his archrivals; for, by accepting such help, he showed his hope that the mutual interest of the clerks would moderate their conduct toward each other even across the barriers of faction.[15]

The clerks of the Buyid period believed in their mutual interest as strongly as had their predecessors under the 'Abbāsids. When the Buyid king Bahā' ad-Daulah arrested Abū 'Alī b. Ismā'īl, his vizier, he ordered Ṣābūr b. Ardashīr, who was then the highest civil official in Baghdad, to arrest the family, associates, and dependents of the deposed official. Ṣābūr, however, first warned Abū 'Alī's relatives and children so that they could flee before he publicly set out to arrest them, as the king had ordered. Ṣābūr's fellow clerks appreciated his courtesy; when, in 392/1002, they were ordered to arrest Ṣābūr, they purposely let him escape to the marshes of southern Iraq. They did so partly, one chronicle tells us, so that the financial claims that Ṣābūr had against them might be forgotten, and partly lest they should be ordered to treat him with violence. Kings did not share the mutual interest of the clerks; so, while clerks could not openly disobey royal orders to harm other clerks, they did have a shared interest in moderating violence directed against their own *ṣinf*, and they often succeeded in doing so.[16]

The Soldiers

The *ṣinf* of the soldiers had, as we have seen in numerous preceding examples, a self-conscious identity that was understood throughout society. In fulfillment of the vows taken while in hiding, Ibn Muqlah, on becoming vizier under ar-Rāḍī, freed two categories of men imprisoned by al-Qāhir: the *kātibs* (clerks) and the *jundīs* (soldiers). A member of this second group, a *jundī* (or *'askari* or *ṣāḥib as-saif*, man of the sword) was as distinct from the rest of the population as a *kātib*. In fact, in many ways he was more distinct, since a man's *jins* or race was considered an extremely important index to the military talent that a man might possess. Many clerks came from Aramaean background, and the factions among clerks did draw some strength from antagonism between clerks from different "races." But the question of *jins* was a covert and secondary issue among the clerks; and clerks of Turkish, Persian, Aramaean, and many other backgrounds can be found in late 'Abbāsid and Buyid administration on both sides of most factional disputes. In the army, however, questions of *jins* were open and of central importance. The bureaucracy, of course, could resupply itself with sons of bureaucrats. The army lacked this advantage; it had to reach beyond the sons of soldiers, and therefore had to have presumptions of ability to guide its recruitment.

There were several reasons why the army could not resupply itself. Some soldiers were eunuchs. Some rulers, moreover, did not think that the sons of slave-soldiers had the same loyalty as their fathers, who had been bought and raised by a patron. Rulers therefore applied the principle of inherited talent less directly in recruiting soldiers; while a large number of the sons of soldiers became soldiers, a considerable number of new soldiers were recruited from one or another *jins* known to produce a high proportion of men of military talent.[17]

The sense of shared interest among professional soldiers was repeatedly demonstrated in the career of Mu'nis, the 'Abbāsid general. The elaborate concern that Mu'nis showed for the welfare of the generals who opposed him in battle was almost a subject of scandal to the caliph and vizier in Baghdad. At the very beginning of the reign of al-Muqtadir,

Mu'nis defeated and captured the Ṣaffārid ruler al-Laith b. 'Alī, who had invaded Fārs. But Mu'nis was loath to arrest Subkarā, the leading general in the army of al-Laith, who was in origin a *ghulām* like Mu'nis. The 'Abbāsid general sent a message to Subkarā to flee, and this warning enabled Subkarā to reach Shiraz and to set himself up as a semi-independent governor of Fārs. When Subkarā then refused to let the caliph's officials administer the taxes of Fārs, the central government sent Mu'nis to coerce him to pay a huge yearly sum or be deposed. But Mu'nis refused to impose such harsh terms on his brother soldier, and demonstrated such concern that the vizier even tried to remove Mu'nis from the negotiations because he suspected Mu'nis of sympathy with Subkarā.[18]

Mu'nis and the sometime rebel general Yūsuf b. Abī 's-Sāj expressed a similar degree of mutual concern. Mu'nis was sent against Ibn Abī 's-Sāj in 304, when the latter had more or less independent control of the northwest Iranian province of Azerbaijan. Ibn Abī 's-Sāj defeated Mu'nis at Sarāt in Azerbaijan, and captured many of his officers; in fact, he could have captured Mu'nis himself, but instead allowed him to escape with three hundred *ghulāms*. "Mu'nis," the chronicle tells us, "was grateful for this service," and soon had a chance to repay it. In Muḥarram 305, he defeated and captured Ibn Abī 's-Sāj at Ardabil in the same province. Ibn Abī 's-Sāj was paraded around Baghdad in chains, and wept at his former impiety in opposing God's caliph on earth. Nevertheless, he now had a powerful friend in court; and partly through the influence of Mu'nis, he was soon forgiven, released, and put in charge of Azerbaijan and Rayy.[19]

If such shared interest could move soldiers to mercy in the period of the 'Abbāsids, when some of the caliph's opponents had little to offer in exchange for kind treatment by the caliph's generals, there was all the more reason for shared interest to move men in the Buyid period. Under the Buyids, soldiers were manifestly the most privileged employees of the government. They had, therefore, a profound interest in controlling the violence they might have used against each other in combat. If they killed each other off too readily, few of them would survive to enjoy their privileges; and those that survived might be replaced by another military people who had continued to be numerous and formidable. This, in 390, when the vizier Abū 'Alī b. Ismā'īl wanted to pursue the campaign against Abū Naṣr b. 'Izz ad-Daulah, the Dailamī generals of the Buyids urged the vizier not to be so vigorous because, as one of them said, if they achieved a final and unambiguous victory over their opponent, the king "will no longer have an urgent need for you and for us; and when this king feels secure, that security will be a reason for him to scheme against us and to cast his eyes on our wealth and situations. The best and most suitable plan is for you to leave things as they are and, having reached this point, to stay where you are."

Similar motives seem to explain the concern of one of Bahā' ad-Daulah's generals for the life and safety of the opposing king in a battle in 384. In this year, Bahā' ad-Daulah's forces defeated those of Ṣamṣām ad-Daulah in Khūzistān, which lies between Iraq and southern Iran. When a general of Bahā' ad-Daulah saw a high officer of the opposing side standing confused and motionless with the reins of the defeated king, Ṣamṣām ad-Daulah, in his hand, the general did not ride over and kill or capture Ṣamṣām ad-Daulah (who was blind and would have been an easy mark). Instead, he shouted in Persian to this high officer: "What are you stopping for, you cupper—take your master and be off" ("cupping" or "bleeding" was a despised profession). By this means, the general saved the opponent of his master, and made sure that the petty warfare which was his principal employment would continue. This general also ensured that if he tried to capture the opposing king but, by some accident, Ṣamṣām ad-Daulah escaped, he would not be punished in return by Ṣamṣām ad-Daulah, if that king ever became his master. The world was full of minor kings who exchanged their kingdoms through the fortunes of battle. Many of these kings were related to one another. A soldier could never tell who might be his master tomorrow, and what other king might be offended if that soldier captured or killed his cousin.[20]

The "group interest" of soldiers was at times so self-evident that it was blamed for the open refusal of soldiers to follow the orders of their masters and, in some cases, for their masters' downfall. In 415, the armies of the Buyid king Abū Kālījār and his opponent (and relative) Abu'l-Fawāris found the valley in Fārs in which they were fighting unbearably hot, and many of them became ill. In spite of the conflicting ambitions of their masters, "the two armies chose peace," and go-betweens picked by the soldiers arranged that Abu'l-Fawāris should have Fārs, while Abū Kālījār would be given Khūzistān. The two kings had no choice but to accept the dictation of their armies.

The comparative weakness of the Buyids has often been explained by the conflict between the Turkish and Dailamī elements in their armies. But surely, of all the elements in Buyid military policy, their efforts to maintain a mixture of "race" or *jins*, and thereby keep control of this kind of group interest within their armies, was the most essential. Miskawaih, in explaining the rebellion against 'Izz ad-Daulah, says that this king, through his bad administration, allowed the Turks and Dailamīs to agree not to oppose each other in demanding what they wanted; consequently, 'Izz ad-Daulah was forced to agree to their every request. 'Izz ad-Daulah had allowed the common interest of his soldiers to override their antagonism of *jins*; and, as a result, the king became the servant of a unified army. Most Buyid kings were not so foolish, and no Buyid kingdom was ever successfully overthrown to the advantage of a non-Buyid ruler by its own army. The weaknesses that afflicted the Buyids as a result of the mutual opposition of their Dailamī and Turkish soldiers were successfully exploited only by their external enemies, such as the Ghaznavids and Saljūqs.[21]

Shared Interest among "Men of the Regime"

Sometimes the soldiers and secretaries were lumped together as a common interest group, and were called by that remarkably flexible word, *khawāṣṣ*. *Khāṣṣ* or *khāṣṣah* (plural *khawāṣṣ*) in its basic sense means "special, distinguished," while the companion term *'āmmah* (plural *'awāmm*) means "common, ordinary." *Khawāṣṣ* and *'awāmm* are, therefore, frequently used together to mean "people high and low." These terms can be used loosely or concisely; they were used by men of the Buyid period with all the precision and imprecision with which men of our time use the terms "proletariat" and "ruling class." *Khawāṣṣ* and *'awāmm* are words that divide men somewhat vaguely according to *ṭabaqah* or "level" in society, and the use of these two terms to express level will be discussed later in this chapter.

Khāṣṣ also means "particular to"; *khawāṣṣ* was, therefore, used to mean "those who were particularly associated with the ruler," that is, the clerks and soldiers. Their particular association gave them a shared interest which, on occasion, transcended the sharp barrier between men of the pen and men of the sword. In 312 the new vizier al-Khāqānī argued that the men in government should oppose the caliph's wish to have the deposed vizier Ibn al-Furāt and his sons executed, even though al-Khāqānī was very much afraid of the Furātids: "It is not appropriate," he said, "that it become an easy thing for kings to kill any member of their retinue; how much more inappropriate that it become an easy thing for them to kill their *khawāṣṣ*." We also see in this remark that the *ḥawāshī*, the "retinue" composed of the king's wives, eunuchs, boon companions, and so on, are distinct from his "special employees." These special employees had a shared interest not only in preserving their privileged position with relation to the other subjects of the king, but also in preserving themselves from the murderous anger of the king.[22]

The Professions

Not only the clerks and the soldiers, but every profession, as identified by the classification of the period, felt a common interest at some moments; and for this reason, every profession was a potential focus for the shared loyalty of mutual interest. The loyalty shared by the members of any profession was no secret to their contemporaries. The third/ninth-century writer al-Jāḥiẓ, in his deliberately provocative treatise, "A Condemnation of the Character of Clerks," tries to explain why, as he claims, clerks are unlike the members of other professions: they do nothing for each other when in need. Except for the clerks, al-Jāḥiẓ argues, men of every profession (*ṣinā'ah*) have mutual sympathy (*ta'āṭuf*) and an esprit de corps (*ta'aṣṣub*) against outsiders. Butchers, for example, will close their shops for a day if they find that one of their number is doing badly. They will do so in order that the distressed butcher may have all of that day's business for their profession. In contrast to this, clerks, according to al-Jāḥiẓ, are like children of different wives by the same father (which, by the way, speaks eloquently against the superficial attempt to describe the loyalties of Near Eastern society as mere extensions of family loyalties). The fellow-feeling in the profession chosen as an example by al-Jāḥiẓ is confirmed by evidence from the Buyid period; one of the two factions in the western Iranian town of ad-Dīnawar at the beginning of the fifth/eleventh century was called "the butchers." Presumably, the actual butchers of ad-Dīnawar did not constitute the majority of this faction; yet, as a group, the butchers pulled together to such an extent that they formed the nucleus or most conspicuous element of this faction, and thereby gave it their name.

Since professions tended to be concentrated in a single neighborhood in any town, loyalty of profession and neighborhood sometimes conveniently coincided. When, in 423/1043, one of the *'ayyārūn* (gallants) entered the house of a cloth merchant (*bazzāz*) in Baghdad and took his money, "the people of his market were strongly partisan on his behalf" (*ta'aṣṣaba lahū ahl sūqihī*). As a result, the *'ayyārūn* returned part of what had been taken.

Al-Jāḥiẓ is, of course, in part right about the lack of cohesiveness among clerks. They, like the soldiers, were so vulnerable to the manipulation of the king that they were forced to divide into internal factions, in contrast to many professions that entered the larger factions of local life *en bloc*. Nevertheless, as we have seen, even the clerks showed strong mutual sympathy of shared interest. They helped each other even in circumstances in which they had the opportunity to harm each other severely.[23]

One other profession appears frequently in the sources, partly because it was collectively the object of government policy: the great merchants, or *tujjār* (singular *tājir*). The term *tājir* was generally not used for the keeper of a small shop or a peddler, for a *tājir* was a substantial man of business who could be assumed to have considerable assets. Even in the largest cities of the period, the *tujjār* were a relatively small and identifiable group, as some of the following examples show. When news of al-Muqtadir's death reached Egypt, there was a riot of the garrison that was kept there to fight the Fāṭimids in Tunisia. The soldiers placed the *tujjār* under guard, and extracted a forced loan from them, in return for which the soldiers offered the *bai'ah* or the oath of allegiance to the new caliph.

The *tujjār* of Baghdad are seen in a somewhat less pliant role in an incident that took place several years later. In 324, the vizier Ibn Muqlah asked the rich *tujjār* to give him ready money in exchange for promissory notes so that he could pay the troops. The *tujjār*, however, refused in the only safe way they knew: they went into hiding. In 362 the Buyid vizier in Baghdad, ash-Shīrāzī, summoned the *tujjār* and tried to be very agreeable and conciliatory toward them, because they felt (probably rightly) that the vizier's agents had set fires that had burned many of the city's markets. At the end of the session, one of the senior *tujjār* said to the minister, "Vizier, you have shown us your power; and we hope that God will show his power over you." The king, who was always eager to seem the agent of God, took the hint; for this and other reasons ash-Shīrāzī was arrested shortly after.

In all these examples, the *tujjār* were an identifiable and relatively small group. It would have been nearly impossible to treat a large group in the same way. For example, the vizier would have had great difficulty in placing the weavers or the porters of the bazaar under guard; and it would certainly have been impossible for all of them to have gone into hiding. The *tujjār* were also a clearly identifiable group; ash-Shīrāzī knew whom to invite, even if he invited only those merchants who were spokesmen for other merchants, when he needed to conciliate them.[24]

As an identifiable group with great wealth, the *tujjār* were able, as we have seen in the case of ash-Shīrāzī, to exert an influence on government policy. Yet this influence seems to have been largely negative, unlike the influence of the court bankers, who were a separate and smaller, though sometimes overlapping group. The *tujjār* constituted an international credit community that the government could abuse only at considerable risk. When the vizier Ibn Muqlah returned to Baghdad in 323 from an expedition to Mosul, the *tujjār* of Mosul from whom he had borrowed money demanded that he repay; and Ibn Muqlah, eager to preserve the government's credit standing, was forced to sell government estates at a disadvantage. He was forced to do this even though his expedition had failed to regain direct control of Mosul.

Shortly after this, when ar-Rādī died in 329/940, the leading officials consulted various important groups in the population, including "the leading merchants" (*wujūh at-tujjār*) as to who should be the next caliph, "so that there should be unanimity (*ijmā'*) [on the person chosen] in order that [Bajkam, the mayor at the palace or *amīr al-umarā'*, and his secretary] should not make this decision alone, or exclude [these important groups] from the choice." The procedure was unusual, and was probably the result of Bajkam's desire to handle his relatively new office of *amīr al-umarā'* in a manner that would be acceptable to the leading men in Iraq; and the merchants were a group important enough to be counted among the leading men. Significantly, the merchants and all the other leading men, instead of trying to emerge as spokesmen for any policy, tried instead to guess what candidate Bajkam and his secretary might have in mind, so that they could confirm the choice of those who really made policy. Collectively, the *tujjār* seem never to have stepped beyond this passive role.[25]

The social style of the *tājir* was just as recognizable as that of the clerk. When a wealthy merchant who was a friend of at-Tanūkhi, a judge in Buyid Iraq, performed the *ṣalāt* (ritual prayer) in an idiotic manner, the merchant excused himself to his friends by saying, "this is the *ṣalāt* as the *tujjār* perform it." The excuse was farfetched, but it was possible for him to offer it because, in matters (unlike the ritual prayer) subject to variation, the *tujjār* did, in fact, have characteristic ways of acting.

Therefore, if the *tājir* wanted to change his profession and become a clerk, he had to labor to convince society that he was not just a *tājir* masquerading as a clerk. One of the shrewdest viziers of the entire 'Abbāsid period had been Muḥammad b. 'Abd al-Malik az-Zayyāt. His grandfather, who came from the Caspian province of Gīlān, made a fortune in the oil trade. His father had been not only a merchant but also a supplier of various practical and ceremonial equipment to the court; and he was so wealthy that some people accepted the rumor that he had financed the abortive rebellion of the early third/ninth century that temporarily made Ibrāhīm b. al-Mahdī caliph. Even though Muḥammad az-Zayyāt was somewhat removed from his grandfather's commercial origins, when he became vizier many people were convinced that the smell of commerce clung to him, and therefore regarded him as an outsider. Some merchants did free themselves from their association with commerce, and transformed themselves into clerks; as with all professions, a man with skill and luck could convince the sceptical public that he had begun to accumulate a new stockpile of *ḥasab* for his descendants to build on.[26]

Ra'īyah

Most categories of *ṭabaqah* or "layer" seem to have lacked the ongoing mutual concerns shown by members of a single profession; instead, divisions of *ṭabaqah* seem in most cases to have emerged only when the interests of the *ṭabaqah* as a whole were threatened. We have seen a partial exception in the *khawāṣṣ*, understood as those particularly associated with the ruler; this category was based both on "level" and on shared interest of profession. In this sense of the term *khawāṣṣ*, the complementary term that denoted those not part of the government, but subject to it, was *ra'īyah*. *Ra'īyah* in its original sense meant "tended livestock," and came by extension to be used for the human flock in the care of the ruler. In this technical sense, *ra'īyah* could include wealthy and prominent men who were not associated with the government.

When, for example, Miskawaih describes the strong control of the southern Iraqi town of Wāsiṭ by a civil official, Abū Qurrah al-Ḥusain ibn Muḥammad al-Qunnā'ī, in the reign of the Buyid king 'Izz ad-Daulah, he calls the population of Wāsiṭ *ra'īyatuhū* "his subjects"; they doubtless included some men wealthier or more learned than Abū Qurrah, who were nevertheless part of the flock he tended. The caliph ar-Rāḍī made a similar distinction when describing his dislike for his first mayor of the palace, or *amīr al-umarā'*, Ibn Rā'iq. When one of the soldiers of the *amīr al-umarā'*, he said, "acted wrongfully to one of the *ra'īyah* or even to one of my dependents (*asbābī*), and I would issue an order, they would not obey." In this statement, the soldiers are distinct from the *ra'īyah*, and the personal dependents of the caliph are either distinct or an easily distinguishable subdivision of the *ra'īyah*.[27]

These distinctions meant, of course, that it was generally understood that the *ra'īyah* reacted to policy and did not make policy, which was the province of the *khawāṣṣ* of the regime. In this respect, the *ra'īyah* (unlike the *khawāṣṣ*, who had a common interest through their common employer) resembled other groups based on *ṭabaqah* in that they acted together only when threatened. When Qirwāsh, the 'Uqailid ruler of Mosul, told the inhabitants of that city in 401 that he intended to recognize the Shī'ī Fatimid caliph of Egypt in the public prayer, "they agreed," says Ibn al-Jauzī, "in the manner of a servile people (*ra'īyah mamlūkah*), and kept secret their aversion and distaste." Ibn al-Jauzī by this statement explains, probably correctly, why the population of Mosul, although often riotous, quietly accepted a dictation by their king to accept a Shī'ī caliph, an action that must have been highly distasteful to them as Sunnī Muslims. They did so because, although the Mosulis were far from servile in many matters, in matters of policy in which their interests were not immediately threatened, they acted as "a servile *ra'īyah*," as the inhabitants of many neighboring communities would probably have done.[28]

Distinctions of Level

Unlike the division between *khawāṣṣ* and *ra'īyah*, which was based on the association (or lack of association) of each category with government, the division of *khawāṣṣ*, the distinguished, and *'awāmm*, the commoners, was a true division of *ṭabaqah*. The division between *khawāṣṣ* and *'awāmm* is, in fact, one of the most pervasive divisions in the history of Islamic social thought in the Near East. It resembled the division between *khawāṣṣ* and *ra'īyah*, however; and the *ra'īyah* are frequently defined as *'awāmm*. It is difficult to know whether even official usage followed the strict or the loose sense of *'āmmah/'awāmm*. When we read, for example, that the caliph al-Mu'taḍid (d. 289/902) ordered the vizier 'Ubaid Allāh to sit for the *maẓālim* court of the *'āmmah*, and ordered the general Badr to sit for that of the *khāṣṣah*, the division may have been between those who served the government and those who did not, or between higher and lower "layers" of the population. In some cases, there is no doubt that the distinction is one of level. When grain and bread prices continued to rise in Baghdad in 307, first the *'āmmah*, and then the *khāṣṣah*, became agitated and participated in demonstrations against the government. In this context, *khāṣṣah* (= *khawāṣṣ*) must refer to the wealthier level of the population, or, at least, to the level of those whose "respectability" restrained them from demonstrating as readily as the *'āmmah*.

In some circumstances, status was more important than wealth to the distinction between *'āmmah* and *khāṣṣah*. In 391/1000, the Turkish troops in Baghdad attacked the highest civilian official appointed by the Buyids to that city; and, Hilāl tells us, the 'Alids (descendants of 'Alī b. Abī Ṭālib) and the *'āmmah* defended his palace by throwing bricks at the Turks from the roof tops. As we know from other sources, there were poor as well as rich 'Alids in Baghdad; and brick-throwing 'Alids were probably not, in majority, men restrained by a great sense of their social dignity. Nonetheless, according to the judgment of many people, to be a descendant of 'Alī gave one a special standing or status in society; and for this reason, a careful historian like Hilāl, who had lived through these events, distinguishes them from the *'āmmah*.[29]

The A'yān

Another pervasive division of *ṭabaqah* was the division between *'awāmm* and *a'yān* (singular *'ayn*). *A'yān* meant the chief or most eminent men of a community, however that community might be defined. Usually, therefore, each one of the *a'yān* owed his position to his influence with the group to which he belonged within this community; he was, for example, the leading "witness-notary" in a certain town, or the like. As we have seen, for some purposes the government had to deal with the community collectively, and the community itself usually had an interest in presenting a collective face to the government. In these circumstances, the government dealt with the *a'yān*, who could reasonably be expected by the government to carry along the groups to which they belonged; similarly, these groups could reasonably expect the *a'yān* to keep the shared needs of that group in mind in any negotiations. The relation of the *'ayn* to his group was, therefore, based on the loyalties of category discussed in this chapter; but the relation of the *'ayn* to the government was usually based on personal loyalties acquired through oath and exchange of benefit, as described in the preceding chapter. Some professions were so lowly that their leading men were not acceptable to other *a'yān* or to the government as spokesmen; in any case, the group with which they had influence might not carry enough weight to be worthy of the government's interest. In contrast, some professions, like that of the *tujjār*, would include several members who would be considered *a'yān* because of the influence and resources at their disposal.

Since the *a'yān* owed their position to an informal consensus of those above them (the government) and those below them (the *'āmmah*), they also had a group interest. Their weight in the community came from their standing with the local groups of which they were leaders. A general social upheaval that would encourage a redistribution of wealth, or encourage their groups to put forward alternative leaders, would threaten the *a'yān* collectively. Similarly, the government recognized the leadership of the *a'yān*, and even restricted many posts and forms of official patronage to the *a'yān*. But if the government should try to bypass the *a'yān* and seek leaders from the *'āmmah*, or, even worse, if the government should cease to support the *a'yān* by the threat of military intervention to control sedition among the *'āmmah*, the *a'yān* might well be destroyed.

The cooperation among the *a'yān* is illustrated by events in Mosul in 379. When news of the death of Sharaf ad-Daulah reached that city, the inhabitants attacked the Buyid garrison in support of the claims of two members of the Ḥamdānid family, the dynasty that had ruled Mosul before the Buyids. When the Ḥamdānids arrived, they saw that the *'āmmah* would be satisfied with nothing less than killing the Dailamīs in the Buyid garrison, and they knew that such a slaughter would have serious consequences in their future relations with the Buyids of Iraq. The Ḥamdānids summoned the *shaikhs* of Mosul and its *wujūh* (leaders, an alternative term for the *a'yān*), and said to them, "If you want us to remain with you, put us in control of your affairs. . . . Our advice is that you should restrain your young men (*aḥdāth*) from any killing, and that these people (that is, the garrison) be allowed to retire from your midst with honor." The *shaikhs* and *wujūh* agreed to do the best they could; and the next morning the two Ḥamdānids and the *mashyakhah* (yet another term for elders and/or leaders) went to the *'awāmm* who had already gathered to attack the palace of the military governor. The *'awāmm* agreed that they would not shed blood, but only plunder the palace, while the army stood on the roofs and the *shaikhs* stood on the steps to keep the *'āmmah* from coming up to the roofs; and this agreement worked. The *a'yān*, as the account makes clear, were not sure that they could restrain the *'āmmah*, but they recognized the collective interest of the city, and probably of their category, in trying to do so, while at the same time helping a different (and, presumably, grateful) regime establish its control over the city. The Buyids did not, in fact, make immediate efforts to retake Mosul.

Sometimes the *a'yān* failed to acquit themselves so successfully. In 305, the military governor of al-Baṣrah carried on a running battle with both of the usually opposed factions in the city, the Muḍar and Rabī'ah, who claimed descent, respectively, from the northern and southern inhabitants of the Arabian peninsula. Eventually, the governor was faced with an uprising so terrifying that he left the city with his soldiers; and the government subsequently sent a new governor to restore order. It is not surprising to read that the *a'yān* of al-Baṣrah left along with the previous governor; presumably, they returned with the next governor. As we have seen, the *a'yān* were dependent for their position on their ability to balance government support with the support of those below them. They also benefited from the variety of sometimes overlapping and sometimes contradictory group interests in the populace. If the populace joined as one group against the government, and the government fled, the *a'yān* had no choice but to flee along with the government.[30]

For all their exposure to danger from above and below, the *a'yān* showed remarkable resilience and a remarkable ability to exert influence on their constituencies, both in their communities and in the court. When the Musāfirid ruler al-Marzubān was besieging Daisam in Ardabīl, an important city in Azerbaijan, he induced Daisam to send out the leading men of the city to mediate between the two opponents. Al-Marzubān arrested the leading men (called interchangeably in the sources *al-a'yān*, *wujūh*, and *ru'asā'*) because he knew that "the people of the city, if their *wujūh* and *ru'asā'* were detained, would unite in opposition to Daisam and allow him no respite." The ploy worked; Daisam was forced to leave the city.

In repeated instances, the people of Near Eastern communities of this period acted as if they would be stripped of all internal control, and of all self-respect before the rest of the world, if they were stripped of their *a'yān*. An army of the caliph had nearly reconquered the southwestern Iranian province of Sīstān from Kathīr b. Aḥmad b. Shāhfūr at the beginning of the fourth/tenth century, when a rumor spread that the caliph's general was carrying chains and shackles for the *a'yān* of the region. The people of Sīstān were horrified, rallied to Kathīr, and defeated the caliphal troops, who were clapped into the very fetters they were carrying. Kathīr wisely wrote the caliph, disclaiming responsibility for the people's act of revenge, and thereby relieved the caliph of the need for a reprisal to defend the honor of Baghdad.[31]

The sources do not tell us much about the way in which the *a'yān* maintained the integrity and position within the community of the local groups to which they belonged. Presumably, if the *tujjār* sometimes pulled together to bail out one of their number, or if they felt a common threat from other elements in the community, it was natural that they should defer to a few members, or even a single member, of their profession who had the dignity of age and of noble lineage and, above all, had the greatest wealth. If the noblest, eldest, and richest *tājir* properly sensed the current of opinion among the *tujjār* and put his very considerable *ḥasab* on the line, other *tujjār* probably felt it was tantamount to surrendering part of their *ḥasab* if they did not follow suit.

In our sources, we seldom meet any of the *a'yān* in this role within the community; we do, however, often meet the *a'yān* in their collective role as spokesmen on behalf of the entire local community before the government. In these examples, it is easy to see the reason for the local communities' gratitude to their *a'yān*. When the Byzantines threatened the community of Arzan, for example, it was—quite naturally—their *a'yān* who came to Baghdad to ask the caliph's help. Similarly, when the people of Bukhārā attacked the general Abū 'Alī b. Muḥtāj in order to restore Nūḥ, Abū 'Alī and his troops rode them down and wanted to burn the city; but the *mashāyikh* or "elders" of the city interceded, and Abū 'Alī forgave them. Examples of this kind of intercession by the *a'yān* are frequently mentioned.[32]

Any regime that wanted to last had to anchor itself in the loyalties of the *a'yān* it ruled by establishing special ties with these *a'yān*. 'Alī b. Būyah ('Imād ad-Daulah) was able to outdistance the Dailamī *condottieri* of his period at least in part because he understood the value of such ties. Miskawaih tells us that after he defeated Yāqūt and started to advance on Shiraz, his future capital, his conduct toward all, including—we are pointedly told—the local police (*shiḥnah*) and the "important people" (*akābir an-nās*) completely allayed their fears. On arriving in his new capital, he properly rewarded them; apparently all the fighting had confused the collection of the taxes of Fārs, and 'Alī farmed out the enormous arrears of the year, four million *dirhams*, to "the leading men of the region" (*wujūh al-balad*). The *a'yān* were, after all, the only "handle" by which a regime could take hold of a local community; otherwise, the regime was obliged either to ransack that community or disregard it. Any form of commitment between the regime and the community had, moreover, to be framed in the context of acquired loyalty, since the subject population did not belong to the *ṣinf* or *ṭabaqah*, or even, in most cases, to the *jins* of its ruler. The ruler had, therefore, to establish personal ties with the right members of the communities he ruled through oaths, *ni'mah*, and the like.[33]

The manner in which a new regime sought to anchor itself in the personal loyalty of the *a'yān*, and in which the *a'yān* sought to advance themselves by virtue of these "special relationships" with the government, is well illustrated in the career of Abū Zakariyā Yaḥyā b. Sa'īd as-Sūsī, from the ancient town of Susa (as-Sūs) in the rich province of Khūzistān, between Fārs and southern Iraq. At the time when the Barīdī family of clerks (later a short-lived dynasty in southern Iraq) had a major role in the administration of Susa and neighboring Jundaisābur, they established cordial relations with Yaḥyā. In 323, they sent him to help the caliphal general Yāqūt when

Yāqūt's army, in crossing Khūzistān, was due to pass through Susa, Yaḥyā's own region (*balad*). As an important man in his home region, Yaḥyā could, presumably, provide this help more readily than any outsider. In 326, however, after Bajkam was defeated by Aḥmad b. Būyah and forced to evacuate Khūzistān, during his retreat he arrested the leading men (*wujūh*) of Tustar (the corner of Khūzistān including Susa), among whom was Yaḥyā. Bajkam took them to Wāsiṭ, perhaps hoping by this means to exert pressure on the people of Khūzistān; in any case, once in Wāsiṭ he demanded fifty thousand *dīnārs* from them.

This event, however, was by no means the end of Yaḥyā's career. Bajkam was, at this time, nominally in the service of Ibn Rā'iq, although preparing to replace him as the *amīr al-umarā'* in Baghdad. Yaḥya correctly gauged the ambition of Bajkam, and decided that he was a very capable but dangerous man. He put himself forward, and took the risk of giving advice to this dangerous aspirant to the emirate. First, he suggested that Bajkam would soon be in charge of Baghdad; then, he said to him, "do you not remember how just yesterday you found fault with the emir Ibn Rā'iq for having offended the people of al-Baṣrah [by insulting their *a'yān* so that their *'awāmm* expelled Ibn Rā'iq]? The *'awāmm* of Baghdad are many times more numerous. You plan to act in our case [that is, in the case of Iraqis and Khūzistānīs] as Mardāwīj [Bajkam's original employer] acted toward the people of the Jabal. But this is Baghdad, seat of the caliphate, not Rayy or Isfahan; and it will not tolerate such behavior (*akhlāq*)." Bajkam relented. Partly through the intercession of two high clerks of the caliph, both of whom were friends of the Barīdīs, Yaḥyā's earlier patrons, Bajkam released Yaḥyā, who in turn "guaranteed" (*kaffala*) the imprisoned *a'yān* of his province, and they too were released.[34]

Yaḥyā had convinced Bajkam that if the latter mistreated the *a'yān*, he would earn the hostility of the *'awāmm*; he now demonstrated that favorable treatment of the *a'yān* could be repaid with concrete help. Aḥmad b. Būyah was still fighting in Khūzistān near Susa; and Yaḥyā arranged for his agent (*wakīl*, probably the steward for his estates), to harass the Buyid army by cutting bridges and similar measures. (This agent, incidentally, was Abu Muḥammad al-Muhallabī, who would one day be an important vizier to Aḥmad b. Būyah.) The harassment did make Aḥmad's position worse, but not decisively so. The rest of Yaḥyā's career shows him moving in court circles and attempting to mediate between the various candidates for control of Iraq, including the Ḥamdānids and Barīdīs.[35]

We do not hear of any further use of his influence in Khūzistān; perhaps he had become part of a higher stratum of politics, and did not again risk using his influence in his home province. The Buyids, once they gained full control of Iraq, do not seem to have held any grudge against him for his role in opposing the Buyid invasion of Iraq. They certainly did not hold the opposition of his agent, al-Muhallabī, against this capable man; for al-Muhallabī eventually passed into Buyid service and rose to the vizierate. Yaḥyā and his agent may not have been individually indispensable to their conquerors, but their conquerors realized that the cooperation of at least some of the *a'yān* was nearly indispensable. In seeking to put themselves forward as the intermediaries between these conquerors and the rest of the population, men like Yaḥyā partly succeeded in taming the conquerors and in enmeshing them in the established loyalties of category in their new territories. Correspondingly, men like Yaḥyā became themselves enmeshed in the new regimes; and they were sometimes less fortunate than Yaḥyā, and paid with their fortunes and even with their lives for this involvement.

Riyāsah *or Leadership*

No description of the *a'yān* would be complete without some discussion of leadership and its relation both to loyalties of category and to acquired loyalties. When the sources describe the leadership in a community as a whole, the leading members of that community, as we have seen, are most often called *a'yān*, although the terms *wujūh* and *ru'asā'* are also used. But when leadership is described in terms of the specific group that is led, the sources usually call the leader *ra'īs* (plural *ru'asā'*), and the leadership he exercised is called by the related word, *riyāsah*. If we could describe the meaning of such leadership for the categories that generated leaders, we would be able to give a far more precise description of the loyalties of category discussed in this chapter. Unfortunately, our sources rarely concern themselves with the ties that reach down from leaders to their local constituencies; such ties involved men too humble and ties too informal to be considered worthy of consideration. The sources do, however, provide some hints as to the varieties of leadership that these self-conscious groups produced, and these varieties reflect the differing nature of these groups and the limitations on leadership that any loyalty of category was capable of producing.

The word *ra'īs* is derived from *ra's*, the Arab word for "head," and was often used in a loose way to designate the "head" of virtually any recognizable group. At-Tanūkhī (d. 384/994) says that Ibn Dīyah, a specialist in *anmāṭ* (textile furnishings of all sorts), was in the time of the author "the head of this trade" (*ra'īs hādhihī 'ṣ-ṣinā'ah*) in Baghdad. Sometimes the leader is called a *shaikh*. Thus, we read that a certain man was *shaikh* of the *bazzāzūn* or cloth merchants in Bāb aṭ-Ṭāq, a major market area of Baghdad, at the time of the Saljūq conquest in the mid-fifth/eleventh century. Leadership of craft and mercantile groups was probably not held through government appointment or even through government confirmation. To be the head of one's trade meant, presumably, to be outstandingly successful at that trade. Such success would encourage the government, if it had any reason to deal with the members of that trade collectively, to deal with them through this outstandingly successful man. Doubtless the trade, if it felt the need to deal collectively with the government concerning a tax or a similar matter, would include such a man in its delegation to the government, and would make such a man its principal spokesman in any meeting with government officials.

When the *ra'īs* (or *shaikh*) of the profession had this role of intermediacy with the government, other factors besides his success might make him an appropriate spokesman—his descent from 'Alī, for example, or his age. *Shaikh* in its original sense meant "elder" and, in the example above in which a spokesman for the *tujjār* voiced the hope of the *tujjār* that God would punish the vizier, the spokesman was called a "*shaikh* of the *tujjār*." It is unlikely that a young man who inherited the largest stock of textile furnishings in his city, for example, would immediately be accepted as *ra'īs* of his profession; but the evidence on this matter is very slight.[36]

At the far end of its spectrum of meanings, the *ra'īs* was a leader with the widest powers of any person in this society; he was the sovereign. A chief of any variety of tribe, whether Arab or Kurdish or Baluchee was, of course, called *ra'īs*. But the leader who claimed sovereignty not by inheritance or the consensus of his tribe was also called *ra'īs*. When Mardāwīj was murdered, his Dailamī and Jīlī followers understood that "if we remain without a leader (*ra'īs*) we are done for," so they agreed to accept Washmagīr, who was in Rayy. Similarly, a group of soldiers who abandoned 'Izz ad-Daulah in 367 gave a Dailamī officer "the *riyāsah* over themselves." Such a *riyāsah* was not a gift of temporary leadership. Before dying, both 'Imād ad-Daulah and Mu'izz ad-Daulah purged their army of officers who "wanted *riyāsah* for themselves" and considered themselves more worthy than the Buyids to rule. For such officers, any position except that of a sovereign was subordinate; and their desire for *riyāsah*, independent sovereignty, might tempt them to set aside the heir apparent and claim kingship for themselves. In a sense, this form of *riyāsah* had an origin similar to the professional leadership described above, even if it had different consequences for the *ra'īs*. When the great majority of kings were soldiers, if a leaderless group of soldiers recognized a man as their *ra'īs*, it had to mean that they recognized him as their king. Subsequently, however, if a leader made this claim to kingship good, he could (and usually did) use a titulature that rested this claim on grander titles; for such titles could exalt him far above his original constituency of brother soldiers.[37]

Leadership in the Buyid family of kings was also described as *riyāsah*. *Riyāsah* in the ruling family, however, should not be confused with the claim to sovereignty described above. *Riyāsah* in the ruling family did imply that, in theory, one member of the family held the lands ruled by members of the family directly, while others held their lands as deputies of this *ra'īs*. Such a theory justified the family cooperation that all members believed would make their family strong. Such a theory also presented the small Buyid kings to the world as participants in a large state, the collective importance of which proved God's intention to grant to their family an impressive *daulah*, or divinely ordained turn in power.

This theory of familial *riyāsah* was consonant with the monocratic style of authority throughout society, and allowed loyalties that were by nature personal to be focused on a single person. Such a theory also fitted in well with the monocratic political theory that had grown up around the caliphate. If divinely granted legitimacy of rule was concentrated in a single man, the caliph, and the caliph (through choice or force) delegated the discharge of this duty, then such delegation was meant to pass to a single person who could be the caliph's alter ego in a way that a group of people could not be. The Buyids had preserved the caliphate partly to extract grandiose bestowals of plenary power from the caliph; and to the very end, Buyid rulers of Iraq tried to pretend that they stood in this special relation with the caliphate.

In the end, since all Buyid kings wanted to claim *riyāsah*, the very appropriateness of having a *ra'īs* in the family helped to destroy the family system. In the first generation, the theory that only one of the Buyids held rule directly from the caliph was maintained; when this generation died, it was in practice abandoned. When Rukn ad-Daulah, the last king of the first generation, gathered his children in Isfahan to settle the devolution of *riyāsah* after his death, he declared that his son ʿAḍud ad-Daulah was his heir apparent (*walī ʿahd*) and his deputy (*khalīfah*) over his kingdom. The implication was that ʿAḍud ad-Daulah would hold the kingdom of Fārs directly only on his father's death (when, presumably, Mu'ayyid ad-Daulah and Fakhr ad-Daulah, who inherited portions of their father's kingdom in the Jibāl, would become deputies to ʿAḍud ad-Daulah). In fact, ʿAḍud ad-Daulah tore the whole system apart.[38]

In government service, the principles of hierarchy and delegation had been, and remained, much more clearly defined than in any other sphere of life discussed in our sources. It was always specified whether a judge held a post directly (*riyāsatan*) or as a deputy (*niyābatan*), since the judge who held by direct appointment could (at least in theory) choose any deputies he wished for his district. An army commander was called *ra'īs* in the same sense; he had full authority over the army by explicit grant from the ruler. In the expedition sent against the western Iranian province of the Jibāl in the 350s, the Sāmānid king appointed Muḥammad b. Ibrāhīm b. Sīmjūr as "the *ra'īs* over all" (*ʿalā al-jamīʿ*), thereby subordinating to him commanders who were not ordinarily his subordinates.[39]

No *ra'īs* appointed by the government appears more frequently than the secretarial *ra'īs*; in fact, in later generations the term *ra'īs* without further qualification often meant "high clerk." In 306, when Ibn al-Furāt was being interrogated, he called ʿAlī b. ʿĪsā, the deputy vizier, *ar-ra'īs*, either as a token of respect or because ʿAlī's very high post carried this title. *Ra'īs* remained a very high bureaucratic title; and in 359, when Ibn Fasānjas was appointed vizier to ʿIzz ad-Daulah, the vizier's powerful rival, the clerk Abū Qurrah, obtained an official grant of the title *ra'īs*. Ibn Fasānjas was annoyed, and ordered that he himself should be called *al-wazīr ar-ra'īs*. As time passed, however, the title was granted somewhat more commonly to high clerks. By the end of the Buyid period, the title had become sufficiently debased so that when the caliph made the overambitious Abu'l-Qāsim 'Alī b. al-Ḥasan b. al-Muslimah his vizier in 437/1045, he granted him the title "the chief *ra'īs*" (*ra'īs ar-ru'asā'*). The early Saljūqs adopted this style of titulature; one of Tughril's viziers, Abū 'Abd Allāh al-Ḥusain b. 'Alī b. Mikhā'īl, had the title *ra'īs ar-ru'asā'*.[40]

Since *ra'īs* was used for high government officials, it came to be used in a loose sense to mean one's superior or, even more vaguely, superior people. A story about the *qāḍī* Abū 'Umar b. Yūsuf conveys the sense in which the *ru'asā'* sometimes designated one's "superiors" who were, nevertheless, superior only through deference, and not through official appointment. Abū 'Umar Muḥammad b. Yūsuf, the chief *qāḍī* in the early fourth/tenth century, refused at an audience of the vizier Ibn Muqlah to take a seat higher than 'Alī b. 'Īsā, even though the vizier urged him to do so. He later explained in a message to the vizier that "this is a man who was once my chief and who, through a turn of fortune, is no longer so. I disliked taking a place above him, lest the vizier regard me as a man who exalted himself above his chiefs (*ru'asā'*). I acted as I did for your sake, and to show respect for [the principle of] directorships (*ar-riyāsāt*)." This continuing respect for men who have fostered one's career is, as we have seen, a common sentiment; it is significant, however, to notice that these two men were from entirely different branches of government service, and Abū 'Umar had never been subordinate to 'Alī in the sense that an apprentice clerk was subordinate to a chief clerk.

Even this vague sense of *ra'īs* as actual or past, or even potential, "director" or "chief" or "superior" gave some kind of group feeling to the men so identified. Miskawaih, himself a moderately important government official, tells us ʿIzz ad-Daulah's vizier, Ibn Baqīyah, had some of the liberality of the "gallants" (*shuṭṭār*) among the common people, but did not adopt the manner of people of nobility (*karam*) and leadership (*riyāsah*). The low-born Ibn Baqīyah never succeeded in proving to his enemies that he could be included in the category of *ru'asā'*; and many of the *ru'asā'*, as we have seen, felt that, by assuming leadership, he had deliberately courted the disaster that killed him.[41]

Leadership among the Ulema

Riyāsah conferred by the informal consensus of a school of Islamic law or theology was very different from the *riyāsah* conferred by government appointment. The two were not totally unrelated; as we have seen, there was a category of men whose ancestors had shown "nobility" and "leadership," and who were, therefore, possible candidates for leadership either in the political world or in the less structured world of religious learning and professional piety. Religious learning remained, in contrast to other avenues to leadership, self-consciously open to talent, regardless of background. Nevertheless, most of the other presumptions of society favored men of inherited distinction, and it was quite natural for the presumptions that conferred leadership in other categories of society to influence the choice of leaders among men of religious learning. In addition, the comparative wealth of men with *riyāsah* made it considerably easier for their sons to pursue careers as private scholars. A very large proportion of the leading men of religious learning, therefore, came from families that had shown talent for *riyāsah*, and—most particularly—from the *aʿyān*.

In contrast, families whose ancestors had exercised *riyāsah* in the bureaucracy or the army of the central government did not produce many leading men of religious learning. Their failure to do so was in part the result of the distance that the men of religious learning wanted to create between themselves and all governments that claimed sovereignty and yet could not live up to religious ideals of justice. Still, the number of men from clerical and military families who became men of religious learning was greater than the number of those from clerical families who became soldiers, or vice versa. The comparative openness to new men of the category described by religious learning and piety has something to do with the widely held belief that a man's piety had self-evident claims that did not need to be buttressed by the presumptive claims acquired through ancestry. It also has something to do with the vagueness of the category itself. Once this vagueness is understood, it becomes clear why religious learning could produce leaders who held their positions through an informal consensus only, and who had very limited authority over those who gave them primacy of honor.

The men of religious learning were generally known as ulema (Arabic *'ulamā'*). It is one of the few categories described in this chapter that have captured the attention and interest of modern scholars. The ulema have consequently been made to bear the weight of historical explanation that the bourgeoisie carry in modern European history, or the "gentry" in the history of East Asia. A typical characterization of the ulema is given in an article by D. B. Macdonald, an excellent scholar of Islamic theology and law, and is worth quoting at length. "The *'ulamā'*," he writes, "as a general body represented and voiced the Agreement (*ijmā'*) . . . of the Muslim people, and that agreement was the foundation of Islam. In consequence, the *'ulamā'*, in whatever stated form they functioned, came to have, in a wide and vague fashion, the ultimate decision on all questions of constitution, law and theology. Whatever the *de facto* government might be, they were a curb upon it, as a surviving expression of the Agreement and of the right of the People of Muḥammad to govern itself. . . . It is plain that the organization of the *'ulamā'* was the solid framework of permanent government behind these changing dynasties."

Macdonald does characterize the method by which the ulema reached an agreement as "vague," and points out that some governments partly succeeded in "controlling" the ulema by giving them "official status and salaries." Nevertheless, he sees the ulema as a clearly defined body with a structure—a group of men who, moreover, command a popular loyalty that makes them the single most important force countervailing the force of government in society. With its internal structure and its power of suasion, the body of ulema could and did, in Macdonald's view, exercise certain functions of government that expressed the will of the people, and that were not interrupted by the change of dynasties.[42]

This view was supported by some scholars even before Macdonald, and has been widely held ever since. For the period and area considered in this book, it is, I believe, largely wrong. It is wrong because it considers the ulema to be a fairly distinct group when, in fact, they seem to have been a vaguely defined body of men whose other identities—as landlords, members of city factions, and so on—often overrode their common identification as ulema. It is wrong because the ulema had very little internal structure; leadership based purely on prestige as the first among the ulema was, as we shall see, very weak leadership. Any further structure among the ulema seems, more often than not, to have been imposed by the central governments. And, since the ulema were so loosely defined and so unstructured, it is wrong to think that they represented the voice of popular opinion; their internal disagreements and their other identities—as members of the *a'yān*, for example—meant that if they occasionally acted as spokesmen for the people as a whole, they usually acted as a spokesman for only a segment of the populace, or even for very limited groups with shared interests. Finally, it is hard to see in what sense the ulema can be said, by virtue of identification as ulema, to have been a "permanent government."

Their collective authority through positive *ijmā'* was only very gradually exerted on any specific issue disputed among Muslims. There is, of course, the well-known negative *ijmā'*, according to which *ijmā'* is said to have taken place if the community is silent on an issue. In such cases, the role of the ulema was even more passive than in questions subject to positive *ijmā'*. Insofar as the ulema did individually participate directly even in local government, they seem to have done so less by virtue of being ulema than by virtue of government appointment, and by virtue of their standing in other categories described in this chapter.

The ulema were not quite as diffuse and unstructured a category as are the "intellectuals" in the history of our time, but they were far from being the institutionalized force that the Christian clergy proved to be in many states in medieval Europe. The ulema regarded themselves as the collective voice of the conscience of society; modern intellectuals may regard themselves in the same light, but their consensus does not have the authority that *ijmā'* possessed in medieval Islam. *Ijmā'* is "consensus" on a matter of law or theology, and is, in practice, one of the most important methods by which the validity of such matters can be tested. Yet not all important Sunnī thinkers assigned the task of *ijmā'* to all the ulema; some assigned it to the entire Islamic community, others restricted it to the *fuqahā'*, men specially trained to reason according to the method of Islamic law. Sunnī thinkers also disagreed about the method of ascertaining when such *ijmā'* had been reached; did it, for example, need the explicit consent of the *fuqahā'*?

In the first two centuries of Islamic history, when the body of men concerned with elaborating the law was comparatively small and concentrated in Medina, southern Iraq, and the capital cities of the caliphs, the informal consensus of "experts" was easier to determine; and this informal consensus played a large role in determining the general outlines of the major schools of Islamic law. In fact, the similarity of those major schools must owe a great deal to the common participation of their founders in a relatively small intellectual community. After this period, the intellectual community became far larger and more widespread; but the collective conscience of this community of "experts" showed itself more in its efforts to adhere to the central traditions of the first two centuries than in a desire to "legislate" for the Islamic community in an innovative fashion.

Insofar as the ulema did elaborate Islamic law (which, of course, they did in all centuries), their positive *ijmāʿ* on disputed questions was expressed by their general acceptance over a long term of some of the answers proposed to disputed questions. Those who had supported positions that were eventually dropped by the majority of Muslims were not—either in their lifetimes or by subsequent generations—considered, by that token alone, to be removed from the category of ulema. As we have said, this glacial process by which the ulema decided disputes had no defined method. Accordingly, the process itself could define only in the vaguest terms who was, or was not, entitled to participate in such decisions.

Ijmāʿ, therefore, gave a weight and dignity to the opinions of the ulema; but it did not make the ulema into an institution in the same sense that a legislative body is an institution. The majority of ulema adhered to the central currents of Islamic thought, and those few Islamic governments that tried to compel them to adopt positions which they had not sanctioned usually found them hard to compel. This was in part because they were not, like the Christian clergy or the members of a guild, narrowly enough defined or tightly enough organized to be amenable to compulsion. In this period, the government in most cases left questions of consensus on private and commercial law to the ulema; and in most cases, the ulema repaid the favor by avoiding any positive consensus on practical questions of public law.

ʿIlm, or "knowledge," was the quality that defined the ulema, whose name was derived from this root. As Macdonald stated, " *'ilm* in the first instance was knowledge of traditions and of the resultant canon law and theology." Traditions (or *ḥadīth*) concerning the sayings and actions of the Prophet were the primary constituent of *'ilm* in the period we are studying, even more clearly than they were in later periods. In our period, the oral transmission of *ḥadīth* involved vast numbers of people who were to be considered, to this extent, ulema. Some of these people devoted a large portion of their time to the study of *ḥadīth* and of other religious sciences; others devoted less of their time, and might be considered ulema for some purposes, and not for others, or accepted by some of their fellow scholars as ulema, and not by others. In a later period when *madrasahs*, the colleges sponsored by the Saljūqs for teaching the Islamic sciences, appeared in western Iran and Iraq, such institutions gave an air of professionalism to the scholars who taught or studied in them. But even in the Saljūq period, as a glance at the biographical dictionaries will show, large numbers of people outside the *madrasah* system were considered ulema.

For all the vagueness with which their category was defined, the ulema were nevertheless a category with a self-conscious identity, and their primary characteristic, their knowledge of *ḥadīth*, created an important bond between them. A pupil who had long and close association with a master would have the kind of apprentice-patron relationship that we have described in the preceding chapter. Yet the ulema in most cases took their identity from more casual contacts; for men who were really interested in *ḥadīth* tried to hear *ḥadīth* from as many qualified transmitters as possible, even if their contact with these transmitters was brief and formal. *Ḥadīth* created a deeply felt sense of community with all previous generations of Muslims who, from the time of the Companions of the Prophet, had made a deeper understanding of the implications of Islam a central concern of their lives. Ar-Rāmhurmuzī, an Ahwāzī scholar of *ḥadīth* from the Buyid period, writes, "*ḥadīth* is fame (*dhikr*) which only strong men (*dhukrān*) love, and genealogy, which is not unknown in any place. It is sufficient nobility for the transmitter that his name be joined with the name of the Prophet and be mentioned along with mention of Him and of His family and His companions. For this reason, when someone said to a nobleman, 'We see you want to relate *ḥadīth*,' he said: 'I want, in the first place, to see my name united with that of the Prophet in a single line.' What better relatives (*'aṣabah*) could be desired than a group that includes 'Alī b. al-Ḥusain b. 'Alī and his descendants that followed him, and the family of the Prophet, and the sons of the Muhājirūn and Anṣār, as well as the generation that succeeded them in piety, and the ascetics and the *fuqahā'* and most of the caliphs, and countless numbers of *'ulamā'* and men of nobility, excellence, distinction, and importance?"[43]

The ties created by *ḥadīth* were no doubt strengthened by the money that students gave to the scholars who taught them *ḥadīth*. In a typical biographical notice for a Nishāpūrī scholar who died in 362, we read that during his stay in Baghdad he spent more than twenty thousand *dirhams* on scholars of *ḥadīth*. In theory, such payments were disapproved; but somehow, considerable amounts of money passed to teachers of *ḥadīth*. Wealthy young men often gave a greater dignity to their "grand tour" of the Islamic world, or to their pilgrimage to Mecca, by studying *ḥadīth* on the way. Such men seem to have told their contemporaries how much they spent on the scholars they met, since records of these sums are often mentioned with admiration by our sources.

Still, the bond of *ḥadīth* was sustained more by the dignity and the sense of family mentioned by ar-Rāmhurmuzī, than by the occasional generosity of travelers. When someone appeared who could relate *ḥadīth* with an unusually short line of transmitters from the Prophet, or with an unusually reliable line of transmitters, enormous numbers of people wanted to say that they had studied with him. For example, when Abū Bakr Ja'far b. Muḥammad al-Firyābī came to Baghdad from

Khurāsān, he was met on the Tigris by crowds of people on boats and rivercraft who had come to do him honor. If it is hard to believe the many sources that tell us that thirty thousand people attended the sessions in which he dictated *ḥadīth*, it is still plausible that, as al-Hamadhānī tells us, he had three hundred and sixteen "repeaters" (*mustamlīs*) who passed on his words to parts of the crowd who could not hear his voice. Probably many of these who attended, however, were only there so that they might count al-Firyābī among their teachers. Abū 'Abd Allāh b. Baṭṭaḥ tells us that "we used to attend the class (*majlis*) of Abū Bakr an-Nīsābūrī [al-Firyābī] which thirty thousand people with inkstands attended. It continued to be held in this manner for a short time; then we attended the class of Abū Bakr an-Najjār in which ten thousand people wrote. People were amazed at that [change] and said, 'in this interval, two thirds have gone away.' "[44]

Since *'ilm*, the "knowledge" that characterized the ulema, was so widely accessible and so highly respected, it could only produce a vaguely defined category with a correspondingly weak form of *riyāsah* or leadership. *'Ilm* formed a real bond among men who pursued it; but it was a bond that, instead of clearly circumscribing any group, extended through more and more tenuous links into the less scholarly portion of the Islamic community. A large proportion of all of the thousands who attended the classes of al-Firyābī and an-Najjār doubtless considered themselves ulema. Most probably, the more learned men of the period would have refused to recognize the majority of those who attended as ulema. Many people fell somewhere in between the extremely learned and the rank amateur; and these "semi-professionals" are often met in the pages of the biographical dictionaries of the ulema of our period. Significantly, when surveying the ulema of the same period, dictionaries written by different authors will differ widely on which "semi-professionals" they include.

The ulema, therefore, are one of the most important and

yet least restrictive categories of self-definition in Islamic society of the Buyid period. Its unrestrictive nature is shown by the number of other categories with which it overlaps. Clerks are almost never soldiers, soldiers almost never clerks. *Tujjār* are almost never soldiers, and only occasionally become clerks. But soldiers, clerks, merchants, and members of almost any category we know about became ulema. Of all these groups, only the clerks come close to having an identity that could not overlap with that of the ulema. In the first three centuries of Islamic history, a very large number of clerks were not Muslim; and those that became Muslim continued to admire the pre-Islamic models of secretarial culture, which had been preserved among clerks. Since many clerks had passed directly from the service of the pre-Islamic empires of the Near East into the service of the new Muslim state, it is natural that their literature should preserve the continuing ethos of imperial service, without strong reference to Islamic motives and purposes. This lack of clearly Islamic reference in their work was offensive to the men who studied Koran and *ḥadīth*—that is, to those who considered themselves ulema; and so, for the first three centuries of Islamic history, the clerks and the ulema had somewhat contrasting and hostile cultural orientations.

By the fourth/tenth century, although this contrast is still noticeable, it had become far less sharp. Aḥmad b. ʿAlī al-Mādharā'ī, for example, who was from a famous clerical family and himself supervised the *kharāj* (land tax) in Egypt for years, was, we are told, "prodigious" in writing *ḥadīth*. The great vizier Ibn ʿAbbād, to give added dignity to the sessions in which he dictated *ḥadīth*, would attach a *mustamlī* or "repeater" to each group of six people who attended his classes. Jaʿfar b. al-Faḍl b. al-Furāt (d. 391/1001) (often called Ibn Ḥinzābah), although he came from a family famous for love of secular literature, dictated *ḥadīth* in Egypt, where he had moved from Iraq as a young man. He was so prominent in the study of *ḥadīth* that ad-Dāraquṭnī, one of the very greatest scholars of *ḥadīth*, went to Egypt, stayed with him, and quoted *ḥadīth* he learned from Ibn Ḥinzābah in his works.[45]

Even kings and military officers appear as serious students of *ḥadīth*. Khalaf b. Aḥmad, the descendant of the Ṣaffārids who ruled Sīstān in the time of 'Aḍud ad-Daulah, went to the mosque in his capital city and dictated *ḥadīth* on Fridays. Abu'l-Qāsim 'Alī b. Muḥammad b. Sīmjūr, the powerful Sāmānid commander who led campaigns against the Buyids and, at one time, defected to the Buyids, wrote a book on the activities, wives, and sayings of the Prophet which was known among later generations of scholars. Muḥammad, the deputy chamberlain to Caliph al-Muqtadir, whose father was the *ghulām* general, Naṣr, gathered and recorded *ḥadīth*. Several military governors of the late 'Abbāsid period were serious students of *ḥadīth*. Al-Ismā'ī (d. 305), for example, who was governor of Fārs, was an *'ālim* (or, simply, "learned"—there is no distinction) and "wrote down *ḥadīth*." Similarly, Badr (d. 311), a *maulā* of al-Mu'taḍid who was also governor of Fārs, dictated *ḥadīth*.[46]

As with the clerks, the association of these soldiers with ungodly and, therefore, "usurping" governments probably made many experts in *ḥadīth*, and many thoughtful people throughout contemporary society regarded such soldiers as morally compromised men. Furthermore, a high officer could, no doubt, gather an audience to hear him dictate on any subject if he unsheathed his sword. Still, generals and viziers were not so compromised that *ḥadīth* told on their authority was to be automatically rejected. When, therefore, they took a serious interest in *ḥadīth*, they were included in the lists of scholars of *ḥadīth*; their names might appear in a subsequent *isnād*, or chain of transmitters. If they were accepted as ulema by some (or perhaps most) of the contemporary ulema, it is hard to see why we should reject them as such.

Insofar as men who were seriously engaged in the study of *ḥadīth* shared a common identity, they produced leadership in their regional community to represent this identity. Al-

Ḥusain b. al-Ḥasan Abū 'Abd Allāh al-Ḥalīmī, for example, who was born in Jurjān and died as a *qāḍī* in Bukhārā in 403, became "the leader of the transmitters of *ḥadīth*" (*ra'īs al-muḥaddithīn*) in that city. Such leadership in matters of *ḥadīth* implied great learning and, sometimes, great piety to which other scholars willingly deferred. It usually also implied that a man had lived long enough to be one of the few scholars who could still transmit *ḥadīth*, without intermediaries, from the best authorities of an earlier generation. The "height of [a man's historical span] in the chain of transmitters" (*'ulū as-sanad*) was the attribute every earnest student of *ḥadīth* hoped to acquire. An elderly man who had in youth heard *ḥadīth* from a generation long dead thereby acquired the "height" that enabled him to reach back over the heads of a younger generation to earlier transmitters. Ibn Taghrībirdī, for example, writing centuries after the man he is describing, tells us that 'Alī b. Ibrāhīm Abu'l-Ḥasan al-Qazwīnī al-Qaṭṭān (d. 345) traveled widely in search of knowledge, heard the great authorities of his period, "and acquired the leadership of knowledge (*'ilm*) and the best chain of transmitters (*'ulū as-sanad*) in these regions." The phrase "acquired the leadership" (*intahat ilaihī ar-riyāsah*) is commonly used for leaders among the ulema. It literally means "the leadership ended up with him," that is, he outlived the most likely contenders for leadership so that the leadership devolved upon him. If we can believe that, as Ibn Taghrībirdī says, al-Qazwīnī was born in 254, his life span of ninety-one lunar years should have left him as the only man in his region who could transmit learning on the direct authority of his distinguished teachers.[47]

The sources describe the same kind of leadership in more specialized disciplines among the ulema, such as law and theology. While virtually all of the ulema had studied Koran and *ḥadīth*, only some of them went on to the specialized study within one or the other schools of law or theology, and these smaller groupings among the ulema produced their own leadership. This leadership was also in large part based on the leaders' unique ability to transmit an autoritative text of recognized classics in each school of law and theology. The system of Islamic learning in this period held that a student had only really studied such a text in an authoritative version if he had studied it with a man who had an *ijāzah*, a "permission" to teach the text, from the author, or from a chain of transmitters stretching back to the author, each of whose members had received a "permission."

This sort of leadership is exemplified by Aḥmad b. 'Umar b. Suraij, who, according to Ibn al-Jauzī, "acquired the leadership of the Shafi'īs [that is, of members of that law school in Baghdad] (*intahat ilaihī riyāsah aṣḥāb ash-Shāfi'ī*)." The meaning of this phrase is evident from the notice of Ibn Suraij's death in the far earlier author, 'Arīb, who was a contemporary of Ibn Suraij. He writes that Ibn Suraij was "the most learned surviving individual of the school of Shāfi'ī (*'a'lam man baqiya bi-madhab ash-Shāfi'ī*)." Ibn Suraij was indeed immensely learned; some even called him the *mujaddid*, the "renewer" of Islam for his century. Yet his leadership seems to have owed as much to his survival as to his learning. We read of such leadership throughout the Buyid period. Ahmad b. 'Ali Abū Bakr ar-Rāzī (d. 370), for example, "continued [to teach Ḥanafī law] until he acquired the leadership [in this discipline in Baghdad]."[48]

This kind of leader could have, at best, only very mild authority over his followers. It is possible that such a leader would be used as a spokesman when the government wished to address his group, or when his group wished to address the government. But it is unlikely that he could offer to deliver the support of his group on any matter of public policy. Such leaders could claim precedence, rather than authority or coercive power. Such a leader is often called (as is, for example, Abū Bakr ar-Rāzī, the Ḥanafī mentioned above) "the *imām* in his time" of scholars of that category. To be *imām* meant, as juridical discussions of this term show, to be the *afḍal*, the "best" or "worthiest," that is, to have a leadership of merit.

Of one such scholar, Muḥammad b. Mūsā Abū Bakr al-Khwārizmī (d. 403), we are told that "he attained the *riyāsah*" of the Ḥanafīs of his time, and "he became the *imām* of the followers of Abū Ḥanīfah," and was "venerated by kings." His practical influence in shaping the world of his time most likely came from this veneration, which made men respect his intercession and pay more attention to his legal opinion (*fatāwā*) than to those of other legal experts in his law school. Ibn al-Jauzī describes one expression of the deference to such a leader when he tells us that on any legal "deposition" (*maḥḍar*) of the period of al-Abharī (d. 375), who "attained *riyāsah*" among the Malikīs in Baghdad in this time, al-Abharī was given precedence (*al-muqaddam fīhī*).[49]

Modern scholars have confused this kind of leadership with the related "leadership in piety," and "leadership in religiously defined local factions." "Leadership in piety" has a certain similarity to the leadership of the ulema, both because of the general esteem given to recognized piety and because of the moral associations of religious knowledge. As Ibn Qutaibah and a multitude of other authors tell us, the only lasting *ḥasab* is *taqwā*, literally "fear of God," or, more loosely, "piety." Many men who actually believed in this principle, or at least gave lip service to it, showed respect to men who lived exemplary and ascetic lives. Kings sometimes accepted the intercession of such men, and they did so not only because they admired men of outstanding piety, but also because such men had a certain following.

Until the advent of the Sufi brotherhoods, however, such followings seem to have been even more loosely defined than were the ulema as a group; if you stopped admiring a certain holy man, you probably did not feel that you were leaving some association of admirers. When Sibṭ b. al-Jauzī, a later author, tells us that Yūsuf b. al-Ḥusain ar-Rāzī (d. 304) was the "*shaikh* (respected elder) of ar-Rayy and the Jipāl in his time," he is repeating the estimate of two Sufi authors of the fourth century, as-Sulamī and al-Qushairī. These two earlier authors themselves speak more about the "sincerity" of Yūsuf than about his learning. In this case, we know that Yūsuf's reputation was restricted to fellow ascetics, because Sibṭ tells us that a traveler to Rayy who asked to meet him was told by everyone he met, "what do you want to do with that heretic (*zindīq*)?"

Individually practiced Sufism seems to have been spreading in western Iran in the Buyid period; and when we read that Ibrāhim b. Shaibān Abū Isḥāq al-Qarmīsīnī (d. 348) was *shaikh* of the Sufis of the Jibāl, it is a fair guess that he had a more respected position than Yūsuf ar-Rāzī had had. Sufi brotherhoods, which became important only at the end of the Buyid period, were well-defined organizations with clear definitions of membership and, sometimes, ceremonial initiation. Such brotherhoods were, therefore, well adapted to a stronger leadership, and the heads of these brotherhoods were often leaders of considerable authority.

Sufism, however, was a special form of piety. The more loosely defined *taqwā*, often associated with asceticism and supererogatory acts of worship, survived as an ideal in Islamic society, with its "leading men" of limited influence. Some leaders of the ulema were leading Sufis (though there was often hostility between men of acquired learning and men of acquired spiritual state). Many leading ulema were widely recognized as leaders in piety, although leaders of the ulema who were not particularly ascetic are also common. Some leaders among the ulema were respected as leaders by all three categories: the categories defined by religious knowledge, by Sufism, and by non-Sufi pietism. These categories often overlap, but are in original definition distinct; and they continued on many occasions to produce distinct leaders.[50]

The moral associations of religious learning also encouraged an association of "leadership in piety" with leadership among the ulema. In many religious systems, men are told that "true" understanding will translate itself into actions. On this basis, men are sometimes ready to question whether "wicked" men who study morally persuasive religious systems can really correctly understand what they study. Beyond this, however, in the Islamic educational system we have described, the "correctness" of religious knowledge (and, most particularly, of *ḥadīth*) was personally guaranteed by the men who transmitted this knowledge. If, therefore, the transmitter was a known liar, the authenticity of what he transmitted was suspect. In the manuals on *ḥadīth* we therefore find an involved discussion as to the degree of probity necessary to make a transmitter "acceptable."

There was yet another reason for the association of piety and the ulema. The word ulema is used only twice in the Koran, once to refer to the learned men of the Israelites, and another time in the famous phrase, "It is the ulema among God's servants who fear (*yakhshā*) God" (35:28). This phrase is frequently referred to. For example, in a patent investing one of the ulema with a judgeship in Gīlān in 390, the caliph wrote, "The fear of God (*khashyah Allāh*) is the special mark of the ulema (*mazīyah al-'ulamā'*)." For all these reasons, leaders of the ulema most probably hoped to be considered leaders in piety. Nevertheless, there were always leaders of the ulema who were not outstandingly pious because, as we have said, the piously minded and the ulema were not identical categories.[51]

Leadership among the ulema is also easily confused with leadership of local faction, since many—though by no means all—the factions of local political life were named after law schools or even theological schools. The loyalty of local faction, or *ṭā'ifah*, will be discussed below. Members of the ulema often rose to leadership in faction, and it is necessary to distinguish between the "leader of the ulema" and the "leader of a *ṭā'ifah* who was also an *'ālim*." The sources tell us when these two leaderships are combined in the same person, and thereby indicate that contemporaries did not automatically assume such a combination of functions. For example, we are told by adh-Dhahabī that the *qāḍī* Yūsuf b. Aḥmad b. Kajj, a great expert in Shāfi'ī law, who combined *riyāsah* in jurisprudence (*fiqh*) and in worldly matters (*ad-dunyā*), was killed by the *'ayyārūn* in ad-Dīnawar in 405. The notice of Ibn Kajj in Sibṭ b. al-Jauzī explains this worldly leadership. There were two factions (*ṭā'ifahs*) in ad-Dīnawar, the "butchers" (*qaṣṣabūn*) and the Abū Khuldīyah. Ibn Kajj favored the Abū Khuldīyah. His judgeship, his association with a faction, and his close relation with members of the Buyid and Ḥasanwaihid court must have constituted his worldly leadership, and made him a target worthy of the anger of the "butchers." The court and his own faction may have thought him a more valuable leader because he was a leading scholar of Shāfi'ī *fiqh*; he would, nevertheless, have been a leading scholar even if he had rejected these worldly associations.[52]

Riyāsah of a Town or a Region

Somewhere between the sovereign authority of the *ra'īs* of an independent government and the vague respect owed to the *ra'īs* of *ḥadīth* scholars, lay the *riyāsah* exercised by one of the figures most commonly met in our sources: the *ra'īs* (plural: *ru'asā'*) or "headman" of a village, town, or town-region. Sometimes the sources speak as if villages and towns did not commonly have *ru'asā'*; but it seems likely that when our sources imply that a village or town had no *ra'īs*, they mean that it had a weak *ra'īs*. Miskawaih, in describing the maladministration of Ibn Baqīyah, the vizier of the Buyid king of Iraq, tells us that in the time of this vizier, "in every village there appeared a *ra'īs* from the place, who took control over it; and they [the *ru'asā'*] quarreled with each other." Yet we have references to *ru'asā'* of quarters of Baghdad, and to village *ru'asā'* in Iraq, well before the time of Ibn Baqīyah. The same is true for the neighboring parts of the Near East; at-Tanūkhī, for example, tells a story about the headman (*ra'īs al-balad*) of Īdhaj, a relatively important town in Khūzistān, in the time of al-Mutawakkil (d. 147/863). Miskawaih presumably describes the emergence of village *ru'asā'* to emphasize that leadership capable of interfering with the government, and capable of leading quarrels between villages against the will of the government, had emerged under Ibn Baqīyah's administration, when, as he claims, the "awe of authority" (*haibah*) had disappeared.[53]

There probably were, in fact, considerable regional differences in the importance of the *riyāsah* for villages and towns. *Riyāsah* is seldom mentioned for towns that were the seat of a king: Shiraz, Baghdad, Rayy, and so on, though there were neighborhood *ru'asā'* in Baghdad. Insofar as a town *riyāsah* represents a self-imposed organization, towns that were the seats of government had less need for such organization. They also probably had less chance to shape such organization for themselves. Nevertheless, villages quite near strong governments had their *ru'asā'*. In 388/998, for example, ad-Dūdamān, a village that was a mere two stages from Shiraz, had a *ra'īs* who had sufficient authority to arrest the fleeing king, Ṣamṣām ad-Daulah, and turn him over to his pursuers, the sons of 'Izz ad-Daulah. Ṣamṣām ad-Daulah's brother, Bahā' ad-Daulah, showed that he held all the inhabitants of the village responsible for the action of their *ra'īs*; for when he captured Fārs next year, he ordered the village burned and all its inhabitants massacred. If the villages of the mountain valleys of Fārs could produce a *riyāsah* of this importance, the rich plain of the city-region of Jurjān quite naturally produced dynasties of *ru'asā'* whose importance is repeatedly mentioned in our sources. In this period Jurjān often changed hands, sometimes seeing three different rulers in a single year. A hereditary *ra'īs* presumably provided the continuity in government that both the people of the Jurjān plain and their rulers desired.[54]

Some idea of the practical function of the *ra'īs* can be gained from a story in at-Tanūkhī. In the first half of the third/ninth century, a group of landlords from Khūzistān in southwestern Iran went to Baghdad to argue with the government about their taxes. In the anecdote they call the *ra'īs al-balad* (presumably, the *ra'īs* of the city-region of al-Ahwāz) "he who speaks on our behalf" (*al-mutakallim 'annā*), and he certainly lived up to this description. At first the caliph turned the landlords down flat. Then, the *ra'īs* went to a former financial governor (*'āmil*) who had recently been in charge of the region. This official knew that the present financial governor was making unjust claims on the landlords, but refused to testify on their behalf. The *ra'īs* told the former governor that if the party of landlords returned empty-handed from the capital, it would mean "the loss of our prestige (*jāh*) and the striving of financial officials after our wealth—and *you* know how much wealth and how many estates you have with us." The *ra'īs* then swore by his marriage to his wife and "by the oaths of the *bai'ah*," that unless the former governor testified on behalf of the landlords, he—the *ra'īs*—would reveal to the caliph the embezzlements of the former governor and expose how, while in office, the former governor had arranged for his own estates to be assessed on the basis of artificially low estimates of their value. "I," said the *ra'īs*, "will gain greatly [by such revelations] because the viziers and important officials will know that I was the cause of your disgrace." So, at the official discussion of the case in the presence of the caliph, the former governor testified on behalf of the *ra'īs*. The landlords succeeded in getting their present financial governor dismissed, and most of their claims were accepted.[55]

In this and similar stories in which effective threats of exposure are made, it is clear that such threats would be less likely to have effect if made by a group. It was appropriate that a group of important landlords go to Baghdad together to plead their case; their number gave dignity to their cause and made it clear that a question of policy and not just personal dislike was at issue. Yet when pressure had to be applied to the ex-governor, it was best applied by one person. In one-to-one negotiation, the ex-governor could correctly gauge the seriousness of his opponent (shown by the opponent's individual oath) and could arrive at some sort of undertaking to which both he and his opponent felt bound. Furthermore, he could have some confidence that the damaging information his opponent threatened to reveal was not likely to leak out, since only one person had made the threat. "The leading man" of these leading men, that is, the *ra'īs*, was, therefore, the logical candidate to press home their claim.

The story also reveals a great deal about the position of the *a'yān* as brokers between the power of the central government and their local constituencies. The *a'yān* would lose prestige in their local community, and would be less able to defend themselves against the officials in their province, if they were sent away empty-handed; the *ra'īs* says this to the ex-governor to show that they are desperate to get some concession. The ex-governor has become enmeshed in the financial interests of the region; and it must have been common for financial governors to acquire estates in provinces that they supervised. A man's identity as a clerk was stronger than his identity as a landlord, so that in spite of the many clerks with large estates, these landed clerks appear to us in the sources more as clerks than as landlords. Yet, as we have seen, unusually capable landlords like as-Sūsī could move into the central administration, even if they lacked the traditional training of clerks. In the end, the *ra'īs* in this story threatened to move toward such a position. There were rivalries among the clerks, and the *ra'īs* threatened to ingratiate himself with the rivals of the ex-governor by exposing this official. To prevent such exposures or challenges, clerks had an interest in accommodating themselves to the *a'yān*.

We know that in the Saljūq period the government appointed the *ra'īs* in some towns, and the "brokerage" of the *ra'īs* was formally recognized. In the Buyid period, the *ra'īs* of a region seems most often to have held that position through the informal consensus of the *a'yān* of that region. The *ra'īs* over all the regional groups does not seem to have been uniformly of one profession. The *ra'īs* of Jurjān in the early fourth/tenth century, for example, is described as "its legal expert (*faqīh*) and its *ra'īs*." The *ra'īs of* Īdhaj, in the story told above, was "one of its leading witness-notaries (*shuhūd*)." To some extent such variation must have represented local custom; but it probably also recognized that the *ra'īs*, the man of greatest influence among the *a'yān*, might have accumulated this influence by his leadership in any (or many) of the categories that produced *a'yān*: landlords, large merchants, legal experts, and so on. Since, however, Islamic governments generally showed better manners when dealing with men of religious learning, many communities deferred to such a man, who acted as their spokesmen.[56]

Riyāsah, therefore, had many varieties, from the weak leadership of admiration and precedence among ascetics to the strong leadership of tribal chieftains. Still other forms of *riyāsah* will be discussed in connection with categories described below. It should be emphasized that the term *ra'īs* was by and large restricted to leaders of recognized categories in society, and not used for the leader in the temporary associations acquired by the methods described in the last chapter. These temporary associations, in fact, were often used within these categories by men who were seeking the leadership of their category. In relations between categories, a strong form of *riyāsah* played a larger direct political role than a weak form. The strong leader could deliver the compliance of his category, while the weak leader could not. 'Aḍud ad-Daulah, when he heard that one of the 'Uqailid tribe had been arrested for a very small act of brigandage, wrote to the 'Uqailid chiefs threatening all manner of horrible punishment "if the great among you do not guarantee *yaḍman* (the conduct) of the lesser." Only strong leaderships could be held to account in this way.[57]

We have, so far, described only the gross divisions of level (or *ṭabaqah*), like *khāṣṣah* and *'āmmah*. The fine divisions were in one sense numberless, and in another sense, did not exist. They were numberless because they could be increased in number to place a group of any size in order of rank. They did not exist in the sense that any of these finer divisions mentioned in our sources were produced by a method of ranking men; the ranks themselves were expressions of that method, and expressed the relative standing of men when viewed as members of a certain group. They were not ranks that adhered to men in all or even most groups in which they might be found. While it was, in a general sense, possible to say that a man was of the *'āmmah* or *khāṣṣah*, his actual standing in (or in between) these groups would depend on the associates with whom he was considered; he was not, for example, indelibly "lower-middle class." Men of the period had similar—but by no means identical—standards of calibration by which they could measure their own standing and the standing of others in any group that needed internal ranking. This system or relational hierarchy was well adapted to the ideas of *nasab* (genealogy) and *ḥasab* (an inherited storehouse of merit to which a man added); men were actually ranking each other according to their relative estimates of each others' *nasab* and *ḥasab*.

A representative view of this system is found in a passage in the Koran commentary of the well-known Shī'ī scholar, aṭ-Ṭūsī, "Shaikh aṭ-Ṭā'ifah" (d. 459/1067), who lived the better part of his adult life under Buyid rule in Iraq. To explain the Koranic phrase "the best of you in the sight of God is the most pious" (49:13), aṭ-Ṭusi quotes a scholar, al-Balkhī, who said, "men are in agreement that if an elderly man and a youth be equal in virtue and religiosity, the elderly man is given preference to the youth and is more revered and honored. The same is the case with the father and son . . . and the master and his slave. This is something that intelligent men do not dispute. Similarly, if two men should be equal in religiosity and one of them has ties of kinship (*qarābah*) with the Messenger of God . . . , it would be necessary to give precedence to the one related to the Messenger of God. . . . Similarly, if one of two people has ancestors (*ābā'*) known for virtue, good character, noble deeds, dignity, bravery, cultivation (*adab*), and learning (*'ilm*), it would be according to men's natures to give him precedence over the other. If it is said: 'It is according to human nature to give precedence to men of wealth, in which case [if your argument is correct] wealth and riches would have to be considered nobility (*sharaf*),' we would answer: 'Just so; we do not deny or reject this . . . though the poorer man who spends his money appropriately is better than the man who does not spend his money. . . . Similarly, a pious man in whom those characteristics [of piety] are evident, would be better than a man who has *ḥasab* and nobility through his ancestors, yet is himself immoral, foolish, and vulgar. The *ḥasab* of that foolish man would be something that increases the bad consequences of his [bad] deeds.' "[58]

This quotation is also valuable in that it explicitly discusses the important role of age in assigning precedence and leadership. We have seen how often the word *mashāyikh*, "elders," is used interchangeably with *a'yān*. We have also seen that leadership among the ulema, though not assigned on the basis of age, went to elderly men because of the way in which Islamic learning was transmitted. Age was important even among groups such as professional soldiers in which the knowledge of an earlier generation or the earlier achievements of an old man no longer had a direct bearing on his skill as a fighting man. In 324, when the elderly general Yāqūt left Baghdad because of a quarrel with the government, letters expressing devotion to Yāqūt reached him from the Palace *Ḥujarī* regiments in Baghdad. Yāqūt was an old Ḥujarī commander, although he had probably only commanded a segment of these regiments. Nevertheless, the Ḥujarīs apparently felt exposed without him, because they wrote to say that they had no "elder" (*shaikh*) left except Yāqūt. Since age and leadership were often associated, when "leaders" like the *a'yān* had collective interests, they could be called *mashāyikh* and considered to constitute a *ṭabaqah*. But like many of these adjustable fine measurements of *ṭabaqah*, age by itself seems less to have created a self-conscious group than to have guided men in choosing leaders of self-conscious groups.[59]

The Aḥdāth or ʿAyyārūn

Another category in society was the *aḥdāth*, the "young men," although this term does not stand in simple opposition to *mashāyikh* or "elders." *Aḥdāth* often meant much more than young men; and it was often a synonym for *ʿayyārūn* (singular *ʿayyār*), the groups of men joined by their own will, not by the government, in gangs that were motivated by certain chivalric ideals. Such gangs were more attractive to young men than to their elders, and their members were probably called *aḥdāth* with some reason. However, I have read nothing in the descriptions of their activity that explicitly states that only young men were members of these gangs. The frequent opposition of *aḥdāth/ʿayyārūn* to *ashrāf*, "noble men," suggests that this is a mixed category defined in part by age, in part by chivalric ideals, and in part by position in the social hierarchy—young men of good family probably did not become *aḥdāth/ʿayyārūn*. Insofar as the *aḥdāth/ʿayyārūn* groups were gangs to which one chose to belong and which permitted one to join, they were associations based on acquired loyalty, and belong in the preceding chapter. Unfortunately, we know very little about how one came to be considered a member of the *aḥdāth* in this early period. What little we know seems to indicate that the *aḥdāth/ʿayyārūn* cover a spectrum in different communities and in the perception of different authors, a spectrum that includes both the gang and all the hardy young men of the *ʿāmmah* of a certain faction.

The *aḥdāth/ʿayyārūn* existed in western Iran, as an example from ad-Dīnawar shows; but we find the fullest account of their activity under Buyid rule in the history of Baghdad. There they were called *ʿayyārūn*; and a brief description of the *ʿayyārūn* in that city will give some idea of some of the various aspects that the *aḥdāth/ʿayyārūn* assumed. In Baghdad not only every quarter, but other groups as well seemed to have had their *'ayyārūn*. The *'ayyārūn* were the element that gave real teeth to factional disputes; at the same time, they were an element that could become powerful enough to threaten the leaders of the factions for which they fought. In 361, for example, 'Izz ad-Daulah's commander-in-chief summoned the Muslims to arms against the Byzantines. A large number of the *'āmmah* came forward with weapons, but instead of giving them officers and training, the commander kept them as a reserve for himself. They soon began fighting one another, however, and thus became the cause of serious disturbances. "Many *ru'asā'* appeared among them," Miskawaih tells us, "so that a number of *ru'asā'* of the *'ayyārūn* developed in each quarter, protecting their quarter, collecting money from its inhabitants, and warring against those who were in neighboring quarters."[60]

Miskawaih does not say unambiguously that all the *ru'asā'* who appeared among the arms-bearing populace were *ru'asā'* of the *'ayyārūn*; but obviously some of them were, and these were either old *'ayyār* leaders who assumed new importance, or new *'ayyar* leaders created by the need of each neighborhood to protect itself. The *'ayyārūn* continued throughout the Buyid period to levy protection money on their own neighborhoods when the central government was weak. Such unwelcome expenses show that in spite of the interdependence that brought the local men of substance and their neighborhood *'ayyārūn* together in such circumstances, there remained a social distance between the two groups that prevented a full identification of neighborhood across barriers of *ṭabaqah*.

Factions

The *aḥdāth* and *'ayyārūn*, as we have said, played an important role in the local factionalism that was nearly universal in the Near East in the Buyid period. Whereas the *aḥdāth* and *'ayyārūn* seem to have been drawn overwhelmingly from the lower *ṭabaqāt*, the factions themselves seem to have included men of all ranks. Factions usually appeared in pairs, and the relative stability and vigor of factionalism when the factions were paired off against each other may have owed a great deal to the roughly even match in composition of the two sides. Faction, therefore, is in the nature of a *ṣinf*. A faction is sometimes called a *farīq*, "division," but is more often called a *ṭā'ifah*.[61]

Factions often had a religious identification. In Baghdad, for example, the two great factions were the Shī'īs and the Sunnīs; in many places they were based on schools of religious law. Nevertheless, there are enough places with nonreligious factions to indicate that law school or sect was not the true basis of faction, even if it provided a convenient focus for factional loyalties. Factionalism seems to have been an instrument more of protection than of mutual help. We frequently read that a faction retaliated against its rival for harm done to it, but almost never read that members of a faction helped each other in the way that, for example, butchers or clerks helped each other in the examples above.

I only know of one example from this period of mutual help within a faction. In 441, the people of the Shī'ī quarter of Baghdad, al-Karkh, built a wall facing the Sunnī quarter of Sūq al-Qallā'īn to protect themselves. The Sunnīs, in response, built a wall around Sūq al-Qallā'īn. Both sides made an elaborate display of their methods of work, wearing the most elegant brocades and carrying bricks to the sound of drums, flutes, trumpets, and tambourines, while rose water was lavished on the foundations. Ibn al-Jauzī mentions an assessment (*taqsīṭ*) for the expenses of the building, presumably some form of self-taxation by each of the quarters. The possibility of such self-taxation suggests that a neighborhood faction, when aroused, had some way of enforcing financial obligations on its members. There was a similar *taqsīṭ* in Qazwīn in 358, although in this case it was used to pay a fine imposed by the central government, and local officials may have participated in the assessment and collection. For our present purposes, however, it is important to notice that my only example of constructive, self-generated cooperation among members of a faction is in the context of stylized competition. This example does not in itself argue that such cooperation existed when competitive feelings were not aroused. Examples of stylized competition in building mosques in Iran are mentioned in our sources for the Saljūq and succeeding periods.

The government even encouraged ritualized competition. Mu'izz ad-Daulah used runners to keep in touch with Rukn ad-Daulah in Rayy, a mode of long-distance postal communication hitherto unknown, but henceforth customary. The *aḥdāth* and poor of Baghdad, we are told, were therefore encouraged to become runners so that they might enter government employ in this capacity. They soon became preoccupied with the new sport, and Mu'izz ad-Daulah further encouraged them by holding matches with musical accompaniment in which the winner was given a considerable prize. The local population began to hold matches in various parts of Baghdad, and soon there was a leading runner of the Shī'ī faction and one of the Sunnī faction. Again, by itself, such ritualized competition argues at most that factionalism was a "negative" loyalty, a loyalty only evoked by the possibility of being bested, either ritually or in a riot, by the opposing side.[62]

Some of the loyalties of category described in this chapter acted as seed crystals around which factions formed. The presence of such seed crystals affected the nature of factions; for even if factions existed largely to express negative loyalties, the positive loyalties that they encompassed must have given them some coherence. Whole professions, for example, were sometimes encompassed in a single faction; and a faction might therefore take its name from one of these professional groups, as did the "butchers'" faction of ad-Dīnawar in western Iran. We have the description of a disorder (*fitnah*) in Mosul in 317 that started with such a professional group, and succeeded in drawing a large part of the population into two opposing factions. The "food sellers" (*ahl aṭ-ṭa'ām*), presumably those who sold prepared food, started quarreling with the people of the quarter called *al-murabba'ah* and the cloth merchants (*bazzāzūn*). The disorder emboldened people whom our source calls "evil men" to become involved; and soon the rag dealers (*aṣḥāb al-khulqān*) joined the cobblers (*asākifah*) against the food sellers. The Ḥamdānid governor was unable to quiet the disorder in which a market was burned and even greater destruction expected. "Then some of the ulema and men of religion intervened and made peace between them." Here we see an antagonism based on professional loyalty, which spreads to draw in the other professions. We do not know if this wider antagonism became an established and lasting identification for factions in Mosul.

Certainly the manner in which one profession had allies of varying closeness, which would be drawn into the fight as it grew more serious, resembles the manner in which larger and larger units of lineage were drawn into fights in Arab society of an earlier period. In the fourth/tenth century in al-Baṣrah, as we have seen, the two factions were still named after the classical Arab distinction of lineage, Muḍar and Rabī'ah. Lineage, therefore, was another crystal around which factions could form, and lineage groups were doubtless often drawn intact into factions, even in places where factions were named, for example, after professions. Factions were also on occasion named after neighborhoods; but they were most frequently named after a religious sect (Sunnī, Shī'ī, and so on) or law school (Hanafī, Shāfi'ī, and so on). Both a shared belief and a shared place of residence could, therefore, act as seeds around which factions could crystallize. The sentiments of loyalty that each of these evoked will be discussed below.[63]

The affection between members of a common law school or a common sectarian belief is something to which many sources bear witness. Ibn Ḥazm (d. 456/1064), a Spanish Muslim, writes at the beginning of his treatise on love, "the most excellent form of love is that between men who love each other in God—He is Great and Glorious—either through some [common] striving to do pious works, or through some agreement on principles of belief (*aṣl al-niḥlah*) and on school of belief (*madhhab*), or by virtue of some degree of knowledge which is granted to men." Similarly, al-Jāḥiẓ points out that the sectarians called the Khārijites came from different provinces, different professions, different ethnic groups; so "when we find . . . all these fighting [together] in spite of the disparity of their lineages (*ansāb*) and difference of countries, we know that it is religious feeling (*diyānah*) that has smoothed out the differences between them (*sawwat bainahum*) and reconciled them in this respect."[64]

The mutual affection of men sharing a common belief was reinforced by patronage, and the closeness of this patronage to matters of everyday life made law schools and religious groups even more attractive as a focus around which factions might develop. Ibn al-Jauzī tells us that people used to bring payments of the poor tax (*zakawāt*) and alms (*ṣadaqāt*) to Abū Ḥāmid al-Isfarā'inī (d. 406), the leading Shāfi'ī scholar of his time in Baghdad, so that he could redistribute the money. He distributed one hundred and sixty *dīnārs* a month to his poor followers (*aṣḥāb*) and gave money to the pilgrimage caravan. Vast sums are not involved, since these were voluntary alms and should not be confused with taxes imposed by the government; nevertheless, some such redistribution of wealth through charity was more likely within a religiously defined group than between groups.[65]

Furthermore, some posts were reserved for men of religious learning; and control of these posts by one law school or another gave the controlling law school an important source of patronage. The *qāḍī* had a clerk, an archivist, and other attendants attached to his court; and, in addition, he appointed deputies who had their own attendants. The court and its appointees acted as wards for orphans and executors of their estates. The *shuhūd*, the witness-notaries, were men whose attestation was important in many legal matters, including matters of commercial law. They were predominantly men learned in the religious law. The *khaṭīb* who gave the Friday sermon was a salaried official, and usually one of the ulema. Patronage also extended to the appointment of *imāms* of mosques, though many of these were Hāshimites, descendants of the clan of Muḥammad. But however appropriate it was in an emotional or psychological sense to give religious labels to factions, and however much a winning religious faction might benefit from the patronage it had at its disposal, factions are not, as some scholars have supposed, everywhere called after religious groups. The many exceptions show that the basis of factionalism is not law school or sect; rather, law school or sect was the most common entity around which faction crystallized.[66]

Neighborhood was also a starting point from which factions could grow. Some factions of the period are named after neighborhoods, such as factions within the towns of Abīward in Khurāsān and Niṣībīn in Iraq. Strangely, this feeling of solidarity among neighbors is seldom explicitly expressed in our sources. More general expressions of love of one's native place (*waṭan*), however, are frequent. For example, ar-Rūdhrāwarī writes, "it is instinctive in people to love their native place and to choose to remain among their family and brothers." Sometimes "native place" seems to mean one's own property, as when Ibn ar-Rūmī says in one poem, "I have a native place (*waṭan*) which I have sworn I will not sell, nor see another possess, as long as it exists."[67]

While loyalty to one's town and its immediately surrounding region is not the basis of local factionalism, factionalism between towns is fairly common, and can be seen as a wider expression of loyalty to native place. Not only was Abīward itself divided into factions based on quarter, as we mentioned above, but its inhabitants were also engaged in a factional dispute with Nishāpūr. This loyalty to town-region (*balad*) is sometimes called *baladīyah*. The explicit references to this feeling of *baladīyah* is one of the many pieces of evidence that Near Eastern cities of this period were not, as some scholars have claimed, merely the sum of the quarters of neighborhoods of which they were composed. At-Tanūkhī tells a story in which the late ʿAbbāsid vizier ʿAlī b. ʿĪsā gave precedence over one judge to another who was originally from al-Anbār. The narrator of the story, who was also from al-Anbār, says that the judge given precedence "was delighted that I personally knew and had witnessed what had happened, because we were fellow townsmen (*li-'ajal al-baladīyah*)." In the Buyid period, a worthless member of the ʿAbbāsid family, al-Wāthiqī, became a witness-notary in Niṣībīn, but because of his disreputable character was brought to Baghdad and eventually put in prison. The poet al-Babbaghā' interceded for him "as a fellow townsman (*li-'l-baladīyah*)." Regional loyalties of units larger than the *balad*, however, are uncommon. Typically, the *ghāzīs* who came to Rayy by the thousands on the way from Khurāsān to Syria in 355 had no overall *ra'īs*, but rather had a *ra'īs* for the people of each *balad* from which they came.[68]

Faction existed, as we have suggested, in large part because of the protection such association offered. While the loyalties of this association can be described as negative, as loyalties against some outside threat, the faction was sustained from within by the positive loyalties it encompassed. Factionalism was also kept alive because it was manipulated from above by the *aʿyān* and the government. A weak ruler or a ruler attempting to govern a remote or border area was likely to make more extensive use of such manipulation than was a strong ruler in his home provinces. But it was always risky to use factionalism in the absence of a strong central government. The murder of the *qāḍī* Yūsuf b. Aḥmad b. Kajj, which we have mentioned above, was to some extent the result of the exposed position of this judge when he tried to use faction during the reign of a very weak king, Shams ad-Daulah. Ibn Kajj had been *qāḍī* in the provinces of the Ḥasanwaihid king Badr, and was considered an eminent expert on Shāfiʿī law. After the death of Badr he went to Hamadhān and took refuge with the wife of Shams ad-Daulah, who had, at that moment, the greatest voice in the policy of her husband. Shams ad-Daulah received Ibn Kajj with great respect and arranged for him to return to his native town, ad-Dīnawar. There were two factions (*ṭā'ifahs*) among the *'ammah* in ad-Dīnawar, the butchers (*qaṣṣābūn*) and the Abū Khuldīyah. "Between the two," Sibṭ b. al-Jauzī writes, "existed the [kind of] fighting and partisanship (*'aṣabīyah*) that only foolish people (*sufahā'*) engage in. The *qāḍī* favored the Abū Khuldīyah. The awe of authority (*haibah*) that had surrounded Badr had prevented either faction from overstepping the bounds. [But] then Badr died; and from fear of the butchers, the *qāḍī* supported his position by relying on his relation with Shams ad-Daulah." One night in 405, people called "the butchers" by Sibṭ b. al-Jauzī, called the *'ayyārūn* by Ibn al-Jauzī, and simply called the *'āmmah* by Ibn al-Athīr, attacked and killed him.[69]

There is an interesting example of a strong ruler who actually incited disorders because he was in control of both factions and therefore could manipulate the disorders to his advantage. When 'Aḍud ad-Daulah came to al-Baṣrah in 366, he made peace between Muḍar and Rabī'ah who had, according to Ibn al-Athīr, been feuding with each other for about a hundred and twenty years. In 369, 'Aḍud ad-Daulah used the understandings he had previously reached with the Baṣran factional leaders (*wujūh*) to arrange a mock factional disturbance in the city, after which the local government fled in pretended fear. The *wujūh* then (as instructed) handed the city over to an ex-official of 'Izz ad-Daulah whom 'Aḍud ad-Daulah had been unable to arrest because this official was inaccessible in the southern Iraqi marshes. The official, as expected, gave way to the temptation to come out; he was arrested, and the charade finished.[70]

Even when we are not told of established factions with which the *a'yān* (or *wujūh*) might associate themselves, we do see the government manipulating the *a'yān* themselves to create ad hoc factions for its own purposes. In 368, the forces of 'Aḍud ad-Daulah besieged an officer of the Ḥamdānids in the northern Syrian town of Mayyāfāriqīn. This officer could not have continued to resist without the support of the *qāḍī* of the town, whose family had traditionally held the judgeship of Mayyāfāriqīn and had great influence with its inhabitants. Since Mayyāfāriqīn was in a relatively unprotected area, subject to Byzantine, Fāṭimid, Qarmaṭī, Ḥamdānid, and Buyid attack, it was quite natural that the town as a whole should have a spokesman with such influence. The besieging general, however, was astute enough to know that rivalries always existed among the *a'yān*. He wrote to a respected and influential *shaikh* (who was a relative of the *qāḍī* by marriage), urging him to win the people away from the *qāḍī*. The *shaikh* was able to do so; and when the *shaikh* felt strong enough, his supporters assaulted the Ḥamdānids, arrested the *qāḍī*, and surrendered the town.[71]

A story of disputed leadership at the beginning of the fifth century in Mayyāfāriqīn illustrates that even if the *a'yān* could sometimes be manipulated to control the *'āmmah*, and even if they often identified with one or another faction in their community, the horizontal division between the *'āmmah* and *a'yān* could always reappear and separate the two groups. In 402 or shortly after, Sharwah gained control of Mayyāfāriqīn by murdering the Marwānid ruler. Abū Naṣr, the brother of this ruler, advanced on the town, camping only leagues away. Because many of the *'awāmm* supported Abū Naṣr, Sharwah and his followers were forced to take refuge in the citadel; but at the same time, he appealed to the *shaikhs* of the town for their help. The *shaikhs* agreed to guarantee Sharwah's safety on the condition that they act as his intermediaries with Abū Naṣr; so Sharwah left the citadel and stayed in the house of one of the *shaikhs*. The *'awāmm* then appealed to Abū Naṣr, who had been raiding the suburbs, but now moved closer and demanded that Sharwah be turned over to him. The *shaikhs* refused.

At this point divisions other than those between the *shaikhs* and the common people became important. The town broke into factions; then the factions agreed on a single leader-spokesman, but after a few days he withdrew. Then a local merchant (*tājir*), Ibn Waṣīf, got the support of his close friend Abū Raiḥān, a man with "clansmen and followers," to assume the role of local leader of Mayyāfāriqīn. It seems that up to this point Ibn Waṣīf had pretended that he was acting on behalf of Abū Naṣr; this pretense was now dropped and he openly fought Abu Naṣr. Sharwah was still lurking in some part of the city under the protection of the *shaikhs*, which shows that some distinction between *shaikhs* and common people continued throughout the hurly-burly of these events. The *shaikhs* then negotiated a compromise: Sharwah could go in peace, Ibn Waṣīf would be made governor of a neighboring town, and Abū Naṣr would have Mayyāfāriqīn. This compromise was accepted. This is not, by the way, an instance of successful mobility from the merchant to the emir class. Ibn Waṣīf's spectacular jump from commerce to warfare does not seem to have created a lasting position for him; he eventually left his new governorship and went to Iraq.[72]

Jins

In addition to the loyalties based on *ṭabaqah* and *ṣinf*, there were the many loyalties to family and its extension, *jins* (race). Family has been made into an all-purpose explanation by some students of the Near East, and its significance in all periods has, therefore, been discussed at length. Both family and race were, of course, the direct social interpretation of *nasab*. Race, as understood in terms of the time, was the basis of almost all the regimes that were the direct heirs to the 'Abbāsids; for these regimes came to power as the leaders of ethnically coherent armies of Dailamīs or Turks, and sometimes even as traditional chiefs of Arab or Kurdish tribes. Certainly, a regime of this period encouraged each element in their armies to keep its ethnic solidarity even if the regime itself (like the Fāṭimids) had a different ethnic identity. Correspondingly, each ethnic unit of an army could at times be held by the government collectively responsible for the conduct of its members. 'Imād ad-Daulah 'Alī b. Būyah used to tell the story of how in his youth, when he was in the service of the Sāmānids, he prevented a Dailamī from attaching the non-Dailamī Sāmānid ruler, Naṣr, since all the Dailamīs would have been killed in retaliation. As we have seen, many units of loyalty based on membership in category—"the merchants of Baghdad," for example—were sometimes held collectively responsible in this manner by the government.[73]

If the importance of ties of family has sometimes been exaggerated by modern historians, they were, nevertheless, ever present in the minds of men of the period when they considered their obligations. Ibn al-Jauzī tells us that as a young man in Baghdad, the prominent 'Alid poet of the late fourth/tenth century, ar-Rāḍī, studied the Koran with Ibrāhīm aṭ-Ṭabarī. The latter was a Mālikī *faqīh*, and the *shaikh* of the witness-notaries (*shuhūd*) who, as his title *al-muqaddam* implies, was "given precedence" among them. When aṭ-Ṭabarī learned that ar-Rāḍī was still living in his father's house, he offered to give his pupil a house to live in. Ar-Rāḍī refused and said, "I have never accepted anything from anyone except my father." Aṭ-Ṭabari replied, "my claim (*ḥaqqī*) over you is greater because I have taught you [to recite] by heart the Book of God." Only a claim of great importance would justify a young man accepting such an important gift—with its attendant indebtedness—outside the family. This story, incidentally, confirms the semiformal nature of the bonds of *ni'mah* that we discussed in the preceding chapter. Similar language is used in the account of the rebellion of the Ḥasanwaihid prince, Hilāl, against his father Badr. Hilāl's mother, mediating between the two, said to her son, "you are dealing with your father, whose claim on you is binding (*ḥaqquhū 'alaika wājib*)." Hilāl was deeply moved, and immediately made certain concessions to his father. The consequences of denying the claim of family were, consequently, very serious. Ibn al-Athīr tells us that the son of the ruler of Sīstān, Alyasa' b. Muḥammad b. Alyās died a miserable death in exile due to "the ill luck (*shu'm*) which came from rebellion against his father, and [which was] the fruit of his ingratitude." From these examples we see that relations of family were understood to be foreordained, and not acquired, channels of *ni'mah*, and are therefore often described in terms of *ni'mah*. Correspondingly, as we have seen in the last chapter, the ties acquired through *ni'mah* to a protégé, that is, *iṣṭinā'*, are sometimes described in terms of foster parentage.[74]

All of these loyalties of category have been presented as if their relative importance was comparatively stable, and as if these loyalties gave their members a relatively fixed position in society. This is not the case. In the fourth/tenth century, for example, the importance of faction itself seems to have grown. Faction undoubtedly existed in the earlier centuries, but was not important enough to play a major political role. In the Buyid period government had become more decentralized, and central governments seem to have tried to conduct their administrations more through the manipulation of existing groups than by direct intervention. The breakdown of strong central government and of the more hierarchical bureaucracy that had accompanied it encouraged this change.

It also encouraged men not to focus their loyalties too directly on the regime above them. The population was becoming in majority Muslim, and the formerly crucial horizontal division between Muslims and non-Muslims, in which the Muslims had had a greater community of interest with their Muslim rulers, was losing its importance. The vertical division of faction, in which faction often had a high-minded Islamic identification with a law school or sect, was providing a new structure of self-defense.

The new regimes fell in with the new pattern. Rulers, as we have seen, manipulated factional disputes and the associated patronage. They also ceased to associate any single group closely with their regimes—except the soldiers. In the late 'Abbāsid period clerks failed in their effort to acquire permanent control of the army officers. Thereafter, most clerks were seen as servants who were not held responsible by a new regime for their activities under a former regime.

Even if the categories described in this chapter had not fluctuated in their relative importance, membership in these categories would still not have given a man a fixed position in society. There always remained a possibility of movement to a new category, though this possibility decreased somewhat in the fourth and fifth centuries. In this period, in an increasing number of places, offices such as judgeships or leaderships of towns became hereditary. The tendency to make offices hereditary and to emphasize hereditary as contrasted with acquired claims to office fitted in well with the more decentralized style of administration in the post-'Abbāsid period.

Still, if there was an even greater need for a self-made man, or for a man changed into a category different from his ancestors, to prove himself, some men throughout the period were able to do so. There was also downward movement, as men failed to live up to the weight of their inherited *ḥasab* and *nasab*. But the possibility of movement came most commonly from the expandable or contractable sense in which a man was considered a member of any of these categories, and from the success a man had in making use of his various potential memberships through oath, *ni'mah*, and all the other means of acquiring loyalty described in Chapter II.

The expansion and contraction in the extent to which a man belonged to a category came, first of all, from his freedom to develop his membership in one category at the expense of another. Khalaf b. Muḥammad al-Wāsiṭī (d. 401), for example, a very learned scholar of *ḥadīth*, after traveling to meet other scholars finally settled in the province of ar-Ramlah, where "he became engrossed in business and abandoned his study of the science [of *ḥadīth*]." His case, incidentally, like the careers of many similar men, shows how difficult it is to claim that the group of transmitters of *ḥadīth* represent a discrete and definable segment of society.[75]

Yet the possibility of expanding and contracting one's potential membership also comes from the fundamental sense in which a person was a member. For most of these categories, membership did not imply participation in a defined organization; it only implied a potential role for the member and the consequent expectations of society as to what that member might be able to do. Even the hierarchical system of *ṭabaqah* that we have examined, did not, in its full and refined form, imply that a man had a fixed "station" in life. Again, the measure of the man was to some extent determined by the company he chose to keep, not by some fixed grading that assigned him a specific status in a system that encompassed all of society. A man could not, of course, thrust himself into the forefront of any group. He could associate with different groups to which he belonged, and calibrate his standing in each of them. His worth would not, however, be estimated in the same way in each of the groups to which he belonged. If membership implied potential role, hierarchy was based on an ever-sliding calibration, and as a man had membership in many overlapping interest groups, there was great possibility of movement without movement into new groups. 'Abd Allāh b. Aḥmad of Marw (d. 417) was a locksmith; he devoted himself to learning only when he reached thirty; he became *shaikh* of the Shāfi'īs of Khurāsān; he led a large party of *ghāzīs*, volunteer fighters for the extension of Islamic rule, to the holy war. Clearly, he was not frozen in any fixed station in life.[76]

Some of the overlapping roles were more restrictive, and

some more conspicuous, than others. Many clerks owned estates, but it was more unusual to be a clerk than to be a landowner. Landowners, moreover, probably did not want to be as closely associated with the government as clerks were. To be a clerk was, therefore, a more conspicuous role, and clerical landowners are usually identified as clerks, and not as landowners. To be a clerk was also a somewhat more restrictive role, since clerks were proud that they were distinguished by the specialized cultural style that they had learned with great labor and could display both in their writing and in their manner of conducting public business. Nevertheless, as we have seen, some clerks were accepted as ulema. And if, in his countinghouse, the clerk accepted a pseudo-Sassanian view of society, while he accepted an idealistic Islamic view at his prayers, such inconsistency is part of the experience of every society. Western Christians, after all, in spite of their beliefs, have remained people of only occasionally pacific temperament. The great majority of roles were much less restrictive than the role of the clerk; and there was not even an unexpressed contradiction in holding membership in several of them at once. Many groups, as we have seen, were defined by shared interest, and each man participated in them according to the priority he gave to each of his interests.

A man was expected to do what he could with his bundle of roles, and here both his ability at the task for which the role was defined, and his political talent, came into play. Membership in these categories was, as we have said, only a presumptive sign of ability; this presumption could be proved right or wrong in differing degrees. A man could also use his political sense to create and accept obligation according to the methods described in the second chapter and could, like Yaḥyā as-Sūsī, remain a landowner, yet create a special relation with the government and with the other landlords of his district. When *riyāsah* was not strictly hereditary, it was most probably won by men with some political talent of this nature. A number of categories, like that of the clerks, were thought to be indispensable to society. Movement between categories was slow; thus, insofar as society or government needed to deal with or through any categories, it did so by encouraging the progress of such ambitious men as were already to be found in the needed category. But if the category was indispensable, individuals were expendable; as we have seen, such ambitious men as emerged did so at great risk to themselves.

The relative stability of Near Eastern society, and of its social style, cannot, therefore, be explained by the stability of its "basic institutions" in the sense in which such institutions are understood by the historian of Western Europe. Some of this stability grew out of the integration of self-classification into a powerful and persuasive system of belief. Modern man estimates his personal worth in great part on the basis of his visible, personal achievement—the *ḥasab* he alone has acquired. Muslims in the Buyid period did not have the advantages of aspirin and the modern psychological sciences, but did have the advantage of being sustained by something more than their personal achievements and by a lively sense of their relation to the unseen world. The *nasab* and *ḥasab* of their ancestors, no matter how humble, gave a man a niche in society that a man of another and different lowly ancestry might not have. Many men, moreover, seem to have felt deeply that "the best *ḥasab* is piety (*taqwā*)." They cultivated a relation with God that they did not necessarily expect other men to recognize; and yet this relation must have sustained their feeling of having attained a stable religious *ḥasab* regardless of the somewhat fluid position they occupied in the categories with which they were associated.

The stability of Near Eastern Islamic society and its style also grew out of a self-conscious understanding that society needed government and yet, by and large, did not want to generate any government of its own. The categories that we have described gave no promise of expanding into full sovereign governments, and were not expected to do so. The faction, for example, was not an incipient city-state; it was a negative loyalty, and its members had dozens of other loyalties. In fact, what men most feared was that any one loyalty might overwhelm other loyalties in the consciousness of its adherents. Then members of the group defined by this overwhelming loyalty would disregard their overlapping interests and would practice "injustice" by coercing society to give men of this loyalty a disproportionate share. To prevent this congealing of discrete interests, Near Eastern society of our period needed a presence that was "out of category," a presence that society did not accept as one of its own categories and that could, by virtue of its distance, preserve the equilibrium and movement that resulted from the overlapping of categories. This presence was government, or, more specifically, kingship; it is the subject of our next chapter.

CHAPTER IV

Justice, Kingship, and the Shape of Society

A widespread modern tradition assumes that a yearning for independence lies within the heart of every man, and that this yearning is either rightfully restrained by a duty to the commonweal, or wrongfully restrained by oppression. Men of the Buyid period assumed that a yearning for independence threatened the rights of every man and, if not held back by authority, would encourage men to oppress each other. The difference between these two traditions reflects their different understanding of the threat of oppression that would face society if the sense of obligation between men broke down. Men of the Buyid period believed that a general sense of mutual obligation would be maintained if loyalties to the multiple categories to which they belonged were maintained. If, however, loyalty to one category overwhelmed their other feelings of obligation, then the interest which created that loyalty would feed itself at the expense of the rest of society, which would be oppressed. Only a loyalty not obligated to any of these categories would be free from identification with these categories, and would, therefore, be likely to maintain impartiality in dealing with these categories. This role of arbiter, distant from the society for which it arbitrated, known to live largely for its own interest and not for any particular interest in society, was the role of the king. The king who fulfilled this role and saw that each interest got its due, but no more than its due, was "just."

This conception of kingship and justice explains why, in many situations in which modern historians might expect

Near Eastern communities of this period to yearn to be free, they instead yearned to be ruled. When Alftakīn was defeated by ʿAḍud ad-Daulah, he proceeded to Damascus, where the Fāṭimid governor had just been driven out. The *aḥdāth* had gained control of the city, and "the *aʿyān* could exercise no authority in relation to them, nor could government command their obedience." When, therefore, Alftakīn drew near the city, the nobles (*ashrāf*) and elders (*shuyūkh*) went to him and asked him to stay with them, rule their city, and "relieve them from the harm done by the *aḥdāth*." Alftakīn "took their oath to obey and help him; and he swore to protect them from being harmed either by himself or by any other." He uprooted "the destructive elements" and drove off the bedouins; and "all the people were in awe of his authority (*hābahū*)" and "gladly obeyed him."[1]

In this period, few communities had the opportunities of Damascus, which lay in a no man's land between kingdoms and had an unusually aggressive group of *aḥdāth*, to seek independence. By adopting Alftakīn, the people of Damascus did not gain any obvious advantage against their outside attackers, since Alftakīn was not accompanied by a sizable troop of soldiers, and even acknowledged that he was dependent on the "lives and fortunes" of the Damascenes. By adopting Alftakīn, therefore, they were not exculpating themselves in the eyes of their attackers for their opposition to conquest, nor were they seeking an army of defenders. Instead, they were putting at the head of their society a stranger without whom their society could not function.

Not many communities ruled by the Buyids had similar opportunities to choose between rule generated from within their communities, and an outsider who would be chosen or accepted as king. When they did face such choices, they followed the example of the Damascenes. In 381, for example, letters came to Baghdad from the people of ar-Raḥbah and ar-Raqqah requesting that the Buyid government send someone to whom the inhabitants could deliver their territories in northern Iraq, which—owing to the confusion of changing regimes in that region—were temporarily without government. It was, in fact, automatically assumed that a town did not have a system of rule that could fill the vacuum left by a departing ruler. If, therefore, a town remained without an outside ruler even for a short period, it was the subject of surprised comment.

When the forces of Mardāwīj evacuated Isfahan in exchange for recognition of the Ziyārids by the caliph, Miskawaih notes, the town remained for seventeen days "rulerless, deprived of an administrator (*shāghirah khālīyah min mudabbir*)" until the appointee of the caliph arrived. The term *shāghir*, used in this last phrase by Miskawaih, is a technical term for just such an empty, defenseless town. While all the dictionaries emphasize that such a town was exposed to outside attack, being "destitute of anyone to protect it," the definition of *arḍ shāghirah*, "an empty land" by Fīrūzābādī (d. A.H. 816) shows that such a town was "exposed" partly because it lacked administration to pull it together from within. "An exposed land," he writes in his *Qāmūs*, is "a land having no one remaining in it to defend it and to manage its affairs with prudence, precaution, or sound judgment."[2]

The role of the king in preventing partisan interests from solidifying or congealing to the detriment and oppression of others is explained indirectly by Miskawaih in his description of the results of the vizier Ibn Baqīyah's injustice (*ẓulm*) and maladministration, and of the neglect of all government business by his employer, 'Izz ad-Daulah. Things reached such a point, he writes, that "respect for authority (*haibah*) was lost, and the *'āmmah* cast off restraint and attacked each other. Various undisciplined passions (*ahwā'*) and hostile designs came into the open, and murder became common. . . . Supplies of wealth were cut off and the distant provinces were ruined along with the capital. In every village there appeared a *ra'īs* from the place, who took control over it, and they quarreled with each other. The ruler (*sulṭān*) came away empty-handed, the *ra'īyah* were ruined, dwellings became desolate, food supplies failed, and the army fell into mutinous disorder." *Haibah*, the "awe of authority" which 'Izz ad-Daulah failed to inspire, was—it should be remembered—precisely what Alftakīn did inspire in the Damascenes.[3]

The king's justice, therefore, consisted in keeping the overlapping and various interest groups in society from congealing as separate and exclusive units. Since society accepted a system of relational hierarchy that calibrated rank differently according to the group with which one was being considered, it was difficult for interest groups based on rank to congeal along lines of *ṭabaqah*. An important part of the king's role, therefore, was to keep people in their place, as 'Aḍud ad-Daulah explicitly said. The king thereby preserved a system that had as many ranks as it had people, and as many ranking systems as it had groups.

The king, however, did not keep them in their places by virtue of his position at the top of the social hierarchy. Rather, he did so as an outsider, the man who was above categories and their associated hierarchies. Because the army was the only category in which the king participated (and he did so at several removes, since his title was based only in part on his military leadership), the army had to consist of men who were, like the king, detached from special interests and not identified with the categories present in the population. Armies recruited from the settled population of the Near East of this period are rare, and of very minor importance. With outsiders at his command, the king had the coercive instrument that allowed him to be the just arbiter that society wanted him to be. The king might not, in fact, turn out to be just in his use of coercive power. But most men of the Buyid period would have agreed with Macaulay that if he were unjust, "so strong is the interest of a ruler to protect his subjects against all depredations and outrages except his own, so clear and simple are the means by which this end is to be effected, that men are probably better off under the worst governments in the world than they would be in a state of anarchy."[4]

The categories of Buyid society, as we have described them, were such that they were not likely to produce even "the worst government"; left to themselves, they would produce anarchy. Only an outsider, separating himself from the interests of society, could be expected to find it self-evidently in his own interest not to favor some party so strongly that it would be allowed to destroy or permanently override other parties. As long as the interests of his subjects were not convergent, but overlapped, he had in these competing interests a powerful means to manipulate his subjects and to prevent the anarchy which would leave his kingdom too barren to be worth plundering.

The earlier definitions of *ẓulm*, a term which modern scholars usually translate as oppression, also show that men in the Buyid period did not believe themselves to be faced with a choice between "freedom" and "oppression." *Ẓulm*, according to most of the early Arabic dictionaries, means "putting a thing in a place not its own"; hence, "acting in whatsoever way one pleases in the disposing of the property of another"; and also, "transgressing the proper limit." The opposite of *ẓulm* was, therefore, putting and keeping things in their proper place, preventing men from impinging on each other, and, especially, on each other's property. The two most common words for justice, *'adl* and *inṣāf*, both etymologically and in actual use, have the sense of "balancing," so that no excess or falling short destroys equilibrium. The government in the Buyid period was often an "oppressor" in the sense that it transgressed the proper limits, took the property of its subjects, and harmed them. But only the government was in a position to maintain an equilibrium that existing categories, if set free to drift, would be likely to destroy. Better, men felt, to endure the limited oppression of the king (for which they felt no moral responsibility) as long as the king's presence restrained men from oppressing each other without limit.[5]

In the 'Abbāsid period, government had hoped to pose as something more than a bitter necessity. The 'Abbāsids had come to power in the middle of the second/eighth century as the leaders of an eschatological movement. Their party or *shī'ah* was an expression of *al-firqah an-nājiyah*, "the group of the saved," which according to common belief would rally to true Islamic rule at the end of time. This role also opened to their subjects the possibility of becoming closely identified with the government by joining "the group of the saved." Soon, however, it was apparent that the 'Abbāsids were not figures of messianic purity, and that many of their subjects had never been remotely willing to accept the 'Abbāsids as such. The 'Abbāsids no longer claimed that they could save their subjects in a direct way, but they did claim a large role in guiding Islamic society to save itself. They attempted by patronage and by decree to guide the development of Islamic law and theology; and they attempted to make obedience to the 'Abbāsids an integral part of Islamic belief.

Even if their subjects did not accept this last claim, in the first century of 'Abbāsid rule the community of duties and obligations shared by Muslims coincided with the community of political power. The caliphate, which encouraged the increasing definition of these rights and obligations, could claim an established place in the fabric that they created. This close but temporary fit, a near identity between moral and political community, was helped by the comparative smallness of the Islamic community at the beginning of the 'Abbāsid period. Muslims were a minority and, by virtue of their greater association with the caliphate, a sort of ruling class. Since ties were largely between individuals and not between strongly defined groups, this ruling class was still small enough and had enough common interest of privilege to maintain its unity in association with the state.

The centrifugal forces that are present in any empire, the stubborn and unpleasant realities of ʿAbbāsid rule, and the expansion of the Muslim community then made it apparent that the identity of moral and political community would not continue. Through conversion and assimilation, the Muslim community had ceased to be a ruling class. Muslims felt pulled by the many horizontal and vertical ties of identity that have been described in previous chapters. The ʿAbbāsid caliph, moreover, seemed to be maintaining power in the interest of the ʿAbbāsid caliph and of no one else. As ʿAbbāsid rule foundered and collapsed, one central strand, which claimed to be the controlling strand, was removed from the fabric of the moral community of duties and obligations that united Muslims. Part of the task of post-ʿAbbāsid society was the redefinition of the Islamic moral community in a way that would account for the new circumstances. New governments, after all, could not claim validation as an integral part of this moral community, and did not, in their geographical extent, coincide with this community.

The Buyid government, which was the heir to ʿAbbāsid rule at its very center, adopted a decentralized system of rule, and this decentralization influenced the manner in which the community of moral obligation and the government redefined their relations. Decentralization was to a certain extent imposed on the Buyids by their military and financial weakness, which in turn encouraged the rapid evolution among the Buyids of administrative practices that would later be imitated in other parts of the Islamic world. The government abdicated a large proportion of its financial rights by assigning them to its servants as *iqṭāʿāt* (government revenue rights, the collection and retention of which were assigned to people designated by the government). Tribes were increasingly allowed to control autonomous areas, and were paid *khifārah* ("protection money"), supposedly in exchange for their obedience, but often, in practice, to restrain them from despoiling the settled subjects of the government. An indivisible office of government, the caliphate, was maintained to validate the actual government by kings who considered their kingdoms and titles infinitely divisible. The southern Iraqi marsh and the tribal regions became areas of refuge, and the caliph's precincts became sanctuary from arrest by the king.

Administration became less hierarchical, and redundancies of function appeared at all levels of administration, from dual vizierates to the administration of local mints. In a decentralized government, it was desirable to have alternate wires to pull in case any wire (as so easily and frequently happened) disappeared. The middle and lower posts in the administration had taken advantage of the decentralized style of Buyid administration to create special relations with the tribes, the *iqṭāʿ*-holders, local leaders, and the like. These special ties made the hierarchical principle in government even weaker.

As the task of each administrative post became less defined and the chain of command more diffuse, the world of administrative status became more decentralized. Titles like *ra'īs* and vizier were the permanent possessions of men who had attained these distinctions, and the status increasingly resided in the man, and could not be withdrawn by the government. Simultaneously, throughout society there was an increasing tendency to consider ability to be hereditary, and to assign posts on this basis. Status, therefore, was less and less in the government's gift, and insofar as men acquired status, it was less and less in the power of the government to take away such acquired status.

If the administration had become less centralized and less hierarchical, central government did not wither into a mere ornament at the top of society, or a remote tyranny imposed on society against its will. Men not only went out to seek a king when they were "exposed" by the absence of a king, but kings could coerce their subjects and, especially, their armies, by threatening to leave them. In the late Buyid period, the Turkish garrison in Baghdad wanted the weak Buyid king Jalāl ad-Daulah to come to Baghdad because the city and its region were being destroyed by the "ambitions" of the *'āmmah* and the Kurds and the Arabs, "and they did not have a government to bring agreement among them (*sulṭān yajma'u kalimatahum*)." Jalāl ad-Daulah, however, was finally so disheartened by his inability to control the Turks, or even to feed his own horses, that in 422 he sent away all his attendants and locked the gates of his palace. As a result, a disorder (*fitnah*) broke out in which the army fought the *'ayyārūn*. Abū Kālījār, a powerful relative of Jalāl ad-Daulah, did not hurry to Baghdad to replace him, even though the two Buyids were opponents; for, as he plainly said, he believed that the ever-growing weakness of the Turks would increase their need for him. The Turks did, eventually, come to support Jalāl ad-Daulah; they had no answer to his argument that, left without a king, they could not produce their own king, or maintain balance in society.[6]

The king maintained the balance, kept loyalties overlapping, and prevented interests from congealing, partly by the wide range of personal loyalties he acquired in the manner described in Chapter II. The principal day-to-day concern of the king, however, was his military power, which gave him coercive power over his subjects. It is surprising how seldom this coercive power was actually used; but its very presence, and the constant threat to use it, was essential to the maintenance of the generally accepted social order.

The ties between central and local governments were to some extent determined by the way in which they presented themselves (and the way in which they were perceived)—both as kingly patron and as punitive outsider. Each of these two faces of central government was, in fact, adapted to the other, and was in a way dependent on the other to have its appropriate effect. Local communities had learned how to become fastened and unfastened to different rulers with a speed suited to their uncertain situations. Nevertheless, they and the rulers, understood the dependency between local government and central rule, and that the "whole" composed of local and central government was, if not greater, at least different from the sum of its parts. The threat of coercive power helped to create the shape of the whole even when coercive power was not used. For many groups, the *ra'īs*, as we have seen, was not a government appointee; but the need for *ru'asā'*—and, more generally, the need for the self-consciously defined category of *a'yān*—was conditioned by the threat of coercion. On the one hand, men were encouraged to arbitrate quarrels without resort to royal judgment, and to accept the results of such arbitration, because they wanted to bring in the coercive arbitration of the government only as a last resort. On the other hand, both the central government and the local community recognized the advantage of settling quarrels through the ties of personal patronage that the *a'yān* created by cultivating both those below themselves, in the local community, and those above themselves, in the royal court. The association of the ruler with the coercive power of an alien army, was—as we have seen—stronger in the Buyid period than in the 'Abbāsid period, so that clerks, for example, were less identified with the regime and to that extent pushed down into society as another category.

This salutary "awe" or "dread," which surrounded kingly authority by virtue of its threat of coercion, was often called *haibah*. It was the *haibah* of the Ḥasanwaihid king, Badr, which, as we have seen, prevented the factions from "overstepping the bounds" (*tajāwuz al-ḥadd*) in his lifetime. In 306, when the caliph hesitated to accept Ḥāmid b. al-'Abbās as vizier, since he had little training in the technical skills of the office, the caliph was persuaded to accept Ḥāmid because of, among other things, "the awe (*haibah*) of Ḥāmid felt by the financial governors." In contrast, in 416, when the *'ayyārūn* went to horrible excesses in their abuse of Baghdādīs, and the government could not restrain them, we are told that the *haibah* of the government was destroyed.[7]

The presence of kings, however necessary, had to be explained in terms of the general values of Islamic society in the

Buyid period. Kingship, after all, had been a morally repugnant feature of the old order that Islam had replaced. Islam, in the view of the overwhelming majority of its adherents, was meant not to create kingdoms but to bring into existence a divinely appointed polity, based on a divine law, which would last until the Day of Judgment. The word for king in Arabic, *mālik*, was associated with the verb *malaka*, "to possess," and any man who pretended to "possess" the world or a portion of it was plainly a usurper. God alone, as the Koran repeatedly says, is "the King, the Truth" and has *mulk*, "possession of [or sovereignty over] the Heavens and the earth," just as he is "Possessor (*mālik*) of the Day of Judgment." God loans this sovereignty to men, yet the title of permanent possession remains with God; as the Koran says, "Say, oh God, Possessor of sovereignty (*mālik al-mulk*), you give sovereignty to whomever you choose and take it from whomever you choose" (3:26). True caliphs were not kings but stewards, who administered their trust in full knowledge that they possessed nothing; for the world, and the judgment of their conduct in it, belonged exclusively to God.

Caliphs, of course, had been in practice indistinguishable from kings; but their claims, which were based on this argument against monarchy, could not be transferred to the Buyids and their contemporaries. The presence of these new rulers seems, from the start, to have been explained in terms of *daulah*, the divinely granted turn in power, an idea that fitted comfortably with the Koranic verse quoted above. The 'Abbāsids had claimed that their *daulah* was synonymous with the *daulah* of Islam and that authority would remain with them until the second coming.

Events had proved this claim false and had opened the way for a more flexible interpretation of *daulah*; and, from the very beginning, men seem to have explained the rule of the Buyids as a new *daulah*. Officially, the Buyids still pretended to be living in the *daulah* of the 'Abbāsids, and therefore accepted titles like Mu'izz ad-Daulah, "Strengthener of the Abbasid *daulah*," and 'Imād ad-Daulah, "Prop of the Abbasid *daulah*." Unofficially, however, men recognized that the turn of the Abbasid *daulah* as a locus of independent authority had ended. Al-Muhallabī, the highly educated vizier of the early Buyids of Iraq, said, "I will be the first memorable man in the *daulah* of the Dailamīs since I escaped becoming the last memorable man in the *daulah* of the 'Abbāsids." However closely the caliphate was associated with the central symbols of Islam, circumstances had proved that actual rule would be less closely associated with them. Al-Muqtadir, one of the last 'Abbāsid caliphs to really rule as well as reign, used the Prophet's staff and cloak, and every potent symbol at his disposal in his test of power with his general, Mu'nis. When al-Muqtadir's head was brought to Mu'nis, one of the clerks present quoted a poem that said, "When fate fixes its talons, all amulets are thrown away as useless."[8]

A century later it was widely accepted that there would be continual new grants of sovereignty, and that—as became the common metaphor—the shirt of kingship would be forcibly removed from one man or dynasty and given to another in accord with some deeper divine wisdom. Al-Muqtadir had said, "I will do as [the third caliph] 'Uthmān b. 'Affān did; I will not hand over a right that God has entrusted to me nor will I divest myself of a shirt (*qamīṣ*) in which God has clothed me." But a century later, al-Baihaqī, the vizier of Mas'ūd of Ghaznah (d. 432/1040) explains the sovereignty of his Ghaznavid masters by saying, "If any defamer or jealous person says that this great house has come from humble or unknown origin, the answer is that God, since the creation of Adam, has decreed that kingship be transferred from one religious polity (*ummat*) to another and from one group to another. The greatest testimony to what I am saying is the words of the Creator: 'Say, O God, possessor of sovereignty, you give sovereignty to whomever you choose and take it from whomever you choose (3:26).' So it should be realized that God's removal of the shirt of kingship from one group and his placing it on another group is in that sense divine wisdom and for the commonweal of mankind, [wisdom] which surpasses human understanding. . . . [God knows] that in such and such a spot a man will appear through whom men will obtain happiness and good fortune." When Mas'ūd wrote the Saljūq Ṭughril Beg a menacing letter shortly before suffering a crushing defeat at the hands of the Saljūqs, Ṭughril turned the argument against the Ghaznavids by the same verse (3:26) from the Koran.[9]

The new understanding of *daulah* not only explained the new monarchies, it also redistributed the moral responsibility associated with government. The Dailamīs had had a rich experience in obeying and betraying petty kings and counter-caliphs by the time they conquered western Iran and Iraq. The Buyids were Shī'īs, but kept their Shī'ism undefined and adaptable to the expediencies of their political lives. They did not claim, as the 'Abbāsids did, that they came to their subjects with some moral truth to teach; they did not pretend, as modern democratic leaders do, that they hoped to learn any moral truth that their constituents might want to teach. True, even in their heyday, the 'Abbāsids were regarded with indifference or even hostility by many of their subjects. But the 'Abbāsids argued that salvation could come through obedience to the truly Islamic society that they were trying to build. The Buyids, at most, were men given a *daulah* for reasons best known to God. The Buyids could pose only as protectors of the attempts that society made to save itself. The full titles of the later Buyids reflect this changed position of the ruler; after the standard title with *ad-daulah*, virtually all the later Buyids had titles that called them protectors of the *ummah*, the *millah* (Islamic community) and of *dīn*, religion itself. The government was the work of a small minority who had been granted a *daulah*. They had to be outsiders and had to be a minority in order to function. They therefore could not pose as an instrument of salvation for their subjects, and could not in this way invite their subjects to identify with their rule. At most, they could claim to protect the community in which their subjects might realize their moral and religious values.

This redistribution of responsibility freed the population of certain moral responsibilities toward the state, and, similarly, freed the state of certain moral responsibilities toward its subjects. Ar-Rūdhrāwarī, commenting on uncanonical taxes imposed by ʿAḍud ad-Daulah, quotes a well-known *ḥadīth* that "whoever institutes a good practice (*sunnah*) shall have the reward thereof and of all who act thereby unto the day of resurrection; and whoever institutes a bad practice shall have the guilt thereof and the guilt of all who act according to it thereafter unto the day of resurrection." Correspondingly, ar-Rūdhrāwarī is shocked that ʿAḍud ad-Daulah should have disgraced Ibrāhīm aṣ-Ṣābī, the head of ʿIzz ad-Daulah's chancery, for having written a letter on behalf of ʿIzz ad-Daulah with phrases offensive to ʿAdud ad-Daulah. "Suppose," says ar-Rūdhrāwarī, " ʿAḍud ad-Daulah had ordered him to do what Bakhtiyar [ʿIzz ad-Daulah] had ordered; when under his power, would aṣ-Ṣābī had been able to resist?"

Most Buyid rulers were more understanding than ʿAḍud ad-Daulah. Jalāl ad-Daulah clearly wanted the title *malik al-mulūk*, "king of kings," even though Muḥammad in a widely accepted *ḥadīth* had called it "the worst of names in my sight." The caliph asked the jurists if such a title were permissible, and the only important jurist to dissent was al-Māwardī. The first time Jalāl ad-Daulah saw al-Māwardī after his dissent, he said, "everyone knows you are the greatest of the jurists (*fuqahā'*) in wealth and prestige (*jāh*) and in my favor. You have opposed the others in opposing what I desired; but you have done so only because of your lack of partiality and adherence to right."[10]

One corollary of the new understanding of *ad-daulah* and the lessened moral responsibility of society for government, and of government for society, was that men felt that the evil consequences of their political ambitions that did not institute established practices fell only on themselves. For scrupulous men, this was an inducement to set political ambition aside. For less scrupulous men, it was an encouragement to take political initiatives. At the very end of the fourth century, an adventurer named Abū Rakhwah almost succeeded in overthrowing the Fāṭimids. When he was finally captured, he wrote to the Fāṭimid caliph, "I have done wrong, but I have thereby oppressed no one except myself and my misconduct has brought me perdition." Accordingly, men often refused to carry out the orders of a dead king (whose authority was, in any case, highly personal), since the moral responsibility could no longer be placed on the king. The governor of Sīrāf, for example, who was ordered by Sharaf ad-Daulah to blind the imprisoned Buyid pretender, Ṣamṣām ad-Daulah, heard that Sharaf ad-Daulah had died. He therefore refused to carry out the operation, since "the authority for this has ceased with the death of Sharaf ad-Daulah."[11]

The lessened moral responsibility between king and subjects also freed the king to practice without embarrassment a kind of law that society hoped to have him practice; and that was, in fact, essential to his position as an arbiter above category. The fourth-century poet al-Babbaghā said in a poem to the Ḥamdānid Saif ad-Daulah, "He whom justice has not improved, because of his extreme unruliness, when he does wrong, oppression (*ẓulm*) will improve." Rough justice had been practiced by caliphs as well as kings; but society felt less moral responsibility for kings, and only hoped for certain functional benefits from their presence. One of these benefits, as we have said, was to prevent any specific interest from monopolizing the attention of those who shared that interest. The king, therefore, was in a sense encouraged to disregard "right" as defined by the divine law, and to apply probabilistic and commonweal solutions. Typically, when Shīʿīs and Sunnīs fought in Baghdad, the king ordered one member of each faction to be drowned in the Tigris. Such exemplary punishment was essential to the *haibah* of the king and to the enforcement of compromise.[12]

By disengaging itself from government and the moral burdens of government, and at the same time giving enormous power to governments, Islamic society of the Buyid period freed itself to maintain a community of duties and obligations in levels of life below the government. Ibn al-Athīr explains that even though Qābūs lost his kingdom in helping the Buyid king Fakhr ad-Daulah, Fakhr ad-Daulah on becoming king did not give Jurjān back to the homeless Qābūs because, as the proverb says, "kingship is bereft of ties (*al-mulk 'aqīm*)." Men expected kings to be above category and to put reasons of state ahead even of important acquired loyalties like *ni'mah*. Among themselves, however, the structure of obligation remained intact, and served functions that a decentralized government was not interested in or capable of serving. The government, by its remote threat and its ties of personal patronage, encouraged local communities to maintain the structure of obligation and of *riyāsah* that we have examined.[13]

Yet even beyond the local community, an "international" community of credit and of law was maintained. A moral community of highly personal and yet endlessly overlapping loyalties had been evolved, which took over many of the functions of government. It was as members of this community that so many people clung to the fiction of a universal Islamic caliphate. In the course of the tenth and eleventh centuries, this community had learned how to define its relations with actual governments so that it might withstand repeated changes of central government. This community understood its constraints and possibilities so well, in fact, that it has never entirely disappeared.

NOTES

Chapter I, Introduction

1. Alexis de Tocqueville, *De la démocratie en Amérique* (Paris, 1951), I, 466.
2. Ira M. Lapidus, "Muslim Cities and Islamic Societies," in a book edited by the same author: *Middle Eastern Cities* (Berkeley and Los Angeles, 1969), p. 49.
3. These two sayings of Muḥammad are given in paradigmatic form; they vary greatly in their original wording. For example, Mālik b. Anas in his *Muwaṭṭa'* (Cairo, 1370), II, 899, quotes Muḥammad as saying: "I have left you two things because of which you will not go astray as long as you cleave to them: the Book of God and the *sunnah* of his Prophet." Aḥmad b. Ḥanbal in his *Musnad* (Cairo, 1313), III, 26, gives one of many versions in which Muḥammad calls his legacy two "important things," which in this quote are "the Book of God . . . and my family." Sometimes, as in the *Sunan* of Ibn Mājah, statements of this nature are put in the context of Muḥammad's address to his followers at Minā during the pilgrimage; but these statements are by no means exclusively associated with this occasion.
4. This and succeeding paragraphs give the explanation of the *sunnah* as understood by Muslims both in the period discussed by the book and in all later periods. Joseph Schacht in his book, *The Origins of Muhammadan Jurisprudence* (Oxford, 1953), argues persuasively that for the first generations of Muslims, the *sunnah* was the usage of the Muslim community as a whole, and was not identified with the sayings of, or about, Muḥammad.
5. *Ḥadīth* quoted by C. van Arendonk, "Sharīf," *Shorter Encyclopaedia of Islam* (Leiden, 1953), p. 531.
6. J. W. Fück, "Ibn Mādja," *Encyclopaedia of Islam*, 2nd ed. (Leiden, 1971); III, 856.
7. See H. Laoust, "al-Barbahārī," *Encyclopaedia of Islam*, 2nd ed. (Leiden, 1960), I, 1039-1040.
8. Miskawaih, *Tajārib al-umam* (Cairo, Vol. I, 1914; Vol. II, 1915), I, 322. This chronicle, its continuation by ar-Rūdhrāwarī, and a fragment of Hilāl aṣ-Ṣābī have been translated by D. S. Mar-

goliouth as *The Eclipse of the Abbasid Caliphate* (Oxford, 1920-1921). In quoting from these sources I have given slightly revised versions of Margoliouth's excellent translation. The pagination of the Arabic text is given in Margoliouth's translation, and I have therefore given references only to the Arabic text.

9. A. J. Wensinck, "al-Ash'arī," *Shorter Encyclopaedia of Islam*, p. 47.
10. Abū Ḥaiyān at-Tauḥīdī, *Kitāb al-imtā'* (Cairo, 1373), III, 194-195.
11. Miskawaih, *Tajārib al-umam*, II, 192-193 (Aleppo); ad-Dhahabī, quoted in a footnote to Miskawaih, II, 200 (tumult); Ibn Taghrībirdī, *Annales* (Leiden, 1855), II, 365 (volunteer fighters).
12. Al-Hamadhānī, *Takmilah ta'rīkh aṭ-Ṭabarī* (Beirut, 1961), p. 190 (Tarsus); Miskawaih, *Tajārib al-umam*, II, 223 (Rukn ad-Daulah).
13. Sunnī religious lawyers (*fuqahā'*) were present in the army of volunteer warriors who passed through Rayy in 355; see Miskawaih, *Tajārib al-umam*, II, 223.
14. I hope to treat the political history of the Buyids in a subsequent book, which will also discuss their attempts to justify their rule in terms of ancient Iranian ideas of kingship.

Chapter II, Acquired Loyalties

1. Miskawaih, *Tajārib al-umam* I, 191. Parts of the letter with variants are quoted in several chronicles; only al-Hamadhānī, *Takmilah ta'rīkh aṭ-Ṭabarī* (Beirut, 1961), p. 59 quotes nearly as much as Miskawaih.
2. Miskawaih, *Tajārib al-umam*, II, 74 (an oath "by the Koran—*al-maṣḥaf*—and [other] solemn oaths"). This book is only concerned with the actual use of oaths; for a survey of the rich theoretical (and, in particular, legal) material on oaths, see J. Pedersen's article, "Ḳasam," *Shorter Encyclopaedia of Islam*, pp. 224-226, and his book *Der Eid bei den Semiten* (Strassburg, 1914).
3. Miskawaih, *Tajārib al-umam*, II, 67-72; anon., *al-'Uyūn wa'l ḥadā'iq* (Berlin ms. 9491), f. 219A.
4. Anon., *al-Uyūn*, ff. 216B-217A, f. 221B (quote); Ibn al-Jauzī, *al-Muntaẓam*, Vols. VI, VII, VIII (Hyderabad, 1357, 1358, 1359), VI, 343. Other rulers were believed to have died because they broke their oath, as did, for example, the Ḥamdānid Sa'd ad-

Daulah in 381; see Ibn al-Athīr, *al-Kāmil* (Vols. VIII, IX, Leiden, 1862), IX, 62.

5. Ibn al-Athīr, *al-Kāmil,* IX, 32 (Sharaf ad-Daulah); Sibṭ b. al-Jauzī, *Mir'āt az-Zamān* (Istanbul ms., Köprülü 1157, Vol. XI), p. 477. Mas'ūd eventually broke his oath, for he married a relative of the Buyid (and, therefore, Dailamī) king, Abū Kālījār.
6. Hilāl aṣ-Ṣābī, *Ta'rīkh* (Cairo, 1919), p. 431.
7. ar-Rūdhrāwarī, *Dhail tajārib al-umam* (Cairo, 1916), p. 308.
8. at-Tanūkhī, *Nishwār al-Muḥāḍarah* (Beirut, 1971-1972), II, 19, 216; cf. also Miskawaih, *Tajārib al-umam*, I, 266.
9. Miskawaih, *Tajārib al-umam*, I, 242 (where the officers first *istaḥlafa*; that is, asks the candidate for caliph to swear an oath); also I, 266.
10. Émile Tyan, "Bay'a," *Encyclopaedia of Islam*, 2nd ed., I, 1113-1114.
11. Miskawaih, *Tajārib al-umam*, II, 82 (Ibn Shīrzād); aṣ-Ṣūlī, *Akhbār ar-Rāḍī bi'llāh wa'l-muttaqī li'llāh* (Cairo, 1935), p. 237 (*bai'ah* to Sāmānids); Ibn al-Athīr, *al-Kāmil*, VIII, 301, 345; aṭ-Ṭabarī, *Ta'rīkh aṭ-Ṭabarī* (Leiden, 1890), III, 2290; ar-Rūdhrāwarī, *Dhail*, p. 78 ('Aḍud ad-Daulah's death).
12. Ibn al-Athīr, *al-Kāmil*, VIII, 142 (Mardāwīj); IX, p. 353 (al-Malik al-'Azīz); Miskawaih, *Tajārib al-umam*, II, 101 (Ibn Muḥtāj); p. 102 (Ibn Muḥtāj makes a compact, *'āhada*, with Ibrāhīm to obey him when they meet); ar-Rūdhrāwarī, *Dhail*, p. 79 (Sharaf ad-Daulah takes *bai'ah* from the *awliyā'*). Presumably, in many circumstances when the sources refer to an oath taken from the army without specifying the *bai'ah*, or when the soldiers are adjured to hold to their oaths, the *bai'ah* (taken in the first instance or "renewed") is the principal oath in question; e.g., Ibn al-Athīr, *al-Kāmil*, IX, 374; ar-Rūdhrāwarī, *Dhail*, p. 231; aṣ-Ṣūlī, *Akhbār*, pp. 87-88.
13. ar-Rūdhrāwarī, *Dhail*, p. 104 (Abū Manṣūr); p. 93 (Ibn 'Abbād); cf. Miskawaih, *Tajārib al-umam*, I, 262 for details of a conspiracy in 321.
14. Ibn al-Athīr, *al-Kāmil*, VIII, 503 (Sabuktakīn); compare p. 336.
15. Miskawaih, *Tajārib al-umam*, II, pp. 85, 105-106; Ibn al-Jauzī, *al-Muntaẓam*, VI, 340.
16. Miskawaih, *Tajārib al-umam*, III, 240; Sibṭ b. al-Jauzī, *Mir'āt* (Köprülü), pp. 349, 483; Ibn al-Jauzī, *al-Muntaẓam*, VIII, 148; VIII, 19 (Musharraf ad-Daulah); p. 27 (caliph offers to write Abū Kālījār).
17. Ibn al-Jauzī, *al-Muntaẓam*, VIII, 66 (Rukn ad-Daulah in the

printed text is a mistake for Rukn ad-Dīn; his retinue may refer either to the emir's, including the vizier, or the retinue of the vizier).

18. Sibṭ b. al-Jauzī, *Mir'āt* (Köprülü), p. 456; Ibn al-Athīr, *al-Kāmil*, IX, 417.
19. Miskawaih, *Tajārib al-umam*, II, 286-287 (ash-Shīrāzī); p. 315 (commander-in-chief); p. 356 (Ibn Baqīyah).
20. For example, *ibid.*, I, 249 (reconciling officials in 321); p. 325 (new vizier releases former vizier on oath in 322); p. 332 (release of a general in 324); II, 124 (al-Muhallabī); p. 284 (oath between officials in 360); ar-Rūdhrāwarī, *Dhail*, p. 308 (official and courtier reconciled in 388); Ibn al-Athīr, *al-Kāmil*, VIII, 233.
21. Miskawaih, *Tajārib al-umam*, I, 286 (322); II, 282 ('Izz ad-Daulah); ar-Rūdhrāwarī, *Dhail*, p. 158; see at-Tanūkhī, *Nishwār*, III, 284 (officials take oaths of Dailamī officers to mutiny and demand the dismissal of the vizier).
22. Miskawaih, *Tajārib al-umam*, II, 299-300 (Baluchees); p. 199 (Ḥarrān); cf. also II, 36.
23. ar-Rūdhrāwarī, *Dhail*, p. 26 (Bukhārā); p. 125 (contingency). Other examples of treaty oaths: Miskawaih, *Tajārib al-umam*, II, 312 (*kitab al-ittifāq*, signed and witnessed); I, 385; II, 108; ar-Rūdhrāwarī, *Dhail*, pp. 15, 184; Ibn al-'Athīr, *al-Kāmil*, IX, 182, 309, 421.
24. al-Hamadhānī, *Ta'rīkh*, p. 86 reading *jazaytuhū* for *jazabtuhū*.
25. Miskawaih, *Tajārib al-umam*, I, 412 (al-Barīdī); Sibṭ b. al-Jauzī, *Mir'āt* (Köprülü), p. 322 (Hilāl).
26. Hilāl aṣ-Ṣābī, *Ta'rīkh*, p. 431 (Abū 'Alī b. Ismā'īl); cf. also p. 441 (again called an *amān*); Ibn al-Athīr, *al-Kāmil*, IX, 39 (example of an *amān* to a rebellious general who returns to allegiance); aṭ-Ṭabarī, *Ta'rikh*, III, 211 (al-Mansūr).
27. Miskawaih, *Tajārib al-umam*, II, 228.
28. *Ibid.*, pp. 141-142; Ibn Khallikān, *Wafayāt al-a'yān*, (Vols. I, II, III, Beirut: 1968, 1969, 1970); II, 119 quotes the better part of the story.
29. Sibṭ b. al-Jauzī, *Mir'āt* (British Museum ms. OR 4169, Vol. II, f. 107A-107B).
30. al-Hamadhānī, *Ta'rīkh*, p. 83 (ar-Rādī); Pedersen, "Ḳasam," p. 224 (*dhimmah Allāh* and *'ahd Allāh* in oaths).
31. al-Hamadhānī, *Ta'rīkh*, p. 156 ('Alī b. 'Īsā); Miskawaih, *Tajārib al-umam*, II, 165 (Nahr Rūfīl). For another example,

among many, of a vow and public works, see Ibn al-Athīr, *al-Kāmil*, IX, 154, and Ibn al-Jauzī, *al-Muntaẓam*, VIII, 246.

32. Ibn Ḥamdūn, *at-Tadhkirah*, quoted in Miskawaih, *Tajārib al-umam*, II, 416, note I (mother of 'Aḍud ad-Daulah); Ibn al-'Athīr, *al-Kāmil*, VIII, 97-99 (dream of Būyah); at-Tanūkhī, *Nishwār*, II, 241-242 (the Ṭāhirids; the Ṭāhirids were suspiciously sympathetic to the 'Alids, as when Ṭāhir refused to fight certain 'Alids); ar-Rūdhrāwarī, *Dhail*, p. 206 (al-Qādir; that al-Qādir himself told his story is confirmed by ar-Rūdhrāwarī, p. 147). The Sāmānid pretender Aḥmad rebelled when the Prophet Joseph promised authority to him in a dream; see Ibn al-Athīr, *al-Kāmil*, VIII, 88. For other political dreams, cf. Ibn al-Athīr, VIII, 483; at-Tanūkhī, *Nishwār*, III, 248-249.

33. See aṣ-Ṣūlī, *Akhbār*, I, 121 for a general *amān* to the inhabitants of Baghdad who had helped Ibn Rā'iqi for a vow to punish a group, whose individuals are not named. See Miskawaih, *Tajārib al-umam*, I, 323, ar-Rāḍī's decree of 323, which ends with "a solemn oath which he [the caliph] surely must repay" that if the Ḥanbalīs persist, he will use sword and fire against them.

34. at-Tauḥīdī, *Mathālib al-wazīrain* (Damascus, 1961), p. 15. Compare aṣ-Ṣūlī's poem of 330/941 (*Akhbār*, p. 221) where his patron's generosity is said to be so great that "time (*az-zamān*) will pay every debt [imposed by his generosity] with a long life, and by giving him leadership," with the words of Ulysses in Shakespeare's *Troilus and Cressida*: "Time hath, my lord, a wallet at his back/ Wherein he puts alms for oblivion,/ A great-sized monster of ingratitudes" (act III, sc. 3).

35. ar-Rūdhrāwarī, *Dhail*, p. 45 (Aḍud ad-Daulah); at-Tanūkhī, *Nishwār*, III, 262 (Abū Taghlib); Miskawaih, *Tajārib al-umam*, I, 156 ('Alī b. 'Īsā). *Ni'mah* can mean personal fortune, since personal fortune comes through the grace of God or of the caliph, and we see the word somewhere between these two meanings in the statement of the son of a judge who offered to pay the caliph if he were appointed to his father's judgeship: "My *ni'mah* and that of my father are from the commander of the Faithful al-Muqtadir, so I shall keep nothing from him" (Miskawaih, I, 229).

36. Miskawaih, *Tajārib al-umam*, II, 169-170.

37. al-'Arīb, *Ṣilah ta'rīkh aṭ-Ṭabarī* (Leiden, 1897), p. 20. Al-'Arīb's

account of this conversation is much better and fuller than the account in Miskawaih, *Tajārib al-umam*, I, 4, where the conversation is to exactly the same effect, although it takes place after al-Muktafī dies. On the date of these negotiations, cf. D. Sourdel, *Le Vizirat* (Damascus, 1957), p. 366.

38. Miskawaih, *Tajārib al-umam*, I, 344 (Yāqūt; *maulāya* probably means the caliph, who was not his immediate enemy, but to whom he would be delivered as a dishonored prisoner if defeated); p. 199 (Abu 'l-Haijā' b. Ḥamdān); Ibn al-Athīr, *al-Kāmil*, IX, 76 (Sīmjūrids). Since the Barīdīs were the greatest liars and ingrates of the fourth/tenth century, correspondence with them frequently discussed ingratitude, as when Ibn Rā'iq told them in 325 that "they had shown ingratitude for benefits (*kufr an-ni'mah*) and paid good treatment (*iḥsān*) with evil, and thrown off obedience" (Miskawaih, *Tajārib al-umam*, I, 358). Similarly, the vizier Ibn Muqlah told the Barīdīs in 323 not to persist in "ingratitude to my favor and my good treatment of you" (*kufr ni'matī wa iḥsanī ilaika*), *ibid*., p. 327.

39. Adam Mez, *Die Renaissance des Islams* (Heidelberg, 1922), p. 331, where the passage is quoted from Yāqūt and Tha'ālibī; cf. also pp. 237-238 for a similar passage from the *Rasā'il* of al-Ḥamadhānī.

40. Miskawaih, *Tajārib al-umam*, II, 302 (vizier and gratitude); at-Tanūkhī, *Nishwār*, II, 21 (al-Munajjim); on the style of commercial loyalty described here see Clifford Geertz, *Peddlers and Princes* (Chicago, 1963).

41. Miskawaih, *Tajārib al-umam*, II, 16 (al-Barīdī); I, 277 (quote on 'Alī's generosity, and Būyids leave Mākān); p. 278 ("Next to the divine decree, the only cause [of 'Alī's success] was his freehandedness and liberality"); p. 280 ('Alī's generosity); Ibn al-Athīr, *al-Kāmil*, III, 143 (Asfār); p. 167 (Mardāwīj's generosity); p. 206 (defeat of Yāqūt); aṣ-Ṣūlī, *Akhbār*, p. 254.

42. Miskawaih, *Tajārib al-umam*, I, 235 (Mu'nis); II, 60 (al-Barīdī).

43. E. W. Lane, *An Arabic-English Lexicon* (London, 1872), pt. 4, p. 1734.

44. S. M. Stern, "Ya'qūb the Coppersmith" in *Iran and Islam*, edited by C. E. Bosworth (Edinburgh, 1971), pp. 542, 545 quoting from Yāqūt, *Irshād al-arīb* (London, 1907), I, 322-323.

45. al-Hamadhānī, *Ta'rīkh*, p. 61; Miskawaih, *Tajārib al-umam*, I, 343 (Yāqūt); compare p. 319 where Yāqūt asks for *tajdīd aṣ-ṣanī'ah*; II, 7 (Bajkam); aṣ-Ṣūlī, *Akhbār*, I, 197 (quote from Bajkam); compare Maḥmūd of Ghaznah's grief at the death of a

Sāmānid in Sibṭ b. al-Jauzī, *Mir'āt* (Köprülü), p. 475. Actually, Bajkam had originally been the *mamlūk* of Abū 'Alī, the secretary of Mākān, and was given to Mākān on the latter's request; see Miskawaih, *Tajārib al-umam*, I, 383.

46. Miskawaih, *Tajārib al-umam*, II, 384-385 (Alftakīn).
47. *Ibid*., I, 298 (*ghulāms* of landlords); II, 326 (*ghulāms* in 363); al-Hamadhānī, *Ta'rīkh*, 33; al-'Arīb, *Ṣilah ta'rīkh*, p. 168 (Mu'nis's *ghulāms*).
48. aṣ-Ṣūlī, *Akhbār*, p. 64 (Mu'nisīya); p. 269 (Tūzūn); al-'Arīb, *Ṣilah Ta'rīkh*, pp. 115-116 (Ya'nis).
49. Sibṭ b. al-Jauzī, *Mir'āt* (British Museum), f. 103A.
50. ar-Rūdhrāwarī, *Dhail*, p. 330.
51. Miskawaih, *Tajārib al-umam*, II, 332 ('Izz ad-Daulah); 162-163 (Mu'izz ad-Daulah); Mu'izz ad-Daulah could not at first believe that Rūzbahān had rebelled against him, since he had fostered Rūzbahān's career (*iṣṭana'ahū*); Ibn al-Athīr, *al-Kāmil*, IX, 257 (Jalāl ad-Daulah).
52. Ibn Khaldūn, *The Muqaddimah*, translated by Franz Rosenthal (Princeton, 1967), I, 276 (the Arabic terms in parentheses are not given in the translation); al-Hamadhānī, *Ta'rīkh*, p. 185 (Ibn Abrūnā).
53. aṣ-Ṣābī, *Kitāb al-wuzarā'* (Cairo, 1958), p. 275 (Ibn Bisṭām); al-Hamadhānī, *Ta'rīkh*, p. 146 ('Alī b. 'Īsā).
54. at-Tanūkhī, *Nishwār*, I, 17 (Ibn az-Zayyāt). Compare in aṣ-Ṣābī, *Wuzarā'*, p. 324, the remark of Nāzūk, the head of police, as he excused himself when al-Muḥassin ibn al-Furāt proposed to torture 'Alī b. 'Īsā: "I do not like being present at the torture of a man whose hand I have kissed for twenty years, and to whom I owe favors and benefits; he is, moreover, an elderly and religious man who fasts in the day time."
55. Miskawaih, *Tajārib al-umam*, II, 32; aṣ-Ṣūlī, *Akhbār*, pp. 41-43.
56. Miskawaih, *Tajārib al-umam*, I, 376 (Bajkam); II, 412 (Muḥammad b. 'Umar); see 'Imād ad-Daulah's remark, p. 113, that al-Ḥasan and Aḥmad "are by blood my brothers; by upbringing my sons; and by what they are invested to govern, my *ṣanī'ahs*." Mu'izz ad-Daulah's favor to Turks instead of Dailamīs is called an *iṣṭinā'*, p. 166. Aṣ-Ṣūlī, *Akhbār*, pp. 259, 276 (*muṣāna'ah*), as also Miskawaih, *Tajārib al-umam*, II, 97.
57. Miskawaih, *Tajārib al-umam*, I, 303-304 (Abū Sa'd); p. 361 (Ibn Rā'iq). Compare the version of this in Ibn al-Athīr, *al-Kāmil*, VIII, 247: "He [an-Naubakhti] has a great claim [*ḥaqq*] on me. He it was who strove on my behalf until I reached my present

situation and I want no substitute for him." Al-Hamadhānī, *Ta'rīkh*, p. 105 (reappointment of an-Naubakhti considered).

58. at-Tanūkhī, *Nishwār*, I, 70.
59. aṣ-Ṣābī, *Wuzarā'*, p. 132 (Ibn al-Furāt); compare aṣ-Ṣūlī, *Akhbār*, p. 69, and Miskawaih, *Tajārib al-umam*, II, 334.

Chapter III, Loyalties of Category

1. al-Jāḥiẓ, "Manāqib at-Turk," *Rasā'il* (Cairo, 1964), p. 73; Ibn Qutaibah, "Kitāb al-'Arab," *Rasā'il al-Bulaghā'*, edited by Kurd 'Alī, (Cairo, 1365), pp. 358-360.
2. al-Jāḥiẓ, "Manāqib," p. 23.
3. *Ibid.*, p. 12; Ibn Qutaibah, "Kitāb al-'Arab," p. 360.
4. at-Tanūkhī, *Nishwār al-Muḥāḍarah* (Beirut, 1971-1972), I, 111; II, 100.
5. al-Mas'ūdī, *Murūj adh-dhahab*, edited by Yūsuf A. Dāghir (Beirut, 1973), II, 28.
6. at-Tanūkhī, *Nishwār*, I, 23; Ibn al-Jauzī, *al-Muntaẓam* (Hyderabad, 1357), Vol. VI; (1358), Vol. VII; (1350), Vol. VIII; VI, 359 (and cf. p. 191, where the remark on Ibn al-Furāt is attributed to another source).
7. Cf. D. Sourdel, *Le Vizirat abbaside* (Damascus, 1960) p. 568 on *awlād al-wuzarā'*; Ibn al-Athīr, *al-Kāmil fi't-ta'rīkh* (Leiden, 1862), IX, 387.
8. at-Tanūkhī, *Nishwār*, I, 279 (Babbaghā); 'Arīb, *Ṣilah ta'rikh aṭ-Ṭabarī* (Leiden, 1897), p. 45 (301/914); aṣ-Ṣūlī, *Akhbār ar-rāḍī bi'llāh wa'l-muttaqī* (Cairo, 1953), p. 142 (judge).
9. aṣ-Ṣūlī, *Akhbār*, p. 154 (ar-Rāḍī).
10. Edward William Lane, *An Arabic English Lexicon* (London, 1874), pt. 5, p. 1827 (primitive sense); D. Sourdel, *Vizirat*, II, 671, 683 (caliphal court); Ibn al-Jauzī, *al-Muntaẓam*, VII, 135 (court *ṭabaqāt* in Buyid period).
11. 'Arib, *Ṣilah*, p. 120; Miskawaih, *Tajārib al-umam* (Cairo, 1914, 1915), II, 301 (Rukn ad-Daulah); p. 411 (al-Muṭahhar); compare II, 83.
12. Ibn Manẓūr, *Lisān al-'Arab* (Beirut, n.d.), II, 568c (s.v. *ṭabaq*); at-Tahānawī, *Kashshāf iṣṭilāḥāt al-funūn* (Calcutta, 1862), I, 839 (logic); Ibn al-Jauzī, *al-Muntaẓam*, p. 292 (three leaders).
13. Ibn Manzūr, *Lisān*, I, 16 (on *jins* as biological species); Ibn al-Athīr, *al-Kāmil*, IX, 178.
14. Ibn al-Jauzī, *al-Muntaẓam*, VI, 82 (lists thrown in Tigris); Miskawaih, *Tajārib al-umam*, I, 11 (Muḥammad b. Dāwūd); p. 27

(Ibn Thawābah); cf. also p. 40 for 'Alī b. 'Īsā's high estimate of Ibn al-Furāt's professional skill.

15. Miskawaih, *Tajārib al-umam*, I, 63 (306); p. 111 (311).
16. Hilāl aṣ-Ṣābī, *Ta'rīkh* (Cairo, 1919), p. 371 (Abū 'Alī b. Ismā'īl); p. 413 (Ṣābūr to marshes).
17. Anonymous, *al-'Uyūn wa'l-Hadā'iq* (Berlin ms. no. 9491), f. 144A (Ibn Muqlah); E. Ashtor, "Essai sur l'alimentation de diverses classes sociales dans l'Orient médiéval," *Annales E.S.C.* (1968), pp. 1017-1053, attempts to show that the Mamlūks were unable even to reproduce their own number.
18. Miskawaih, *Tajārib al-umam*, I, 17, 19, 25 (all on Subkarā).
19. *Ibid.*, pp. 47-48.
20. Hilāl aṣ-Ṣābī, *Ta'rīkh*, pp. 354-355 (Abū 'Alī b. Ismā'īl); ar-Rūdhrāwarī, *Dhail tajārib al-umam* (Cairo, 1916), p. 256.
21. Ibn al-Athīr, *al-Kāmil*, IX, 238 (Abū Kālījar); Miskawaih, *Tajārib al-umam*, II, 236-237 ('Izz ad-Daulah).
22. Sibṭ b. al-Jauzī, *Mir'āt az-zamān* (British Museum ms. Or. 4619) f. 78B; other versions of this remark in Miskawaih, *Tajārib al-umam*, I, 137 and aṣ-Ṣābī, *Kitāb al-wuzarā'* (Cairo, 1958), p. 70.
23. al-Jāḥiẓ, "Dhamm" *Āthār* (Beirut, 1969), p. 59; Sibṭ b. al-Jauzī, *Mir'āt az-zamān* (Köprülü ms. no. 1157), p. 365 (ad-Dīnawar); Ibn al-Jauzī, *al-Muntaẓam*, VIII, 62 (cloth merchant).
24. ar-Rūdhrāwarī, *Dhail*, p. 59 (peddler); 'Arīb, *Ṣilah*, p. 186 (Egypt); as-Sulī, *Akhbār*, p. 76; al-Hamadhānī, *Takmilah ta'rīkh aṭ-Ṭabarī* (Beirut, 1961), p. 212 (quote); Ibn al-Jauzī, *al-Muntaẓam*, VI, 60 (confirms that the elder of the *tujjar* is talking about the fire).
25. Miskawaih, *Tajarib al-umam*, I, 326 (Mosul); aṣ-Ṣūlī, *Akhbār*, p. 187 (Bajkam).
26. at-Tanūkhī, *Nishwār*, III, 134 (prayer); D. Sourdel, *Vizirat*, pp. 254-255 (Muḥammad az-Zayyāt).
27. Miskawaih, *Tajarib al-umam*, II, 260 (Abū Qurrah); aṣ-Ṣūlī, *Akhbār* (ar-Rāḍī).
28. Ibn al-Jauzī, *al-Muntaẓam*, VII, 348.
29. aṣ-Ṣābī, *Ta'rīkh*, p. 7; Miskawaih, *Tajārib al-umam*, I, 72 (307); Hilāl aṣ-Ṣābī, *Ta'rikh*, p. 387 (391/1000).
30. ar-Rūdhrāwarī, *Dhail*, pp. 175-176 (Mosul); Ibn al-Athīr, *al-Kāmil*, VIII, 80 (Baṣrah).
31. Miskawaih, *Tajārib al-umam*, II, 36 (Ardabīl); Ibn al-Athīr, *al-Kāmil*, VIII, 77 (Sīstān); cf. p. 50 on Fatimid use of *a'yān* of Tripoli as hostages; p. 312, where a Ḥamadānid punishes the

people of ar-Raqqah by carrying off the *ru'asā'* of the city of Aleppo.

32. Ibn al-Athīr, *al-Kāmil*, p. 146 (Arzan); p. 346 (Bukhārā).
33. Miskawaih, *Tajārib al-umam*, I, 383, 300 ('Alī b. Būyah).
34. *Ibid.*, pp. 320, 378-379 (Miskawaih at first calls the arrested *a'yān* Tustarīs, then later calls them Ahwāzīs, presumably because Tustar and Susa are in the province of al-Ahwāz-Khūzistān); Ibn al-Athīr, *al-Kāmil*, VIII, 252, where the people called *wujūh* in Miskawaih are called *a'yān* and the words of Yaḥyā are somewhat different; for example, he says, "Did you see [Ibn Rā'iq] mistreat all [the people of al-Baṣrah]? No, by God, he mistreated some of them and all were angered at him."
35. Miskawaih, *Tajārib al-umam*, I, 282, 412.
36. at-Tanūkhī, *Nishwār*, I, 311; Ibn al-Jauzī, *al-Muntaẓam*, VII, 72 (shaikh al-Bazzāzīn).
37. Miskawaih, *Tajārib al-umam*, I, 353 (tribal *ra'īs* of the Qufṣ and Balūs); p. 403 (after the death of Lashkarī in Azerbaijān, his army gave *riyāsah* to his son Lashkarsitān); II, 112 (Mu'izz ad-Daulah); p. 121 ('Imād ad-Daulah); p. 135 (remnants of al-Marzubān's army went to Azerbaijān, and gave Muḥammad b. Musāfir *riyāsah* over themselves); p. 334 (Turks rebelling against 'Izz ad-Daulah in 364 gave Alfatakīn *riyāsah* among the Turks); p. 300 (*ra'īs* of Qufṣ and Balūs); p. 382 ('Izz ad-Daulah); Ibn al-Athīr, *al-Kāmil*, VIII, 226 (Washmagīr); aṭ-Ṭabarī, *Ta'rīkh aṭ-Ṭabarī* (Leiden, 1890), III, 2290, Isḥāq, the Sāmānid rebel, invited the people of Samarqand to take the *bai'ah* to his *riyāsah* over them, that is, to recognize his claim to independent rule.
38. Miskawaih, *Tajārib al-umam*, II, 113 ('Imād ad-Daulah assigns *riyāsah* in 336); p. 166 (al-Marzubān, ruler of Azerbaijān, makes a will giving *riyāsah* in the Musāfirid family to his brother Wahsūdhān); p. 363 (Isfahan in 365). The statement in Miskawaih, II, 158 that in 344 Mu'izz ad-Daulah gave *riyāsah* and the office of *amīr al-umarā'* to his son Bakhtiyār is confirmed by Ibn al-Jauzī, *al-Muntaẓzam*, VI, 377, and by Hamadhānī, *Takmilah ta'rīkh aṭ-Ṭabarī*, p. 170, but contradicted by other sources. It may indicate that some contemporaries believed that one line of *riyāsah* descended among the sons of Mu'izz ad-Daulah, and another among the sons of Rukn ad-Daulah. According to Miskawaih, II, 364, 'Izz ad-Daulah in 366 got Fakhr ad-Daulah appointed to his provinces

directly—*riyāsatan*—by the caliph to support him against 'Adud ad-Daulah. Presumably 'Izz ad-Daulah would have done this only if he held his own province *riyāsatan*, and since we do not hear that he was granted this privilege after his accession, he may have held it *riyāsatan* automatically as the successor to Mu'izz ad-Daulah. In any case, confusion as to the office given 'Izz ad-Daulah in 344 certainly does indicate that the idea of *riyāsah* was vague and not of great importance. Either the assignment of 344 is a confused understanding of the assignment of the heir apparency to Iraq, or else it was a gesture so unimportant that we hear no protest from the other side of the Buyid family.

39. at-Tanūkhī, *Nishwār*, I, 246 (example of a *qaḍī riyasatan*); Miskawaih, II, 233 (Sāmānids); aṭ-Ṭabarī, *Ta'rīkh*, III, 2286 (al-Qaffāl was *ra'īs* of the army of Subkarā, the ruler of Fārs).
40. Miskawaih, *Tajārib al-umam*, I, 64 ('Alī b. 'Isā); II, 263-264 (before he became vizier, Ibn Fasānjas had been called *ra'īs*, either by royal directive or at his own initiative, as head of the most important *dīwān* in Iraq); Ibn al-Athīr, *al-Kāmil*, IX, 362 (caliph); p. 359 (Saljūqs).
41. Miskawaih, *Tajārib al-umam*, I, 310 (Ibn Baqīyah); at-Tanūkhī, *Nishwār*, III, 96; Ibn Taghrībirdī, *an-Nujūm aẓ-ẓāhirah* (Cairo, 1933), IX, 145 mentions that in 374 in the correspondence between Ṣamṣām ad-Daulah's vizier, Ibn Sa'dān, and Ibn 'Abbād, the latter called Ibn Sa'dān *al-ustādh ra'īsī*, "the master, my *ra'īs*." Here *ra'īs* can only be the form by which Ibn 'Abbād flattered Ibn Sa'dān, who was never his superior and had never even served the same king.
42. D. B. MacDonald, " 'Ulamā'," *Encyclopaedia of Islam* (Leiden, 1934), IV, 994.
43. ar-Rāmhurmuzī, *al-Muḥaddith* (Beirut, 1971), pp. 161-162.
44. Ibn al-Jauzī, *al-Muntaẓam*, VII, 62 (ten thousand dirhams spent on *ḥadīth*; VI, 124 (al-Firyābī said here to have three hundred and thirteen *mustamlīs*); al-Hamadhānī, *Takmilah*, p. 16 (al-Firyābī); Sibṭ b. al-Jauzī, *Mir'āt* (British Museum ms. f. 113B) (quote from Abū Bakr b. Baṭṭāḥ); various dates between 301 and 324 are given for al-Firyābī's death.
45. Sourdel, *Vizirat*, p. 570; Ibn al-Jauzī, *al-Muntaẓam*, VII, 180 (Ibn 'Abbād); VII, 215 (ad-Dāraquṭnī). On traces of the continuing contrast between the clerks and the ulema cf. Adam Mez, *Die Renaissance des Islams* (Heidelberg, 1922), p. 75.
46. ar-Rūdhrāwarī, *Dhail*, p. 189; Hilāl aṣ-Ṣābī, *Ta'rikh*, p. 340, n.

4 (quote from adh-Dhababī and reference to *Kashf aẓ-ẓunūn* on Ibn Sīmjūr); 'Arīb, *Ṣilah*, p. 121 (Muḥammad the deputy chamberlain); p. 69 (al-Mism'ī); Ibn al-Jauzī, *al-Muntaẓam*, VI, 180 (Badr).

47. Ibn al-Jauzī, *al-Muntaẓam*, VII, 264 (al-Ḥalīmī); Ibn Taghrībirdī, *Annales*, II, 324 (al-Qazwīnī).
48. Ibn al-Jauzī, *al-Muntaẓam*, VI, 149 (Ibn Suraij), VII, 105 (ar-Rāzī), Sibṭ b. al-Jauzī, *Mir'āt* (British Museum ms. f. 67B) (quoting al-Khaṭīb on Ibn Suraij); 'Arīb, *Ṣilah*, p. 76.
49. Ibn al-Jauzī, *al-Muntaẓam*, VII, 266 (al-Khwārizmī); p. 131 (al-Abharī).
50. Ibn Qutaibah, "Kitāb al-'Arab," p. 356; Sibṭ b. al-Jauzī, *Mir'āt* (British Museum ms. f. 64B) (Yūsuf); Ibn al-Jauzī, *al-Muntaẓam*, VI, 390; Mahmūd b. 'Uthmān's *Firdaus al-Murshidīyah* (Teheran, 1333) describes the growth of cenobitic Sufism in Buyid Fārs.
51. Ibn al-Jauzī, *al-Muntaẓam*, VII, 208 (patent).
52. ar-Rūdhrāwarī, *Dhail*, p. 305 n. 1; Sibṭ b. al-Jauzī, *Mir'āt* (Köprülü), XI, 365.
53. Miskawaih, *Tajārib al-umam*, II, 314 (Ibn Baqīyah); at-Tanūkhī, *Nishwār*, II, 77 (*ra'īs* of a village in Iraq); II, 9 (Idhaj).
54. ar-Rūdhrāwarī, *Dhail*, pp. 314, 327 (ad-Dūdamān); Ibn al-Jauzī, *al-Muntaẓam*, VII, 231, (Jurjān's hereditary *riyāsah*); VI, 288 (Jurjān).
55. at-Tanukhi, *Nishwār*, II, 19-20.
56. *Ibid.*, p. 10 (witness-notary); Ibn Taghrībirdī, *Annales*, p. 279 (Jurjān).
57. ar-Rūdhrāwarī, *Dhail*, p. 56 (quote).
58. aṭ-Ṭūsī, *at-Tibyān* (Najaf, 1382), IX, 352-353. For a discussion of this and similar passages of commentary on this verse, see Roy P. Mottahedeh, "The Shu'ūbīyah," *International Journal of Middle Eastern Studies*, 7 (1976), 161-182.
59. Miskawaih, *Tajārib al-umam*, I, 343.
60. *Ibid.*, II, 305.
61. ar-Rūdhrāwarī, *Dhail*, p. 272 (where *ṭā'ifah* and *farīq* are used interchangeably).
62. Ibn al-Jauzī, *al-Muntaẓam*, VIII, 140-141 (Sūq al-Qallā'in); VI, 340 (runners); Ibn al-Athīr, *al-Kāmil*, VIII, 425; Roy Mottahedeh, "Administration in Būyid Qazwīn," in *Islamic Civilisation 950-1150*, edited by D. S. Richards (Oxford, 1973) p. 37 (on factions and their leadership).

63. Ibn al-Athīr, *al-Kāmil*, p. 157; p. 89 mentions a *fitnah* in Mosul between the food sellers and cobblers; al-Muqaddasī, *Aḥsan at-Taqāsim* (Leiden, 1906), p. 138 identifies the section of *al-murabba'*.
64. Ibn Ḥazm, *Ṭauq al-ḥamāmah* (Algiers, 1949), p. 18; al-Jāḥiz, "Manāqib," p. 51 (reading *waqqafat bainahum*, "reconciled them" for *waffaqat bainahum*); Abū Tammām, the early third/ninth century poet, emphasizes the importance of fraternity of belief when he writes, "[He is my true] relative in opinion (*ra'y*), learning (*'ilm*) and school (*madhhab*), even if our genealogical ties are remote in origin" (lines rhyming in *ma-nāsibū*).
65. Ibn al-Jauzī, *al-Muntaẓam*, VIII, 277.
66. I discuss this question with further examples in a review of R. Bulliet's *The Patricians of Nishapur* in the *Journal of the American Oriental Society*, 95 (1975), 491-495.
67. al-Muqaddasī, *Aḥsan*, p. 336 (Abīward and Nisā); ar-Rūdhrāwarī, *Dhail*, p. 120 (quote); Ibn al-Ahtīr, *al-Kāmil*, III, 164 (Nisībīn); Ibn ar-Rūmī, line rhyming in *mālikan*.
68. Ibn al-Athīr, *al-Kāmil*, IX, 296 (Abīward); at-Tanūkhī, *Nishwār*, I, 259; Hilāl aṣ-Ṣābī, *Ta'rīkh*, p. 394 (al-Wāthiqī); Miskawaih, *Tajārib al-umam*, II, 222 (*ghāzīs*).
69. Sibṭ b. al-Jauzī, *Mir'āt* (Köprülü), p. 365; Ibn al-Jauzī, *al-Muntaẓam*, VII, 275; Ibn al-Athīr, *al-Kāmil*, IX, 176; ar-Rūdhrāwarī, *Dhail*, p. 305 n. 1 (quoting adh-Dhahabī). The vocalization of Abū Khuldīyah is uncertain to me.
70. Ibn al-Athīr, *al-Kāmil*, VIII, 496; Miskawaih, *Tajārib al-umam*, II, 413.
71. Miskawaih, *Tajārib al-umam*, II, p. 389; see Ibn al-Athīr, *al-Kāmil*, IX, 50 for a reference to the *shaikh al-balad* of Mayyāfāriqīn in the 350s.
72. Sibṭ b. al-Jauzī, *Mir'āt*, IV, 261 on Sharwah, the vocalization of whose name is uncertain to me. Ibn al-Athīr, *al-Kāmil*, IX, 51 tells a similar story about 'Āmid.
73. Miskawaih, *Tajārib al-umam*, II, 122.
74. Ibn al-Jauzī, *al-Muntaẓam*, VI, 223 (aṭ-Ṭabarī); Sibṭ b. al-Jauzī, *Mir'āt* (Köprülü), p. 323 (Hilāl); Ibn al-Athīr, *al-Kāmil*, VIII, 434 (Alyasa').
75. Ibn al-Jauzī, *al-Muntaẓam*, VII, 254.
76. Ibn Taghrībirdī, *an-Nujūm*, IX, 265.

Chapter IV, Justice, Kingship, and the Shape of Society

1. Ibn al-Athīr, *al-Kāmil fi't-ta'rīkh* (Leiden, 1862), VIII, 483 (quote); cf. p. 436 and IX, 6 (on the military capabilities of the Damascene *aḥdāth*); the alienation of the *ashrāf* and the *ahdāth* is seen in all three of these references and in ar-Rūdhrāwarī, *Dhail tajārib al-umam* (Cairo, 1916), p. 227 where the Fāṭimid general on coming to Damascus is met by both the *ashrāf* and the *wujūh al-aḥdāth*.
2. ar-Rūdhrāwarī, *Dhail*, p. 239 (ar-Raḥbah and ar-Raqqah); Miskawaih, *Tajārib al-umam* (Cairo, 1914-1915), I, 265 (Isfahan); E. W. Lane, *An Arabic-English Lexicon*, pt. 4 (New York, 1956), p. 1566 (quote from Fīrūzābādī). The *ahdāth-'ayyarūn* had coercive authority, which was essential to any rule, but were not acceptable sources of rule to the rest of the community, as we have seen in the case of Damascus. They acted only in the interest of certain levels of the community, and of one or another of its *ṭā'ifahs*. When, therefore, Miskawaih, *Tajārib al-umam*, II, 200, says that in Ḥarrān in the 350s a Ḥamdānid retainer "left the town empty (*shāghir*) without government (*sulṭān*) and the *'ayyārūn* gained power (*tasallaṭ*) over it," it is clear that he does not see the rule of the *ayyarūn* as the equivalent of a "real" government.
3. Miskawaih, *Tajārib al-umam*, II, 314. I am grateful to Mark Cohen of Princeton University for calling my attention to the frequent references to *haibah* in the sources of this period.
4. T. B. Macaulay, "Southey's Colloquies," in *Critical and Historical Essays* (New York, 1965), pp. 50-51; compare Dr. Johnson's: "Better to have one plunderer than many."
5. Lane, *Lexicon*, pt. 5, p. 1920 (definitions of *ẓulm*).
6. Ibn al-Athīr, *al-Kāmil*, IX, 254, 286A; Ibn al-Jauzī, *al-Muntaẓam* (Hyderabad, 1357-1359), VIII, 64.
7. Miskawaih, *Tajārib al-umam*, I, 58 (Ḥamīd); Sibṭ b. al-Jauzī, *Mir'āt az-zamān* (Istanbul ms., Köprülü 1157, Vol. XI), p. 365 (Badr); Ibn al-Jauzī, *al-Muntaẓam*, III, 21 (416).
8. aṭ-Ṭabarī, *Annales* (Leiden, 1879), III, 29-33 (on the 'Abbāsid *daulah*); al-Hamadhānī, *Takmilah ta'rīkh aṭ-Ṭabarī* (Beirut, 1961), p. 186 (al-Muhallabī); Sibṭ b. al-Jauzī, *Mir'āt az-zamān* (British Museum ms OR 4619), II f. 104A.
9. Sibṭ b. al-Jauzī, *Mir'āt az-zamān*, II f. 92A; al-Baihaqī, *Tā'rīkh*

(Teheran, 1324), pp. 97-98 (*ummat* is the Persian form of *ummah* discussed in Chapter II); Ibn al-Athīr, *al-Kāmil*, ix, 336 (Ṭughril).

10. ar-Rūdhrāwarī, *Dhail*, p. 72 (the *ḥadīth* is in al-Bukhārī); p. 23 (aṣ-Ṣābī); Ibn al-Athīr, *al-Kāmil*, ix, 313 (al-Māwardī).
11. Ibn al-Athīr, *al-Kāmil*, ix, 143 (Abū Rakhwah); ar-Rūdhrāwarī, *Dhail*, p. 150 (Sīrāf).
12. at-Tanūkhī, *Nishwār al-Muḥāḍarah* (Beirut, 1971-1972), i, 103. As R. Brunschvig shows in his article "Bayyina," *Encyclopaedia of Islam* (Leiden, 1960), i, 1150-1151, Islamic jurists wanted to accept evidence that made possible probabalistic and commonweal decisions, but were limited in their ability to do so.
13. Ibn al-Athīr, *al-Kāmil*, ix, 98 (Qābūs).

INDEX

The numbers set off by solid carats (▶ ◀) refer to the pages on which the fullest definition of each Arabic term will be found.

Library of Congress Cataloging in Publication Data

Mottahedeh, Roy P. 1940–
Loyalty and leadership in an early Islamic society.

(Princeton studies on the Near East)
Includes index.
1. Islamic Empire—Social conditions. 2. Iran—Social conditions. 3. Iraq—Social conditions. 4. Social groups—Case studies. I. Title. II. Series: Princeton studies on the Near East.
HN656.A8M67 309.1'55 79-3224
ISBN 0-691-05296-4